Acclaimed mixed-media artist Mike Bernard has been at the forefront of collage painting for decades and his work has a sought-after vitality. This practical guide to his unique work brings together his latest guidance, ideas and techniques on a subject about which he is passionate: coastal painting.

From his home near the Devon coast, he and co-author (art writer) Susie Hodge, cover all aspects of mixed-media painting. From considering composition and looking for contrast to reducing elements for greater impact (and even moving towards abstraction). From working with limited palettes to incorporating imaginary colours. From collaging with torn magazines, tin foil, plastic and newsprint to combining inks, oil pastels, PVA, acrylic and watercolours. From playing with proportion to create mood to using thick and thin acrylics for effect. And, of course, how to capture the mood and atmosphere of coastal life, from quiet stretches to busy harbours around the world.

A masterclass from a popular artist with stunning artwork of coasts from around the globe, step-by-step projects are included to demonstrate the techniques, plus a series of experimental exercises to help you try something new.

EXPERIMENTAL COASTS
IN MIXED MEDIA

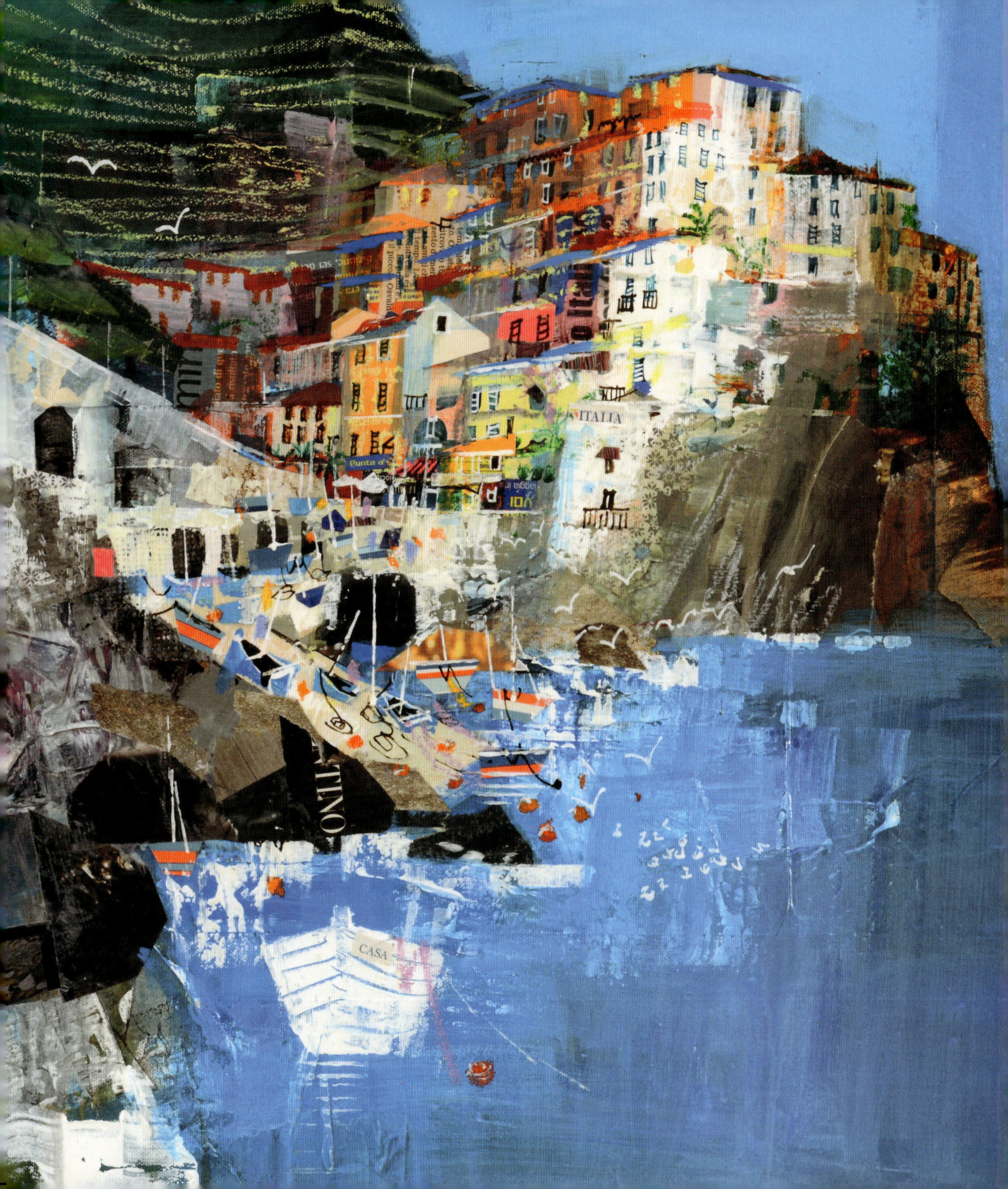

ITALIA
CASA

EXPERIMENTAL COASTS
IN MIXED MEDIA

Mike Bernard and Susie Hodge

BATSFORD

Previous page: **Manarola, Cinque Terre**
Mixed media, 46 x 61cm (18 x 24in)
Bright colours create a sense of
warmth and result in a lively painting.

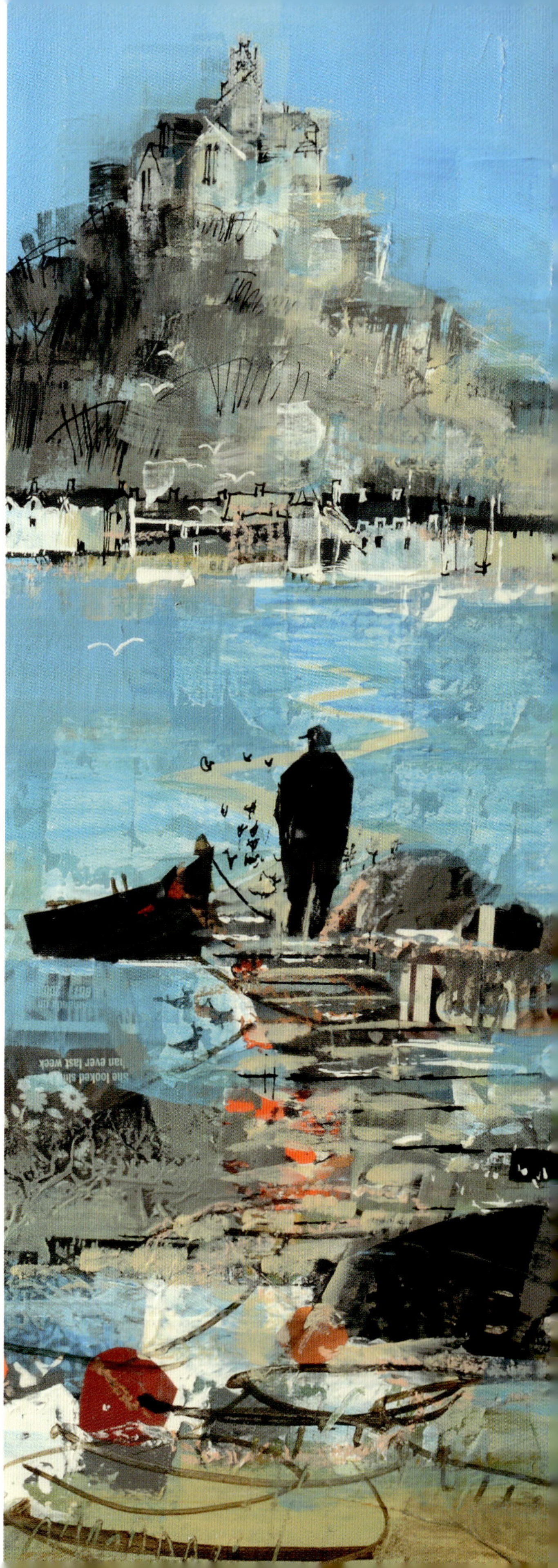

Right: **St Michael's Mount, Summer**
Mixed media, 40 x 61cm (16 x 24in)
This bold composition leads us straight
to the focal point (see page 47 for the
complete painting).

First published in the United Kingdom in 2021 by
Batsford
43 Great Ormond Street
London WC1N 3HZ
An imprint of Pavilion Books Company Ltd

ISBN: 9781849946612

A CIP catalogue record for this book is available from the British Library.

30 29 28 27 26 25 24 23 22 21
10 9 8 7 6 5 4 3 2 1

Reproduction by Rival Colour Ltd, UK
Printed by 1010 Printing International Lt, China

This book can be ordered direct from the publisher at the website
www.pavilionbooks.com, or try your local bookshop.

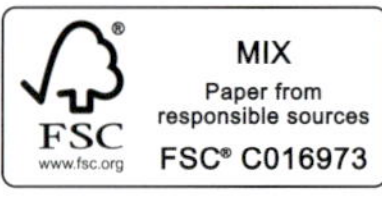

Contents

Foreword

Mike Bernard is renowned for his rich and varied interpretations of lively coastal scenes in mixed media that blend figurative representations with some abstraction, using a combination of collage, acrylics, inks and pastel. Mike has experimented with media, colour, techniques and imagery for several years and his unique, dynamic and colourful style has evolved out of his constant experimentation, inherent talent and experience.

A member of the Royal Institute of Painters in Watercolour since 1997, Mike is especially stimulated by light, space and particularly by the country and coast around his home in Devon as well as by Cornwall, Italy and the south of France. Inspired by his surroundings, his painting process is a continuous push-pull between subject matter and pattern, reality and abstraction, always keeping things free and flexible.

'I enjoy the way textures, shapes, colour and "happy accidents" steer the direction of my paintings,' he says. 'What attracts me most is the pattern of buildings, boats and similar features in a scene. I build a painting by putting in blocks of colour to develop a pattern which is pleasing to my eye, in colours which are harmonious, bringing in feelings of spontaneity, freshness and freedom.'

Born in Dover, Kent, Mike trained fairly locally at Medway College of Art and the West Surrey College of Art and Design in Farnham, followed by postgraduate studies at the Royal Academy Schools in London. Since then, he has exhibited at the Royal Academy Summer Exhibition, the Mall Galleries, Royal Festival Hall and many other galleries in the UK and abroad. He has also received awards and prizes for his paintings, including the Stowells Trophy, the Elizabeth Greenshields Fellowship, Silver Longboat Award, the Laing Award and the Kingsmead Gallery Award. He now lives and works in North Devon, having moved there in 2008 from his previous home in Hampshire. From here, Mike will take over the story.

Susie Hodge, 2020

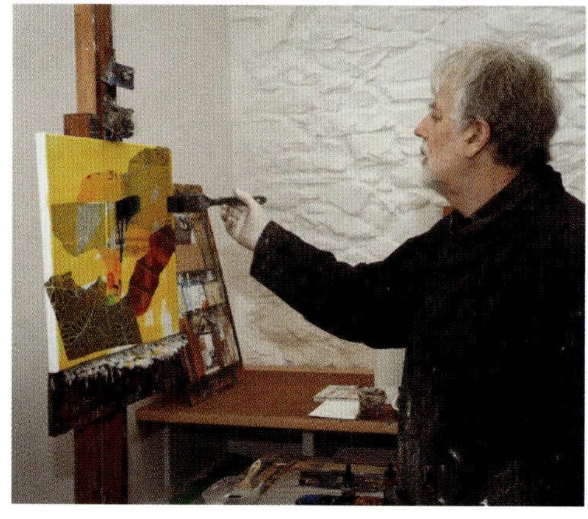

Mike Bernard
in his studio.

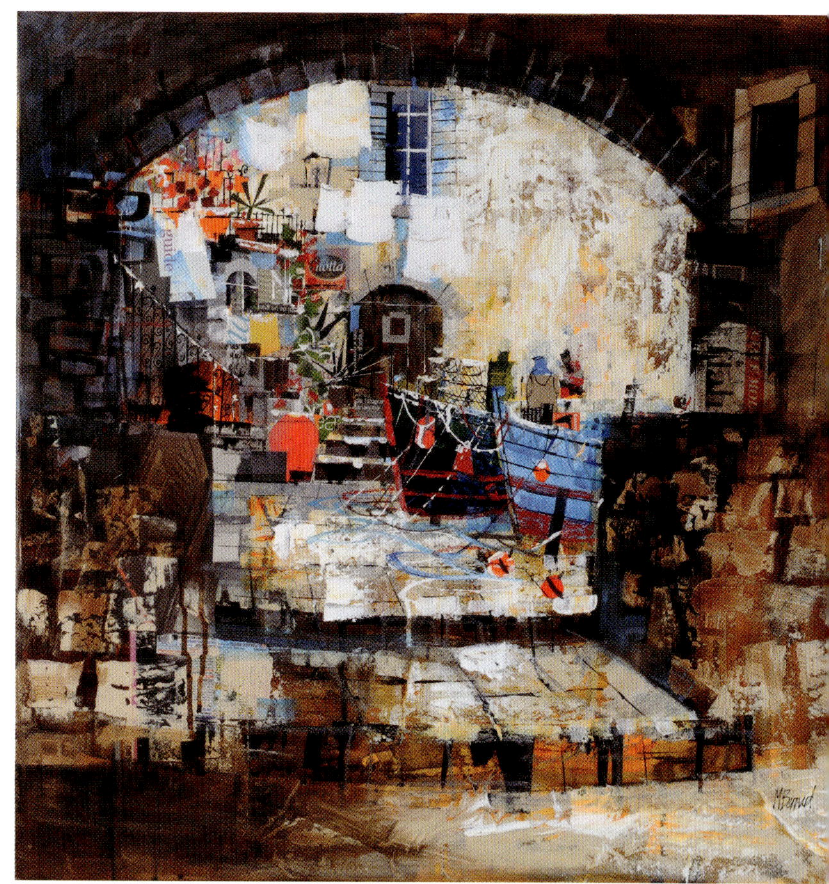

Italian Fishing Village
Mixed media, 71 x 71cm (28 x 28in)
Compositions that lead the viewer to look
through something are always appealing.

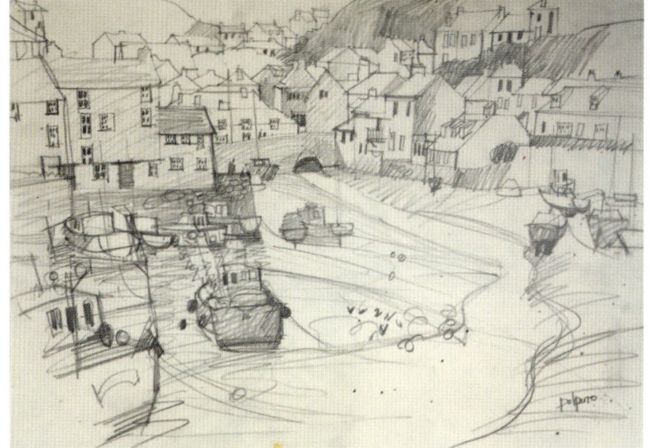

Cornish Fishing Village
Mixed media, 91 x 122cm (36 x 48in)
Selection and simplification result in abstracted images of real places.

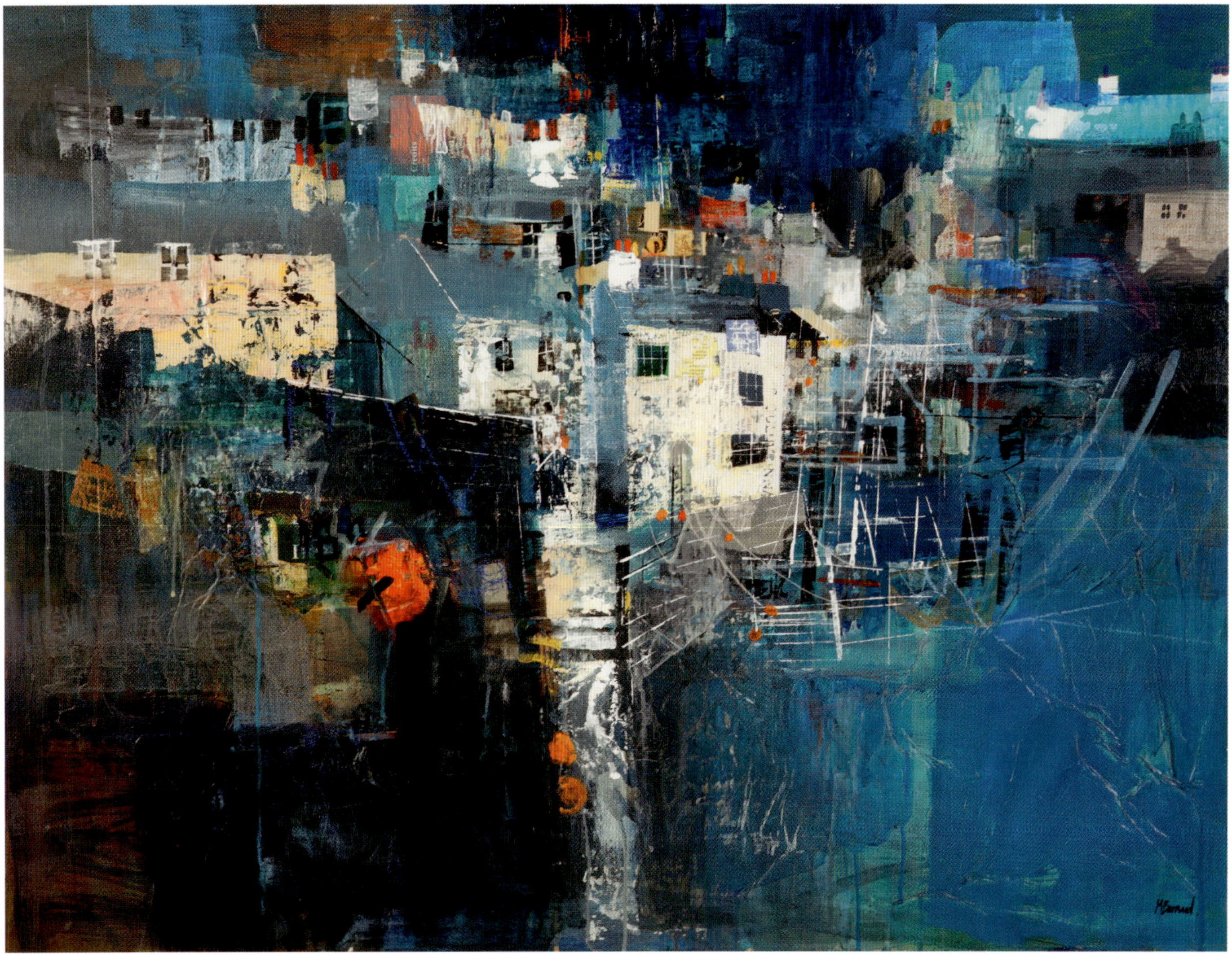

The first step is often a simplified sketch made on the spot in front of the scene before returning to the studio.

Developing a style

Growing up, I had two advantages that helped me to become an artist. Firstly, I had an older brother who was already at art college when I was at primary school. He inspired me to follow in his footsteps, and knowing from his experience about the path though art school made things easier for me. Also, believing that I could have a career in art made it an exciting prospect. My other advantage was that art was the only school subject I was good at! At secondary school, I had two art teachers who encouraged me and helped me get my O and A levels so that I could get into art college. I went to Medway College of Art and a major turning point came as I neared my final year; the staff encouraged me to do fine art rather than graphics as my brother had done. I had thought I would follow him and perhaps could get a job in illustration; I couldn't think how I would earn a living as a fine artist. But I took their advice and have never looked back.

Throughout my seven years at art school from 1974, I was considered quite a conventional painter, attempting to paint landscapes much as I saw them. I found it difficult to invent or create my own vision – it was 'safer' to paint regular, straightforward views. But, on reflection, I do think that landscape, seascape and townscape paintings should be more thought-provoking; and should create a sense of each place while also generating interest, excitement and impact. Every artist should have his or her own personal form of expression or style. However, I've learned through my own development and through teaching art that one of the trickiest factors when learning to draw and paint is to find one's own original approach. It was only when I left college and began to teach amateur painters that my own work began to radically change and develop. Because

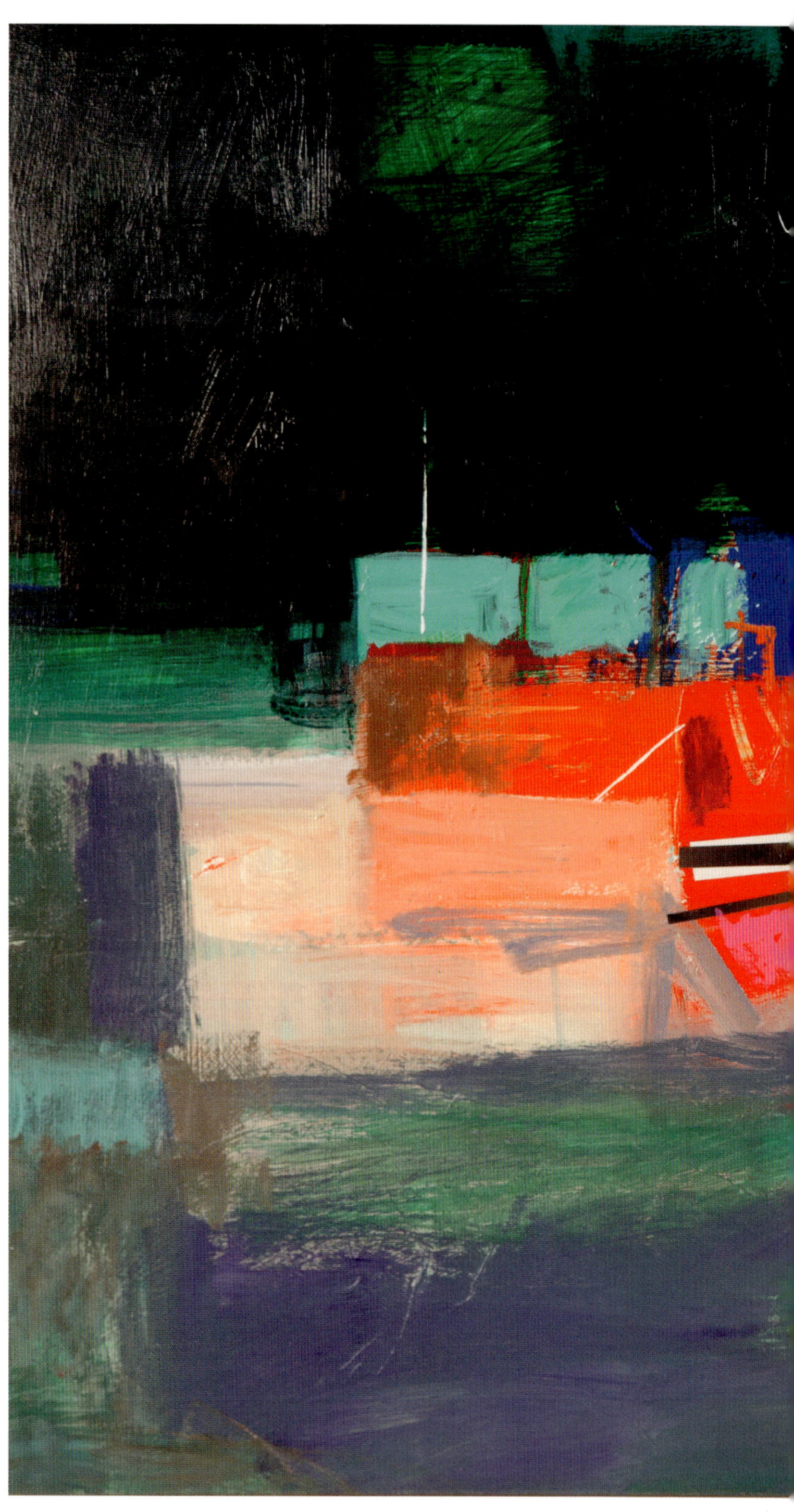

Kentish Harbour
Mixed media, 51 x 102cm (20 x 40in)
Bright colours that don't necessarily follow nature help to make this painting vibrant and arresting.

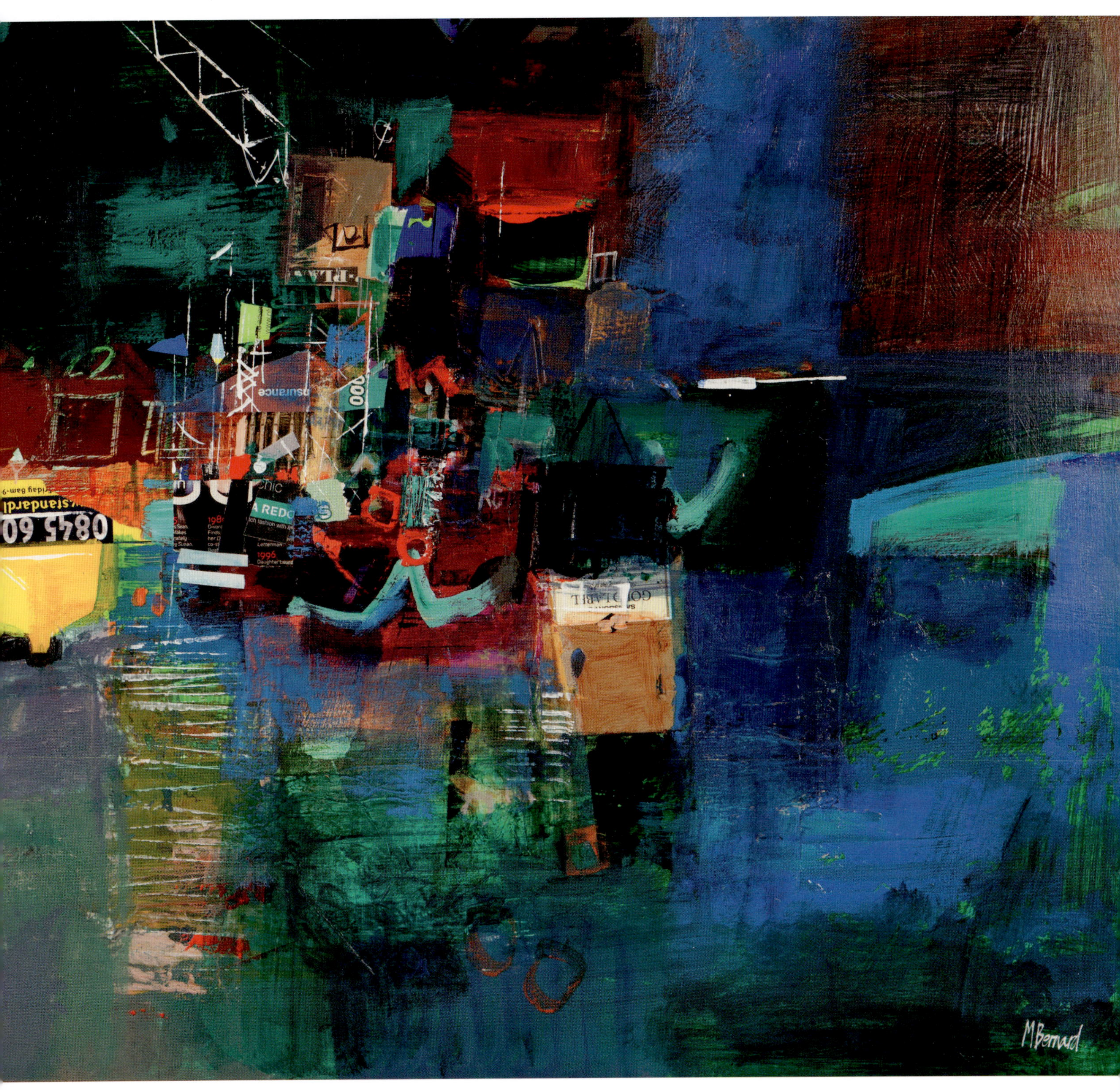

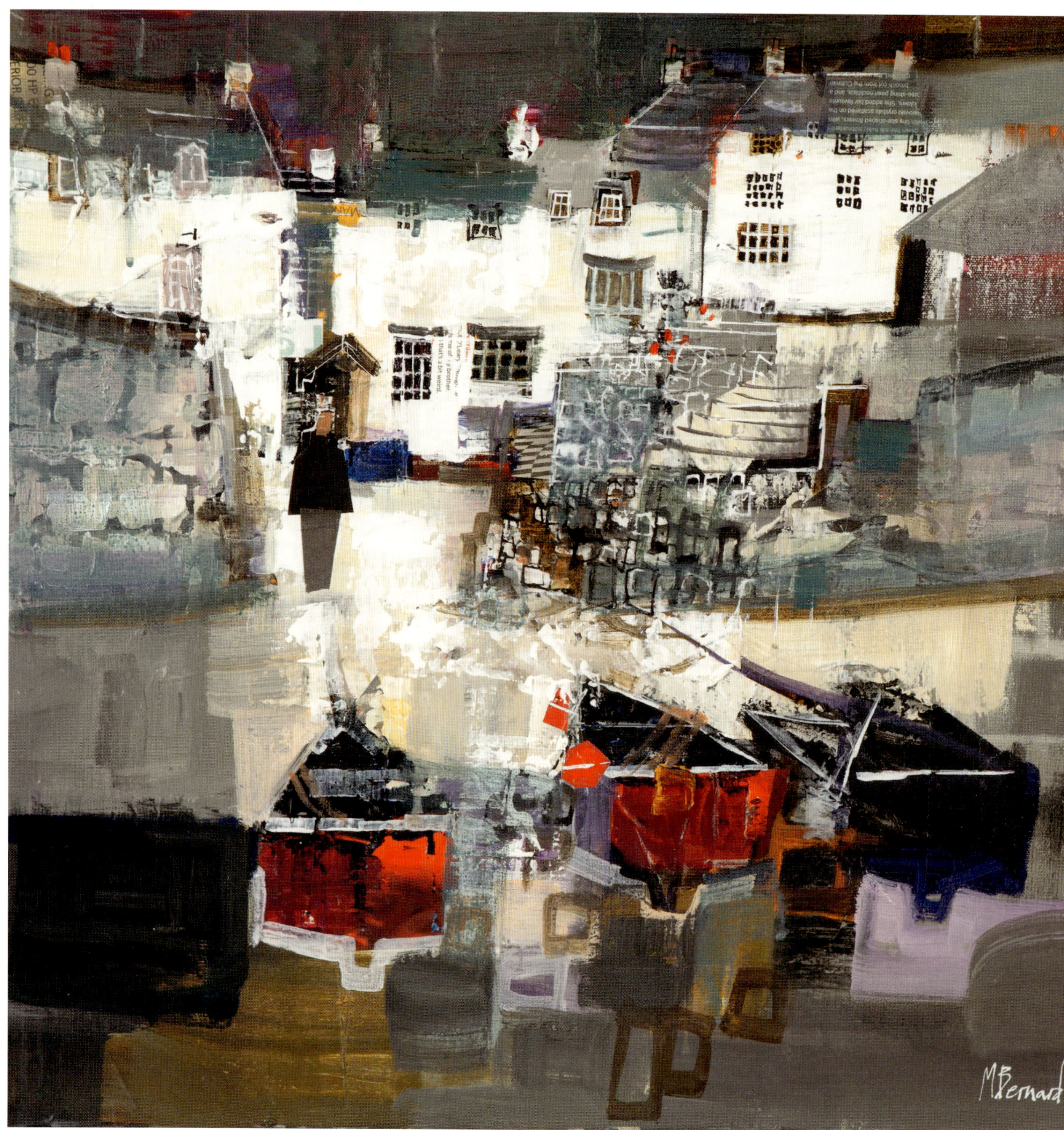

M Bernard

most of my students lacked confidence and were fearful of the white paper in front of them, I encouraged them to experiment with techniques and media. Then, as I watched them, I became excited by the results they were achieving, and I too began to experiment with my own work. It released a 'new me'. I became looser and my work became more abstract and textural. I was able to capture the essence of a scene without getting bogged down by details.

Most artists become proficient by learning the basics. Accuracy, perspective, tone, shape and colour are among the main fundamental skills, and as competence in these areas develops, so does a measure of confidence, but often it is difficult to break away from conventional painting styles and approaches; attaining individuality can be challenging. From the moment we pick up a pencil or paintbrush, we all naturally have our own personal approach, and rather than suppress this, it should be expanded upon through investigation and a certain amount of risk-taking. Risks are always worthwhile. Even if you are not completely happy with some of the art you produce as you work through ideas, you will discover something fresh, such as exciting new processes and pathways, or colours you particularly enjoy, textures that work well or ways of reducing details to convey the essence of a scene. So allow yourself to explore and experiment; plunge right in; make a mess and mistakes, and you will be pleasantly surprised.

However, I'm not advocating that you move into complete abstraction. I always encourage everyone to work with the aim of creating a recognisable likeness of their subject. From that, you can build on creating a more personal expression, which can be generated through the use of a range of materials and techniques. I believe that the best paintings are the least complex; those that allow viewers to use their imaginations when looking at them.

With this in mind, I generally avoid including too many details and I also restrict my palette of colours. Although I use a range of media, even this is fairly limited for each painting. I find that by confining my colours, materials and details in this way, I can experiment with greater freedom of expression.

From the moment you start a painting, you can influence its final outcome. My advice is not to prepare too much and not to have too fixed an idea of what you want for your end result. As I saw with my students, I understand how daunting the white of the paper may seem before you begin, and overcoming this anxiety is one of the first things I will show you in the following pages. But before you even start putting marks on your paper or other work surface, the beginning of any painting is *inspiration*. What I mean here is that you need to see a place and want to express what you see. To be enthused and motivated by something in front of you. This might be a location, or it might just as easily be the light or the weather, the colours or the shapes. And although you might be selecting a particular place to depict, don't allow its exact appearance to overshadow your procedure; don't worry whether or not you are going to get a true likeness. I hope that my fairly spontaneous, free approach will also inspire you to work quite unreservedly and to experiment, and from this, that you build your own style, gain confidence, increase your creative enjoyment and convey your personality.

My highly textured semi-abstract paintings are built up with collage and acrylics, sometimes also in places with watercolour, oils, ink and oil pastels. Whatever the view, whether it's Venice or Polperro, my work is full of colour, character and vitality, and I always aim to capture the atmosphere of each location. The ways I do this are explained in this book.

Low Tide, Mousehole
Mixed media, 51 x 51cm (20 x 20in)
Sometimes I introduce an abstract quality
to my paintings by reducing elements and
flattening the appearance of a place by
simplifying tonal contrasts.

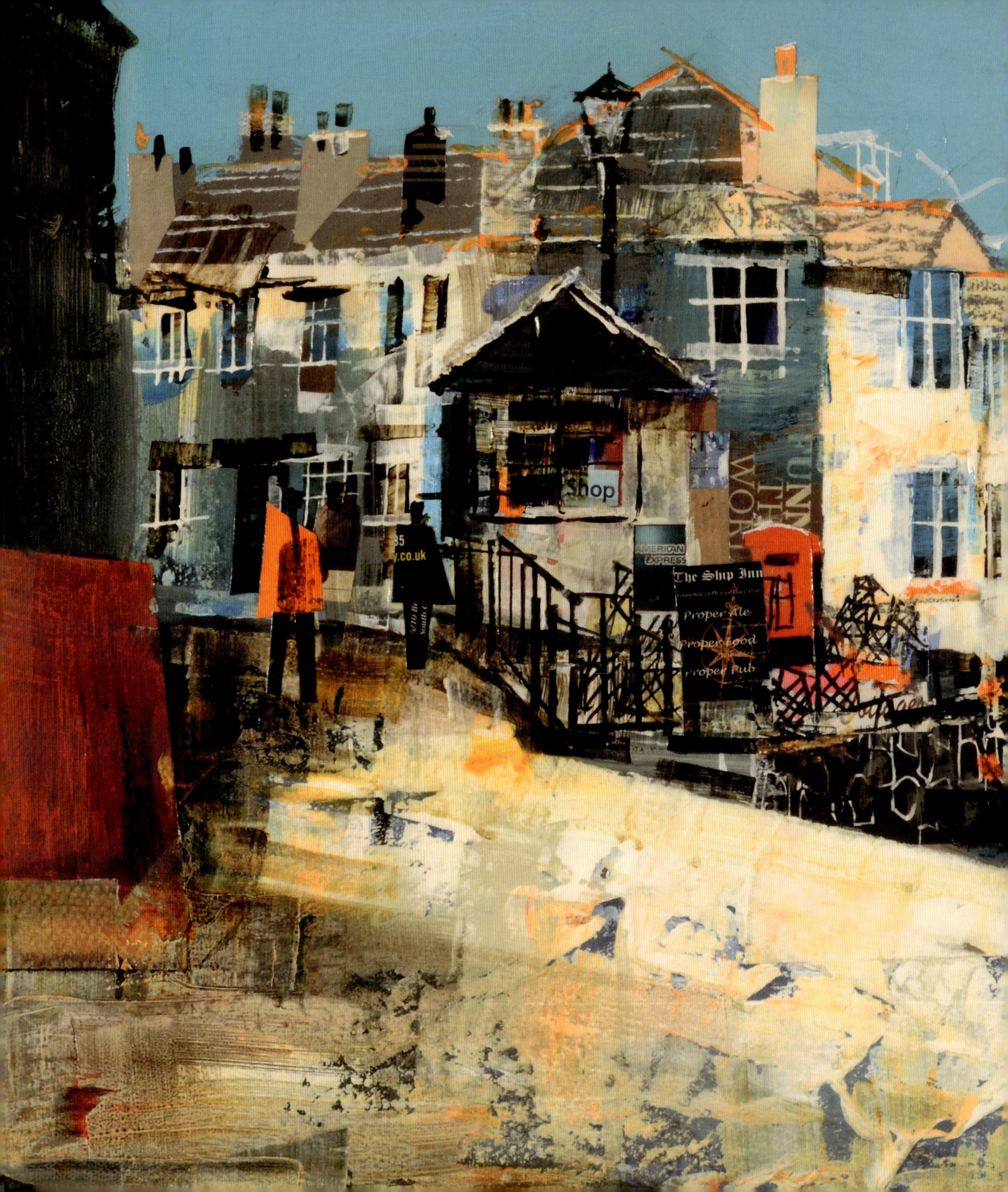

Shop
FUN
THE
WORL
AMERICAN EXPRESS
The Ship Inn
Proper Ale
Proper Food
Proper Pub
.co.uk

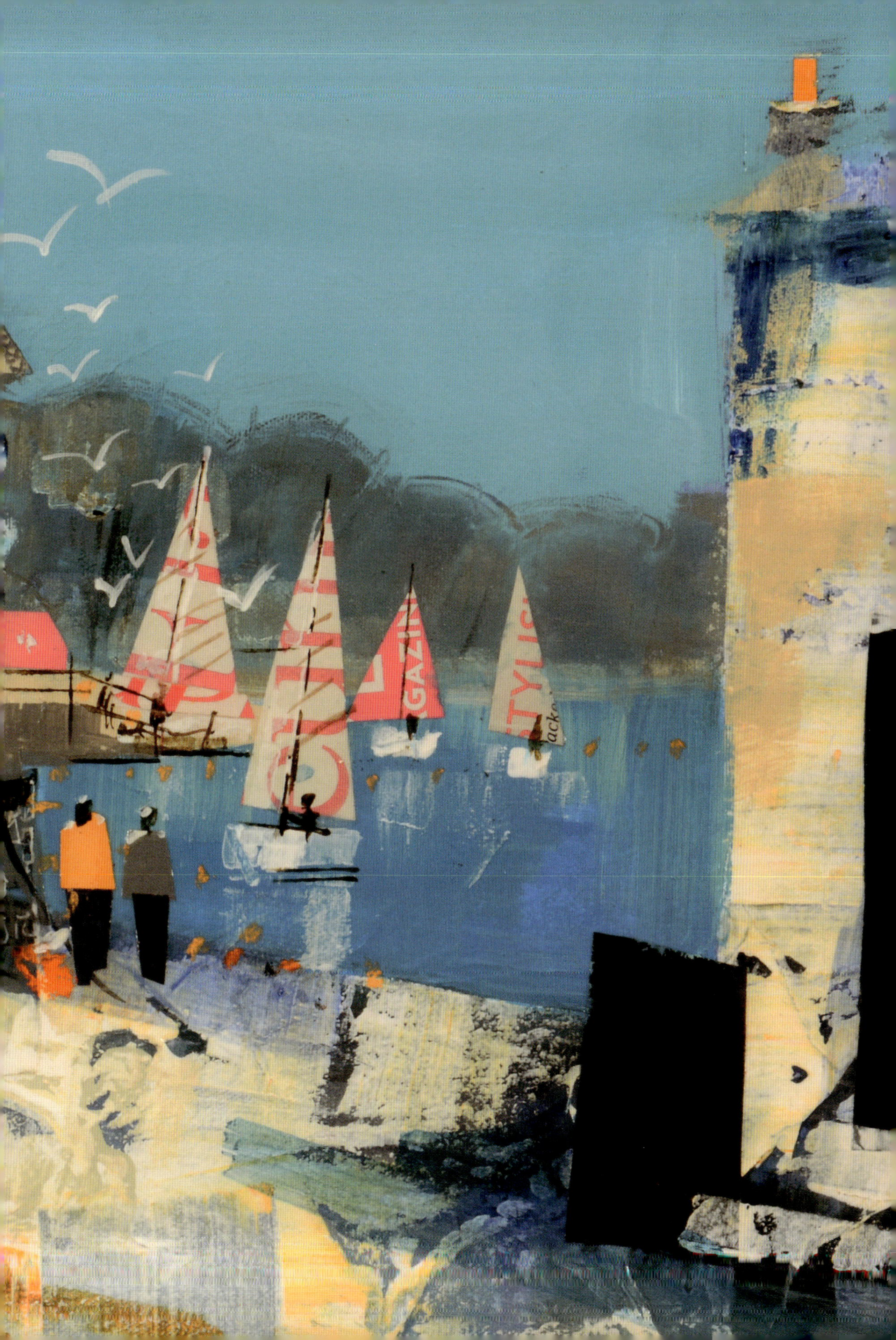

Before You Paint

Faced with a sheet of white paper, plain canvas, card or another surface, it's natural for most of us to be at least a little daunted. Beginning a painting is one of the hardest parts of the whole process of creating art, and when you're about to start, paintbrush in hand, it's easy to stall, to believe that you have nothing new to express, no original ideas. But believe me, there is always something original inside each of us, and always ways that we can motivate ourselves and reinterpret what we see. In this book, I show you many of the ways in which I work, and that will hopefully give you ideas and the momentum to create a fresh approach to painting for yourself.

Over my career, I have explored a multitude of ideas, methods and materials. At times, I also felt that I was grasping for ideas that never came. But by exploring and experimenting, I eventually found an approach that I'm happy with, that I can work with instinctively and continually, knowing that I will never repeat myself. I'll always be able to create original paintings and, yes, they may all have a familiar style, but each one will be different. Because I'm always exploring and experimenting, I never tire of the way I work or the paintings I produce. I hope that after you have read this book, you will feel the same about your own art.

Previous page: **Passage Street, Fowey**
Mixed media, 40 x 61cm (15½ x 24in)
Looking through the buildings to the water, the predominant colours of cream and pale blue are livened up with pink and orange and anchored with black and grey.

Harbour Lights, Salcome
Mixed media, 61 x 76cm (24 x 30in)
Drama is created with deep Prussian blue contrasted with white and bright colours. Small details and reflections are added with fine ink lines.

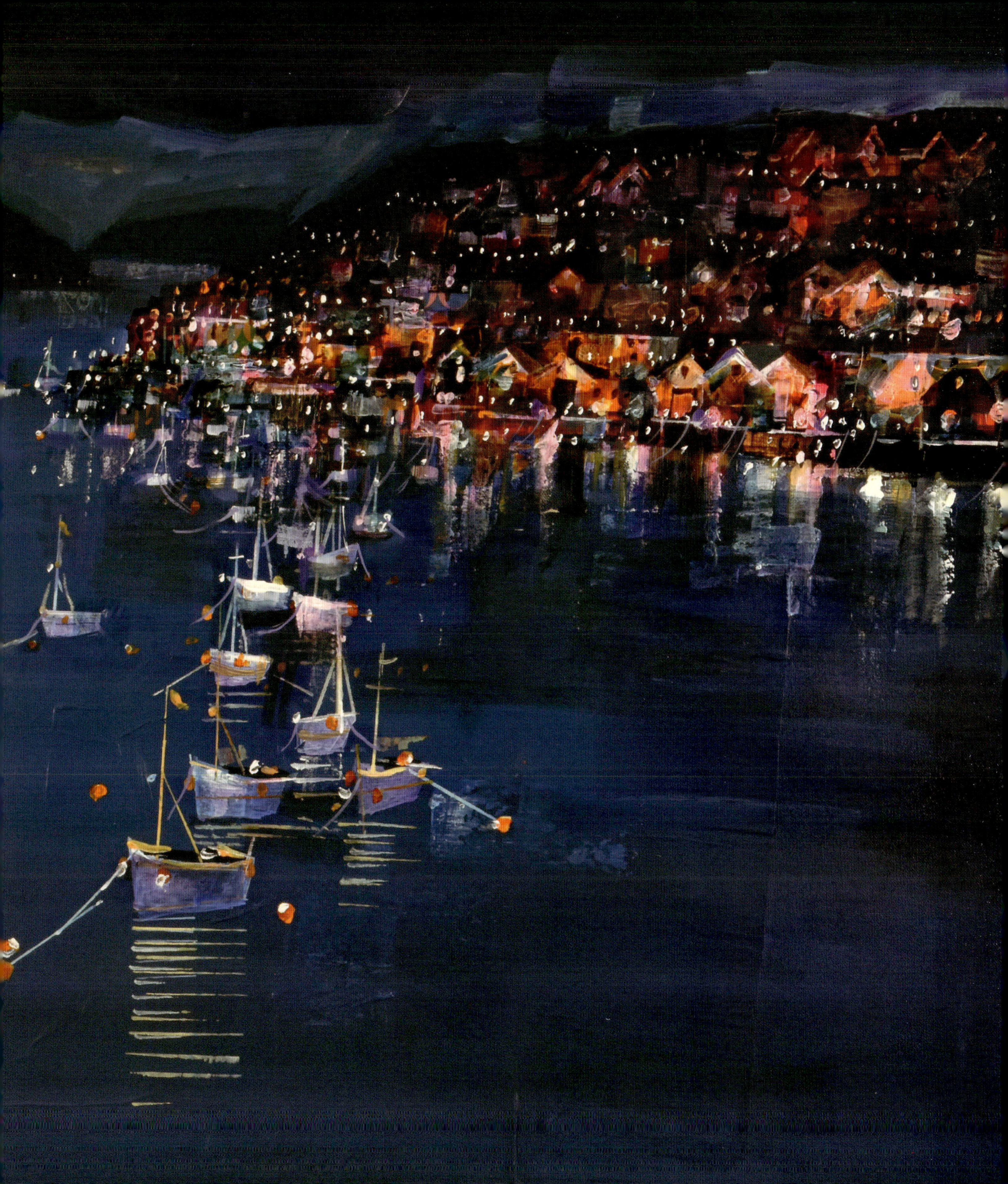

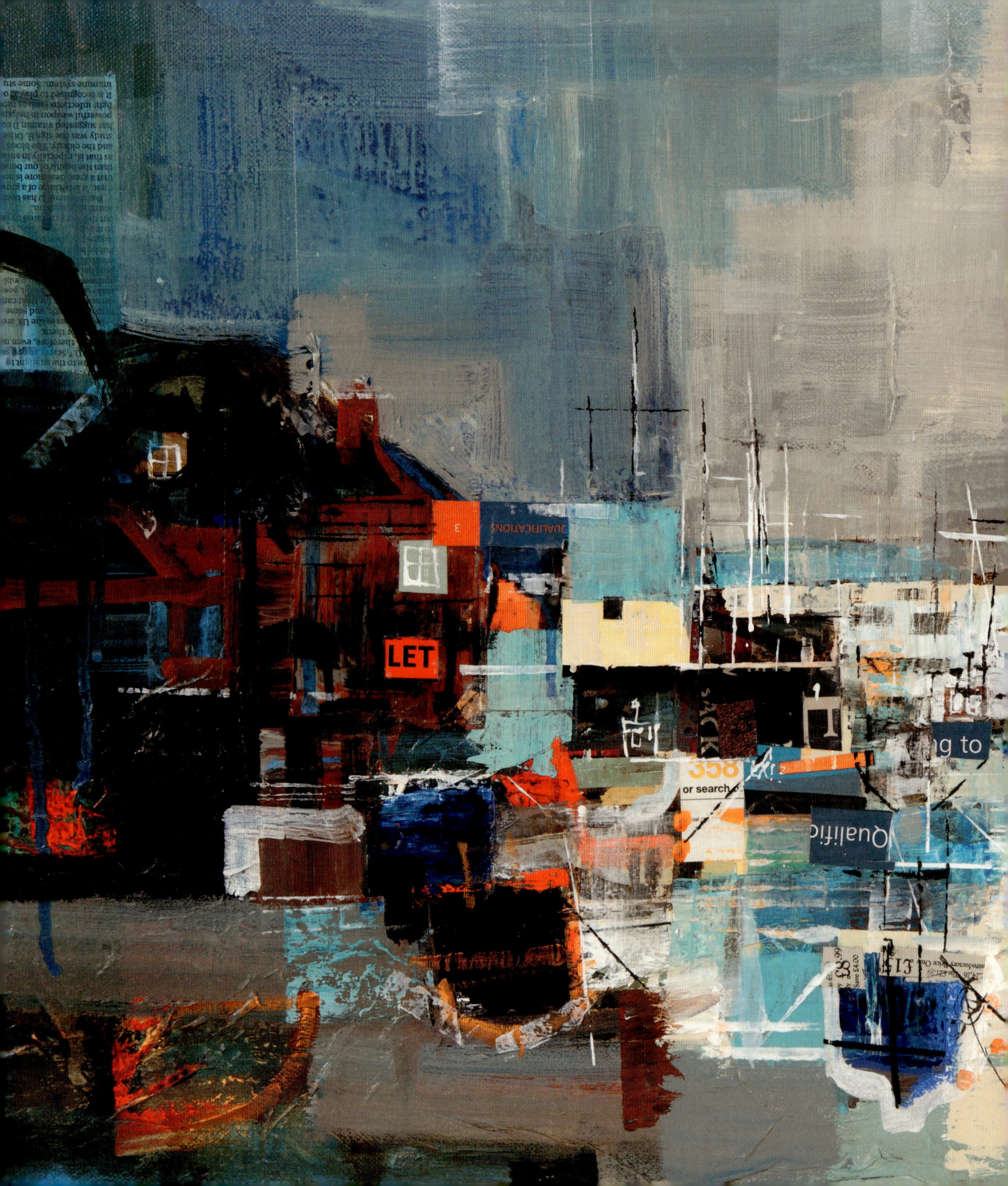
LET
QUALIFICATIONS
358
or search
ng to
Qualifi

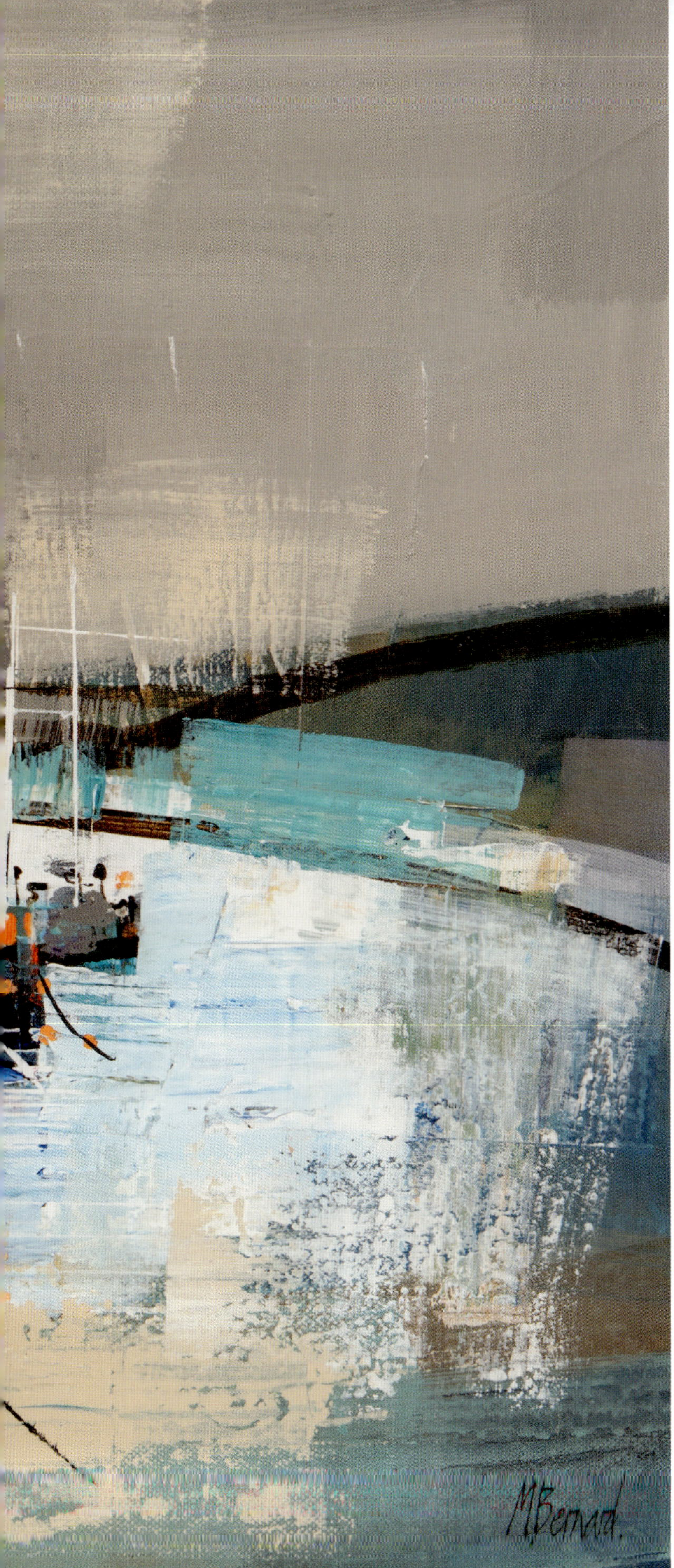

Motivation

So how do you motivate yourself? I motivate myself every day by painting what I love. I set myself challenges – I don't allow the white paper (or card) to overpower me! I also discipline myself, persevere – never give up – and, above all, I believe in myself. It's not always easy and some days are more difficult than others, often for no apparent reason, but every time I complete a painting, or one is going well, I feel a great sense of fulfilment and pleasure. Within these pages, I hope that I can convince you to also challenge the norm as I do, to find ways of expressing yourself without labouring over it, and to believe in yourself. Hopefully, this book will give you the tools, knowledge and confidence to experiment and explore subjects and techniques that appeal to you in order to create some fantastic art of your own. All you need is a determination to work through any doubts you may have, to appraise and evaluate experiments that you may feel haven't worked, and to push on with those that have, exploring and experimenting as you go.

Painting and drawing always take time and perseverance to get right, and self-discipline is needed for this. Often things become easier as you keep working; one rather pleasing painting will motivate you to try another and, even if this doesn't work, you will keep on trying out ideas until they work for you more regularly. We all have off-days or produce paintings that haven't worked out as we intended, but if things aren't working well, don't despair; you will have better days. Similarly, if a painting isn't going too well, put it aside, start another or leave things completely for a day or more and come back to it at a later date. You will be amazed at how much more objective you can be when you look at your work with fresh eyes. More on this later (see page 120).

Morning Light, Axmouth Harbour
Mixed media, 40 x 56cm (16 x 22in)
Colours and textures need to work within
a painting, but also independently to create
areas of interest across the composition.

So first of all, ignore fixed ideas about how you think things should look, forget what you think you should be painting. Through the ideas I am going to share with you, you will hopefully cast your net that bit wider and your creativity will become that bit more exploratory. You will be excited by your achievements, which in turn will give you the drive to continue experimenting and making more paintings that please you.

Two of the first artists ever to use collage in fine art were Pablo Picasso and Georges Braque in the early twentieth century. They were taking a big risk when they began using such unusual materials, as until then, painters only really used oils and watercolour (or, even earlier, tempera). Mixed media was not a 'thing' in fine art. You couldn't go into a major art gallery or museum, for instance, and see work created with mixed media. Experimentation was usual, however, and I have always had a soft spot in particular for certain British artists, from the Norwich School of Painters, through to J.M.W. Turner, Walter Sickert, John Piper, Graham Sutherland and Henry Moore, who all worked in unconventional ways to produce stunning and original works of art. More recent influences for me have been John Blockley, Fred Cuming and Barbara Rae. Every one of these artists – mainly landscape painters – allowed, or allow, themselves to experiment, and in doing so, created and discovered unique, beautiful and innovative personal styles and methods.

So how do I motivate myself? Well, sitting looking at your paper is a difficult way for anyone to begin. For me, ideas for paintings come from my surroundings, and I love boats, harbours and other coastal scenes, probably because I grew up in Kent, near Dover. There's something about the atmosphere, colour and light surrounding the water and sky, the contrast of natural and manmade elements, and the interactions and patterns that can be seen in such things that inspire me. So I'll tell you what I tell all of my students: pick subjects that you love, that mean something to you, or that uplift or stimulate you. Try to see your own familiar surroundings with fresh eyes; always take several photos of places you visit, make sketches, notes, anything that means you will recall what you liked about the place when you're about to start your work of art.

Look for colours, shapes, patterns – repeats and contrasts – in landscapes or wherever you are. As I've mentioned, coasts and harbours always inspire me with their colours, water, skies, contrasts, atmosphere and often drama or busyness. Think about different times of day and changing shadows and light, how colours are affected, the general atmosphere of a location. Use a viewfinder (two 'L'-shaped pieces of paper or card) or your camera to frame a view. Move it around so you see different views and gauge the compositions that inspire you the most. If you do this regularly, you will train yourself to quickly spot great scenes for painting and this will also motivate you to experiment more.

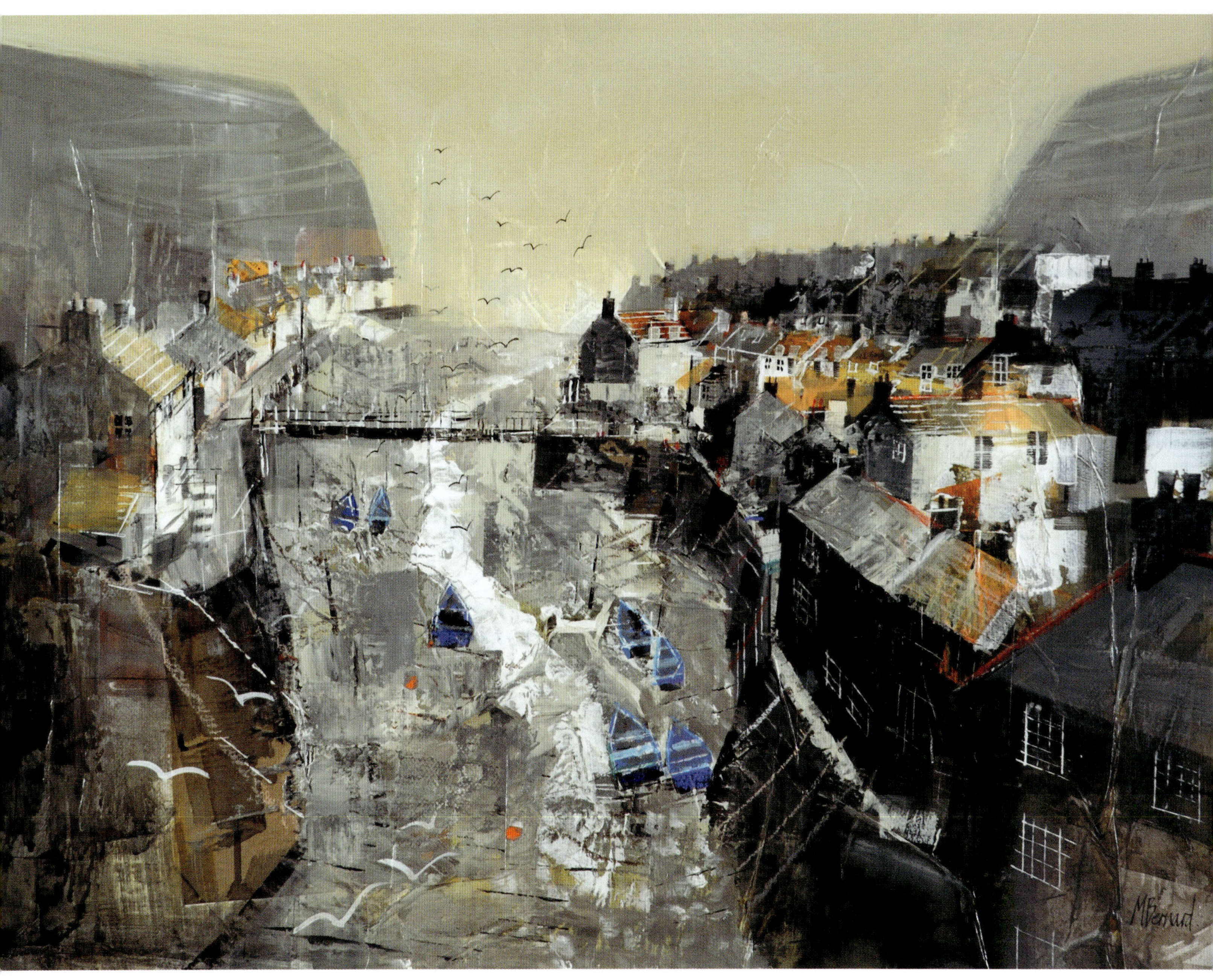

Low Tide, Staithes

Mixed media, 51 x 76cm (20 x 30in)

To capture the particular light and mood of
this scene, I worked with a more subdued
palette than usual.

Inspiration

A much-used word, inspiration is quite illogical and uncontrollable. Moments of real inspiration come with a burst of energy, a thrilling feeling of excitement and a happy glow. As I've already mentioned, for me, ideas or inspirations for paintings are evoked by my surroundings, and one of my favourite locations is Cornwall, a place to which I return regularly. There, I find some of the most inspirational places are the many small fishing villages and harbours that huddle around the wild, rocky coasts. Other inspiring locations for me are parts of Italy and the south of France; even there, it is the harbours and colourful coastlines that usually inspire me the most.

Although inspiration arises from the unconscious part of our minds, you can help yours by visiting different places and looking out for new views; look with fresh eyes for scenes that appeal to you. Allow your gut instinct to choose first of all, then consider and analyse *why* you like them. Your reasons for your choices could stem from the atmosphere or the local people, or it could be that colour, pattern, light, textures, shapes or contrasts appeal to you. For me, it can be any or all of these, depending on the location. Although I often find that several elements inspire me, I try to keep things uncomplicated and simplify aspects of the scene once back in the studio.

So whatever it is that inspires you, hold on to it and take courage and conviction that you will be able to make something out of it. Retain these thoughts as you work – in other words, keep your aspirations in mind. When you are working, refer back often, reminding yourself of your original stimulus and what you found exciting about it. If you lose track of your early intentions, you will probably end up with something that lacks structure, intensity and integrity. It's all too easy to be led off at a tangent, but try to resist this, as your initial inspiration is important. Also, put aside preconceived ideas of how things should look. Be curious and nurture your creativity. Explore and experiment, keep your mind open and follow your instincts.

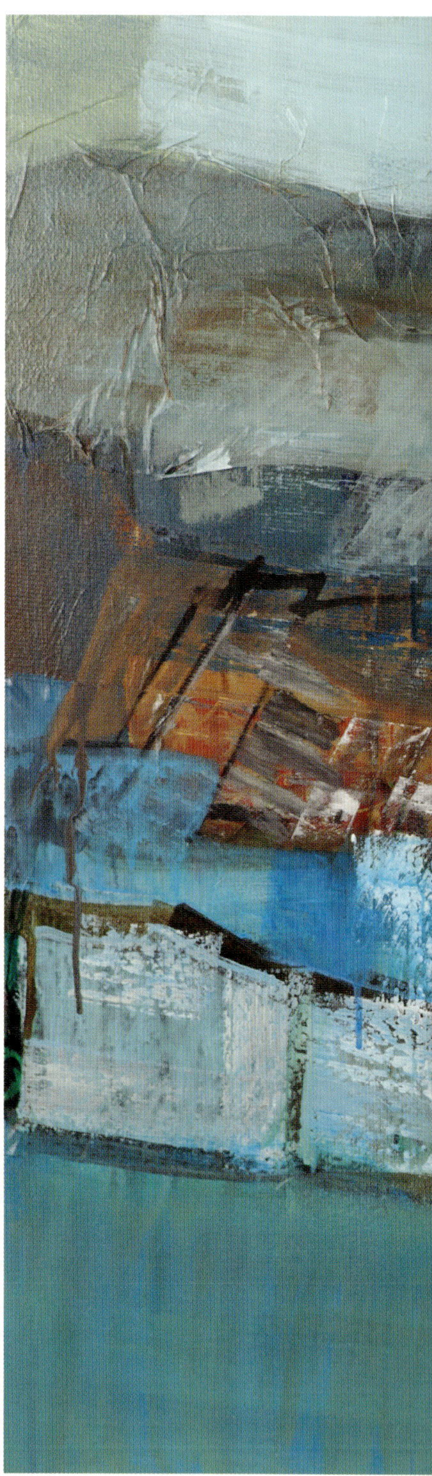

Port Looe Harbour

Mixed media, 81 x 122cm (32 x 48in)

I am always looking for new subjects to paint, but often the most everyday subjects can keep giving. This was a familiar place to me, but by raising my viewpoint and using brilliant turquoise blue and red, I think I gave it a new vibrancy and it took on a new atmosphere.

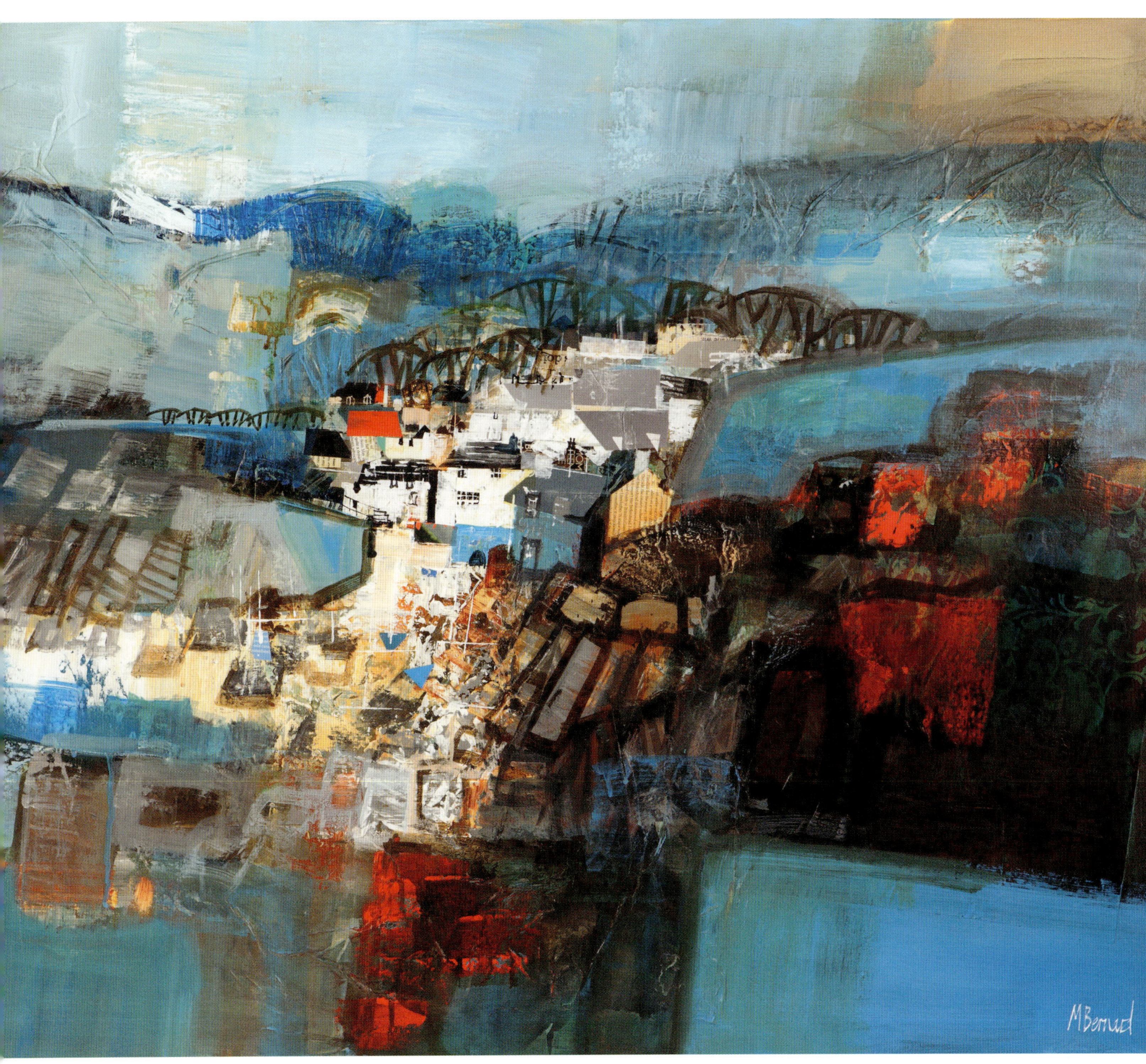

Location

While we all love to discover beautiful new places – and, for me, the lively coasts of Cornwall, Devon, northern Italy and the south of France are always breathtaking and inspiring – don't ignore locations you know well. For example, if there are areas that are familiar to you, go there and observe them as if for the first time, and appreciate them once more. Of course – as the Impressionists exploited so well – different seasons, times of day and weather effects will change the look of any scene, altering the colours, light and atmosphere, but also our attitudes towards these places will change. As artists, we need to view everything with fresh eyes. Returning to a place over and again and rediscovering it can be just as exciting and stimulating as discovering somewhere new. Even if you paint from the same spot, your paintings will look different because no two paintings ever look exactly the same. Think of works by Claude Monet, Camille Pissarro, Alfred Sisley or Paul Cézanne – they painted the same scenes over and over again and never lost their verve or enthusiasm for those locations – and we never lose our love of looking at them.

So how to capture this – or to harness the image and see it with renewed or fresh eyes? When you are on painting excursions, look for interesting angles, contrasts, or whatever it is that inspires you. When I'm on painting trips, I take plenty of photographs, make sketches, notes and anything else that I think I'll need to work from when I return to the studio. Often, these information-gathering visits are planned, but similarly, I frequently find myself somewhere that inspires me for a painting, which is why I always recommend keeping a sketchbook and a camera to hand – much easier now we nearly all have cameras in our smartphones. Use these as reference later to inspire and inform you when you are in front of your paper or whatever surface you are painting on. But don't let the

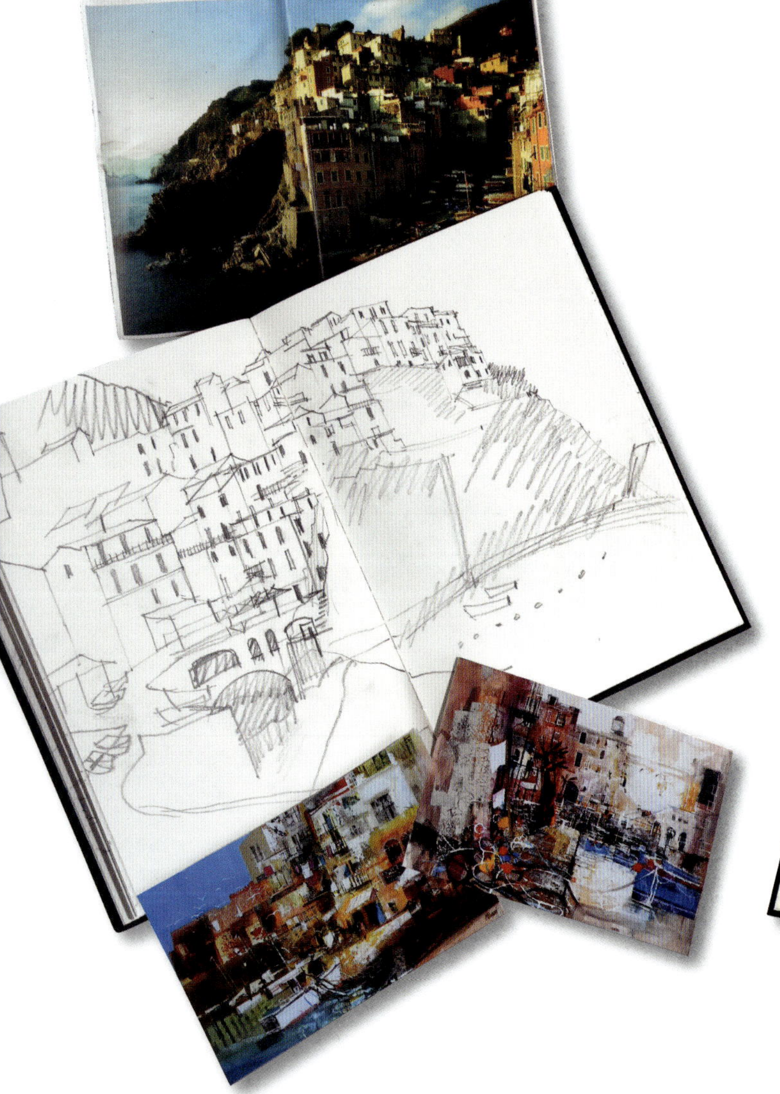

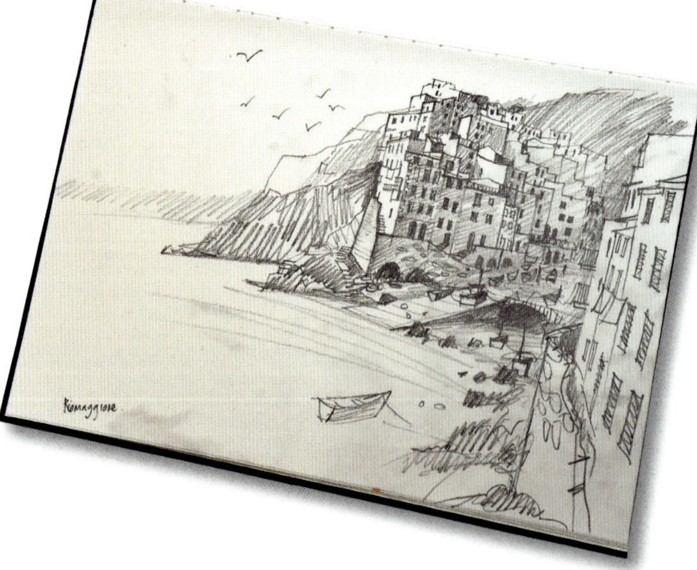

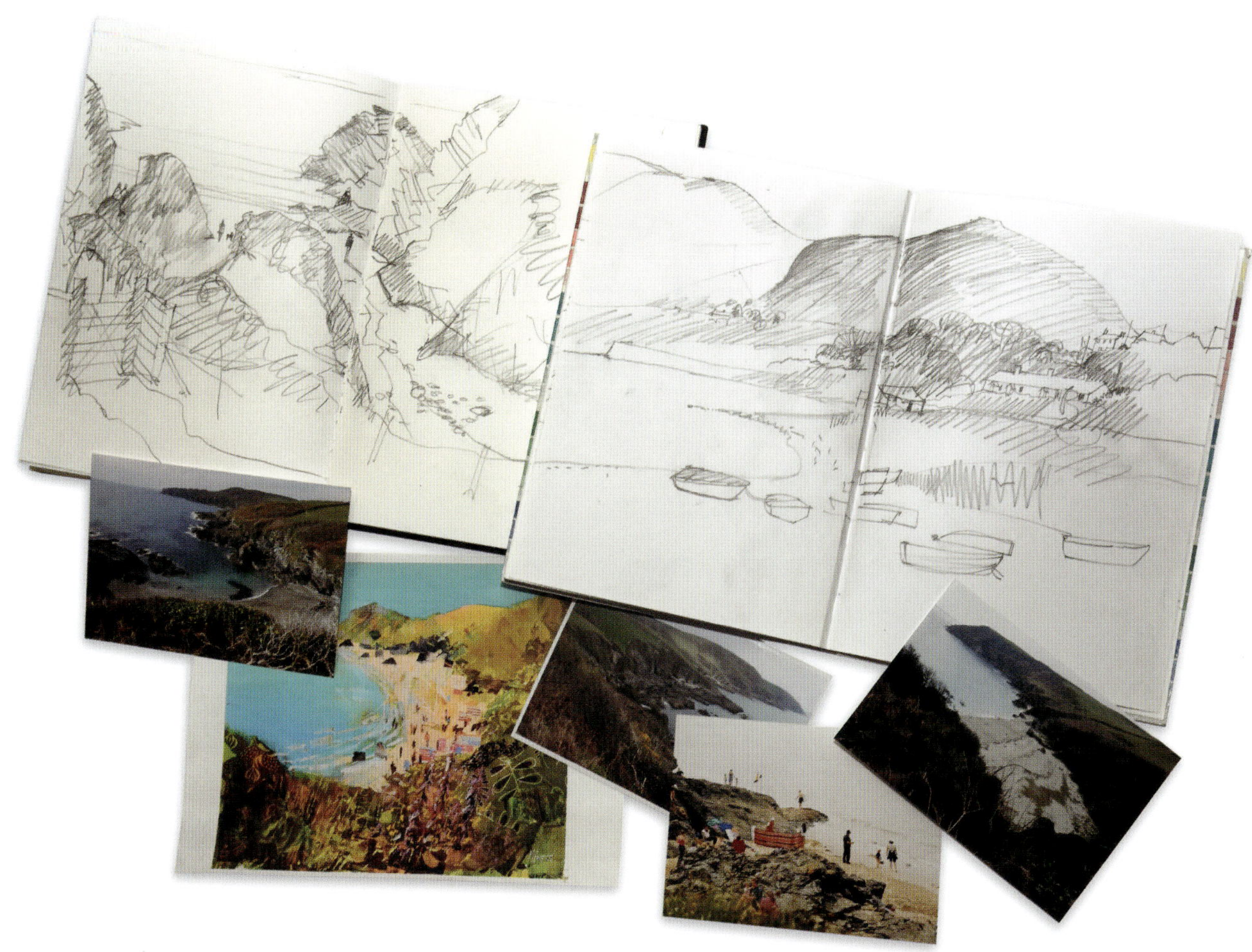

photos or sketches dictate too much. You are not going to copy everything literally, but to use the images you have gathered as points of departure.

My initial starting point is to collect on-the-spot sketches or photographs. While my subjects vary, I am selective when describing detail, as I want to portray only the essence of what I see. I begin every work by making sketches directly in front of the view I've chosen, but when I create the final image, I am discriminating over which details and elements I include, as I aim to distil each subject. Too many details in my images would take away from the liveliness and dynamism I aim for. My paintings are more about evoking moods and atmosphere than about capturing a traditional scene. Although I make some reference to the location sketch, as a beginning, I am only thinking of basic shapes, angles and spaces at this stage.

Above and opposite: For my pencil sketches on location, I usually work in line and tone, quickly noting the most important elements of a scene and omitting any extras that don't immediately jump out at me. I also take photos and sometimes buy postcards to take back to the studio for inspiration later.

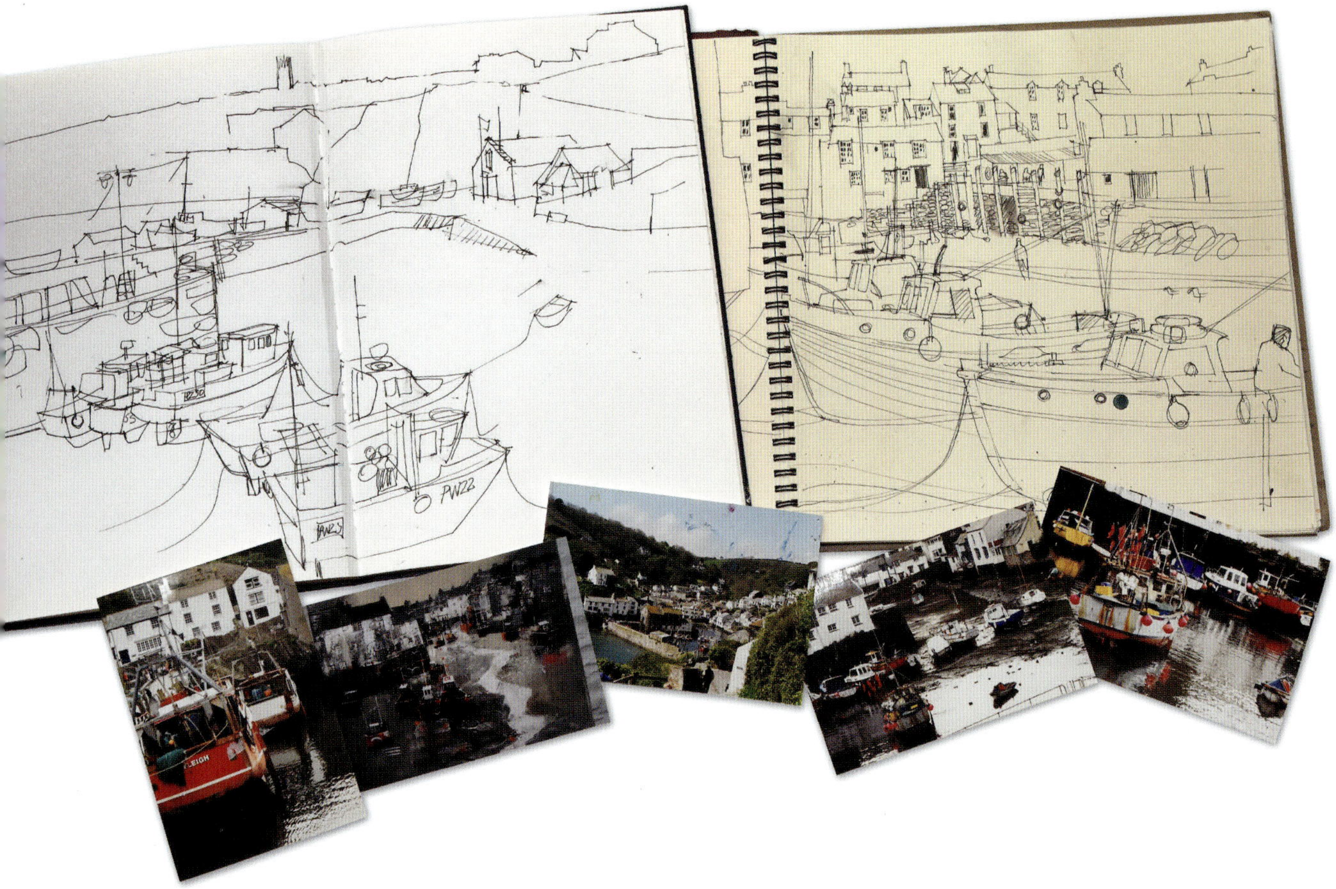

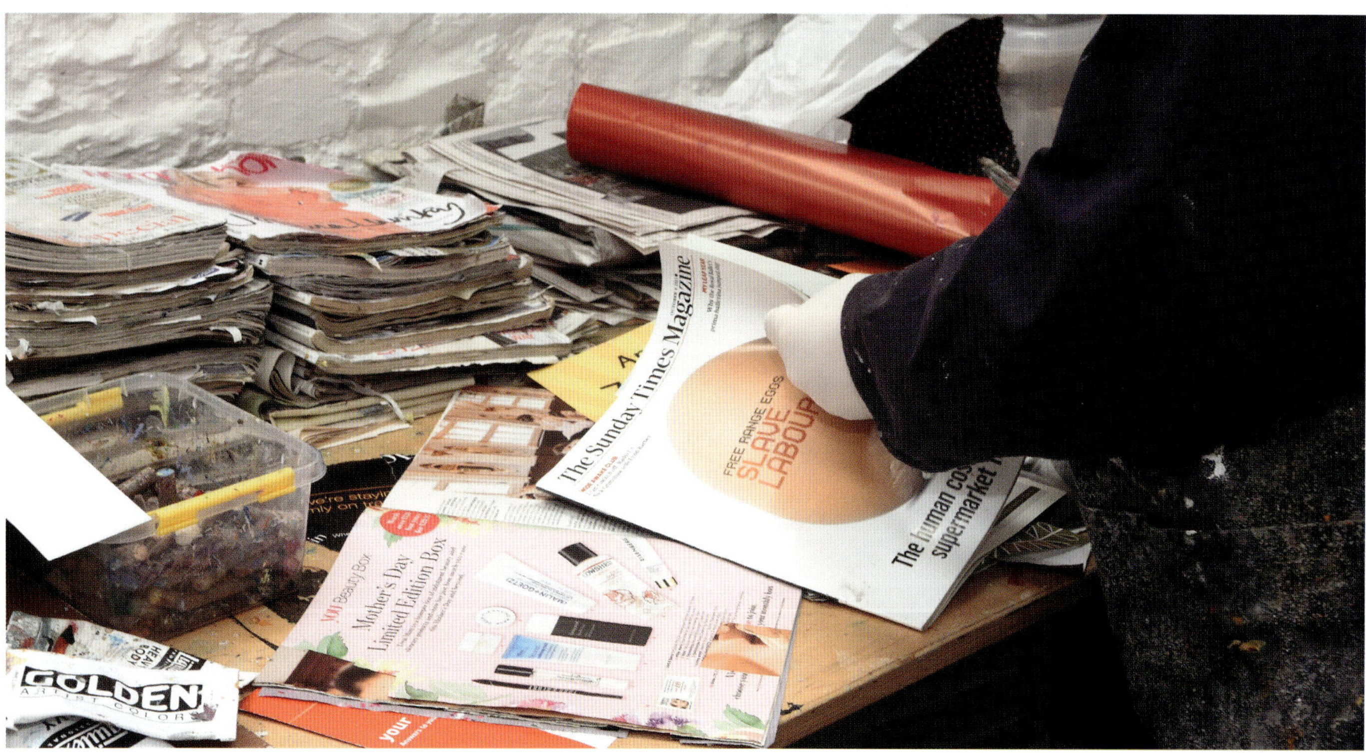

Focal point and other considerations

The focal point of a painting is the area or object within it that creates a focus of interest, drawing the viewer's attention, and this is one of the most important considerations for me when I begin a painting. As I am finding the subject and then gathering visual notes, I think about the design, focal point and emphasis of my image. For this, I often use a viewfinder to see the scene before me as an image within a frame. Note that the focal point is rarely in the centre of the composition.

Before I decide on a composition, I have to make sure that the focal point is where I want it to be, as once my painting is in progress, I keep it in the same place. As I develop the painting, I might change the object that was intended to be at the focal point, but the composition remains the same. For instance, when I plan the image, the focal point might be a boat, but as I progress, I might abandon the boat and change it to a shaft of reflected light. These sorts of decisions come with experience and confidence; when people are new to painting, they tend to try to represent exactly what they see, and some might find it hard to break away from this habit. If you're in this position, you might feel nervous about changing or substituting things, and unsure about what to rearrange, but it won't take you long to become used to 'seeing' how you want your image to turn out. After a few paintings, you will find you instinctively know what is needed – or perhaps simply what you would like – so you will make this work. From the start, you need to use a certain amount of artistic licence as you create your compositions and you will naturally consider what to include and what to omit.

From the moment I start planning, I simplify everything, paring down what I will include, but I don't strip out every element; a certain amount of depth, interest and character is necessary. This isn't an exact science, so I can't give you a formula, but hopefully, after looking at my demonstrations and having a go yourself, you will be comfortable with the concept and will find that it comes to you naturally.

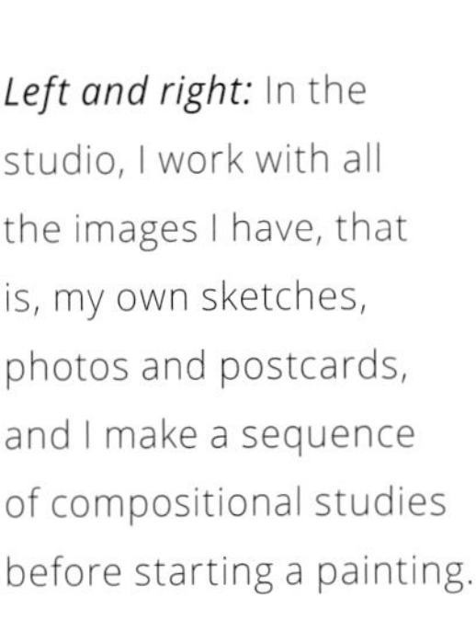

Left and right: In the studio, I work with all the images I have, that is, my own sketches, photos and postcards, and I make a sequence of compositional studies before starting a painting.

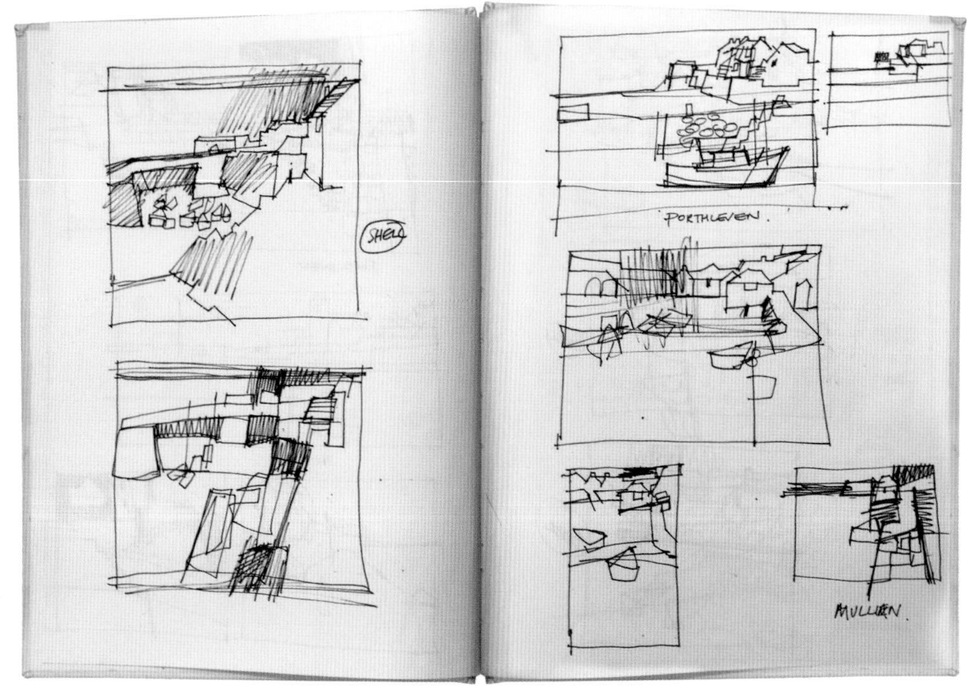

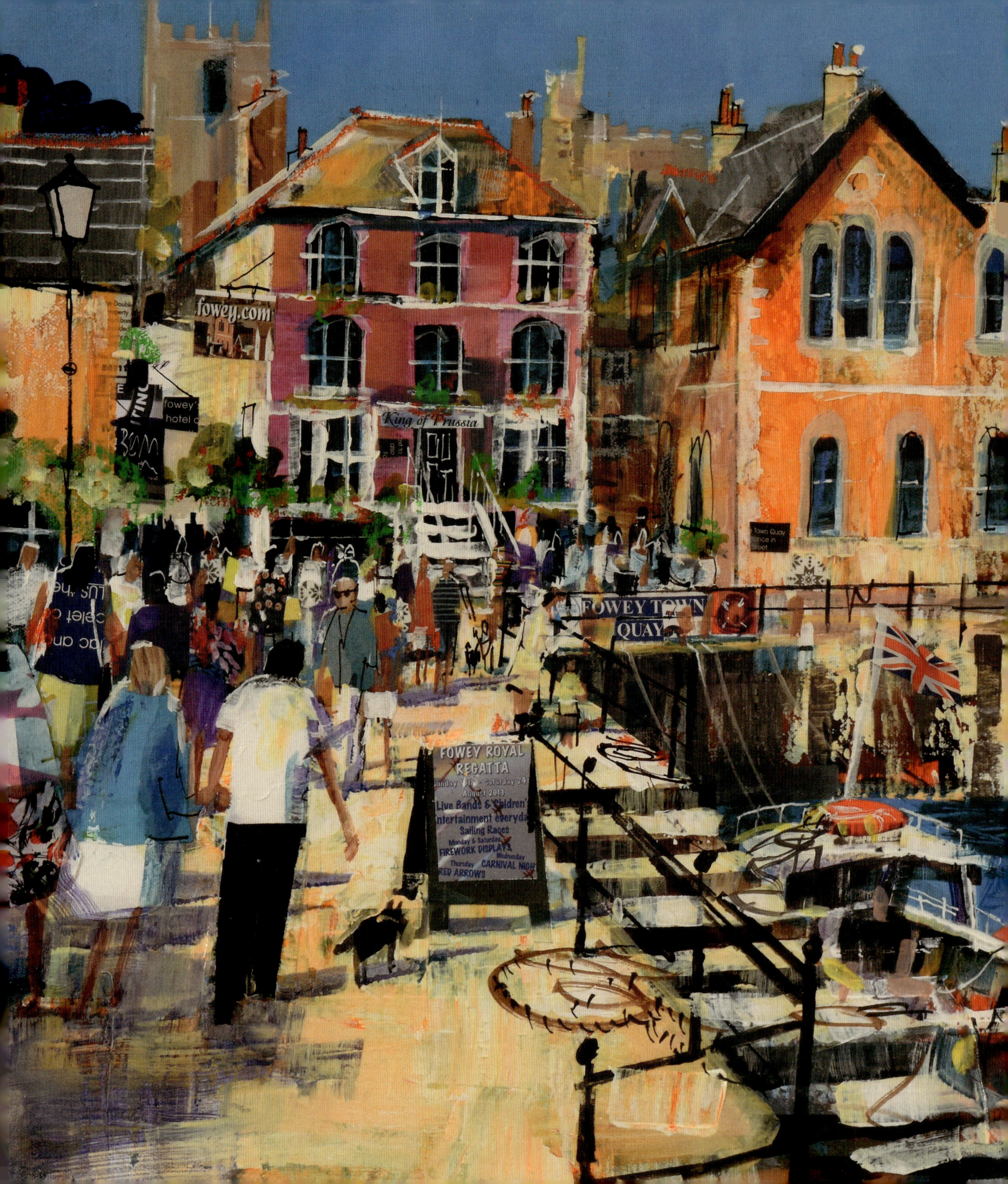

fowey.com
fowey's
hotel c
King of Prussia
FOWEY TOWN QUAY
Town Quay
FOWEY ROYAL
REGATTA
Live Bands & Children's
Entertainment everyday
Sailing Races
FIREWORK DISPLAYS
CARNIVAL NIGHT
RED ARROWS

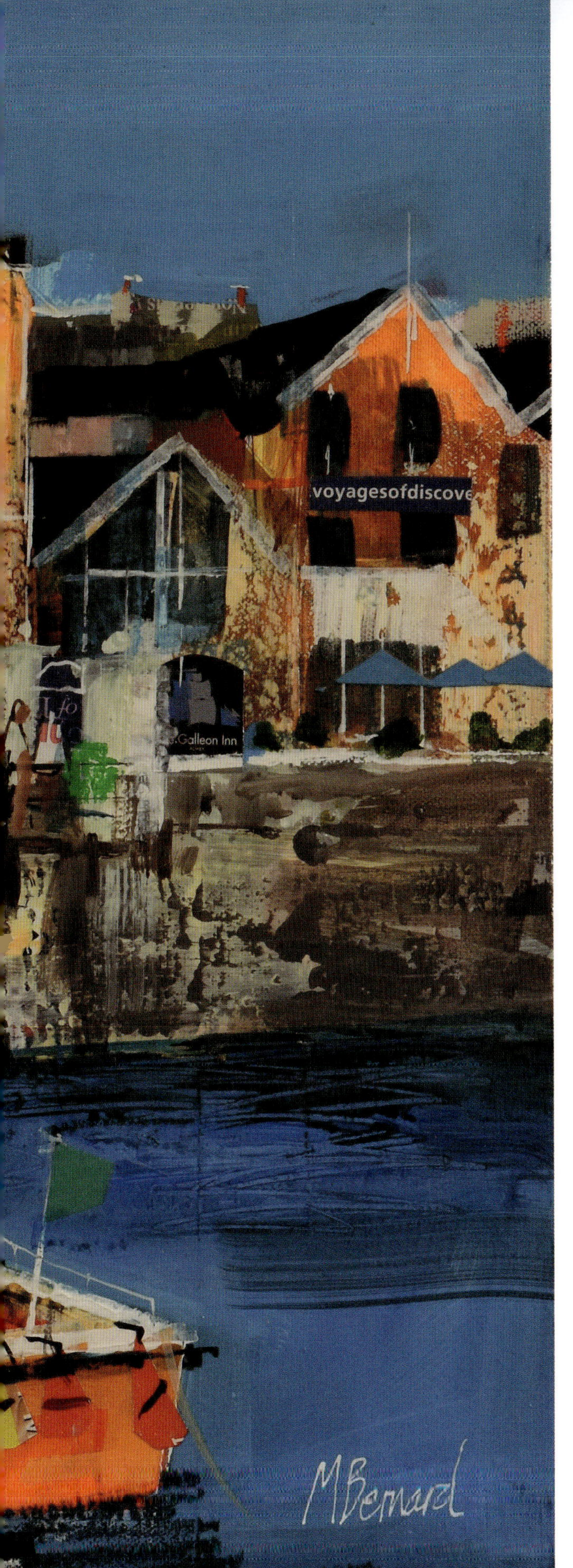

Colour and contrast

Wherever I am, I look for contrasts: in colour, shapes, tones, textures and patterns. For me, colour and contrast are two of the fundamental considerations that I concentrate on to create compelling, captivating paintings. There has to be a certain element of contrast to create a sense of drama in a painting, and I achieve this both through my use of colour and different collage materials. The range of possible papers and other materials I use for collages includes newspapers, magazines, tissue paper, wrapping paper, wallpaper and different handmade and art papers, as well as other textured, coloured and interesting surfaces such as corrugated paper, foil paper and fabrics.

As contrast is so important to me, I like to offset more exciting textural surfaces with plain papers, such as brown wrapping paper, pastel papers or white tissue paper, to incorporate both lively and calming aspects in the work. Creased, transparent, reflective or obviously textured papers will provide other interesting surface qualities to exploit – always counterbalanced by 'calmer', smoother areas. The shapes can be cut or torn. On the whole, I prefer a torn edge, as it is more in keeping with the spontaneity and expressive nature that I aim for in my paintings. I sometimes make use of the trimmed edge of a newspaper or magazine to suggest a particular vertical or horizontal division in the composition, but I seldom actually cut out shapes, because this usually results in outlines that are too rigid and defined.

Sunny Town Quay, Fowey
Mixed media, 40 x 71cm (16 x 28in)
The contrast of colours here create
a sense of vitality. In my collage, I
used words from a local magazine
to highlight the location.

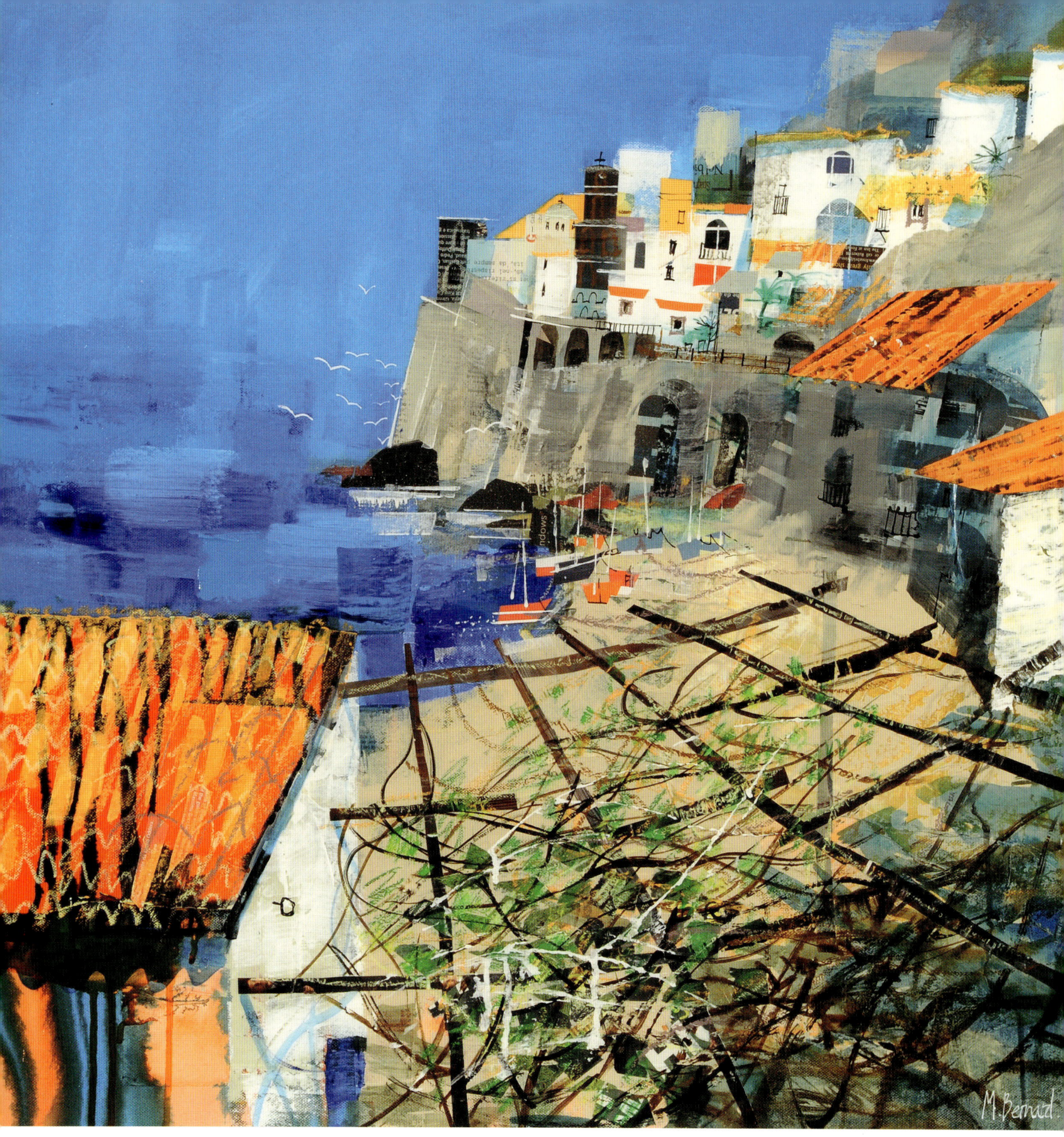

Identification of shapes and pattern

The first things I look for on arriving at a spot with the potential for a painting are the shapes rather than the actual objects. It is largely the fact that coasts provide a rich variety of interesting shapes that makes me return to these over and again. What interest me principally are angular shapes – flat shapes that are capable of being rendered in an abstract form. These are quite different from those found in a garden, for example. They are harder, with straight lines and angles rarely seen in nature. As appealing as natural shapes may be, for me they do not provide the spur that I need, and do not, in my view, lend themselves so readily to abstraction as man-made objects do.

I look particularly for boats, especially in clusters, harbour walls, jetties, silhouettes, skylines, the outlines or contours of buildings, including rooftops and chimneys, masts and sails – plus any bright colour that particularly stands out. I look for these things, not because of what they are as objects, but because they may help to create exciting patterns. So I also look for: shapes that will create a pattern, repetition, individual patterns that will combine into larger patterns, diagonals, effects of light and shade, and negative shapes, that is, the shapes between objects.

Where possible, I do a fairly representational sketch on the spot, but the design of the painting will be finalised in the studio. It is here that I will study my drawing – or photograph if I've not had time to do a sketch – to see what needs to be left out, moved or brought in to make a satisfactory composition.

Church Still Life, Fowey
Mixed media, 34 x 34cm (13 x 13in)
Don't think just in terms of the angular shapes of buildings. Here, for example, the fruits and flowers add a pleasing contrast of curves against the angles.

Amalfi Drive
Mixed media, 71 x 71cm (28 x 28in)
If a shape is needed to balance your painting then go ahead and add one. Boats, rocks, birds, shadows and so on can all be added as desired.

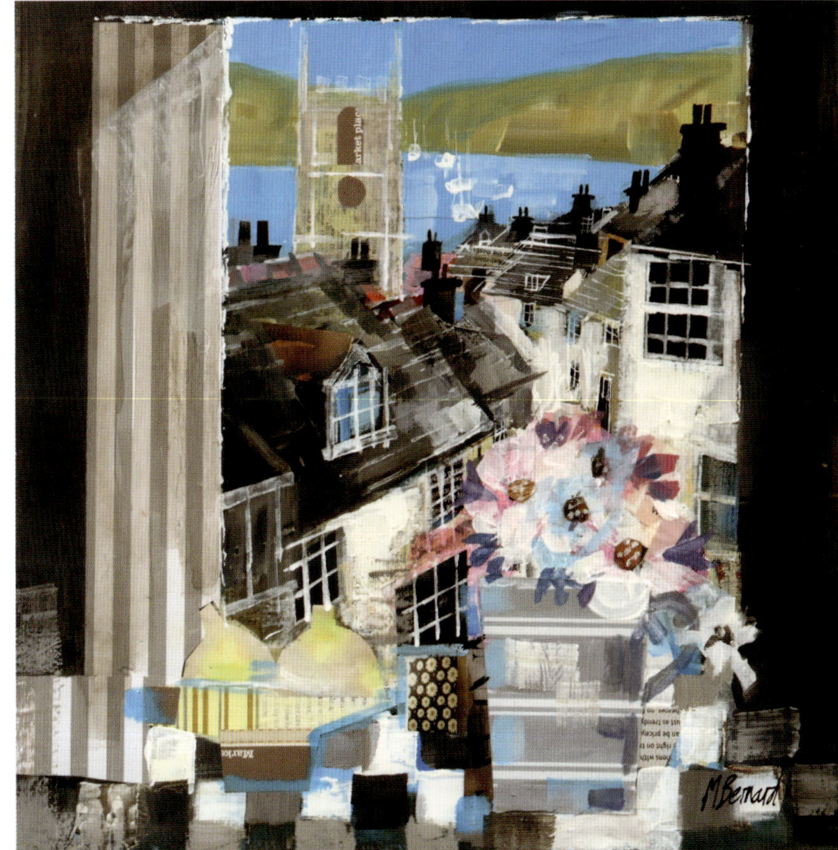

Simplification

While sketching on site helps you to connect with the scene you have chosen, it also forces you to be selective and extract information that is meaningful to you. In transferring what you have seen into a painting, you will make further choices, reducing elements and creating personal interpretations.

Simplification in art involves taking the complex details that we see around us and abridging them into works of art. Your colour palette is one place you can easily simplify your paintings. The more colours you use, the more complex they are to manage. Every additional colour on your palette introduces a vast range of colour-mixing opportunities. Sometimes this is an advantage, but in most cases, simplification of some elements allows you to create greater impact. Just a few colours on your palette is referred to as a reduced or limited palette, and working with such a palette forces you to use and manipulate every colour you can without spreading into a complicated, busy range.

When I return to the studio with the sketches I have made on location, I look at them with fresh eyes and decide which ideas look the most promising for developing into one of my mixed-media paintings. I consider what details are important, looking at each sketch in turn. For each sketch that appeals to me, I make a sequence of small studies as shown above.

Here, I use just the main elements of the subject, trying out different sizes and shapes for the painting and exploring how I can create the most effective composition. Sometimes I decide to focus only on part of the sketch, cropping out aspects and developing a painting from that, or conversely, I will expand on a place, adding or expanding on the original idea in some way.

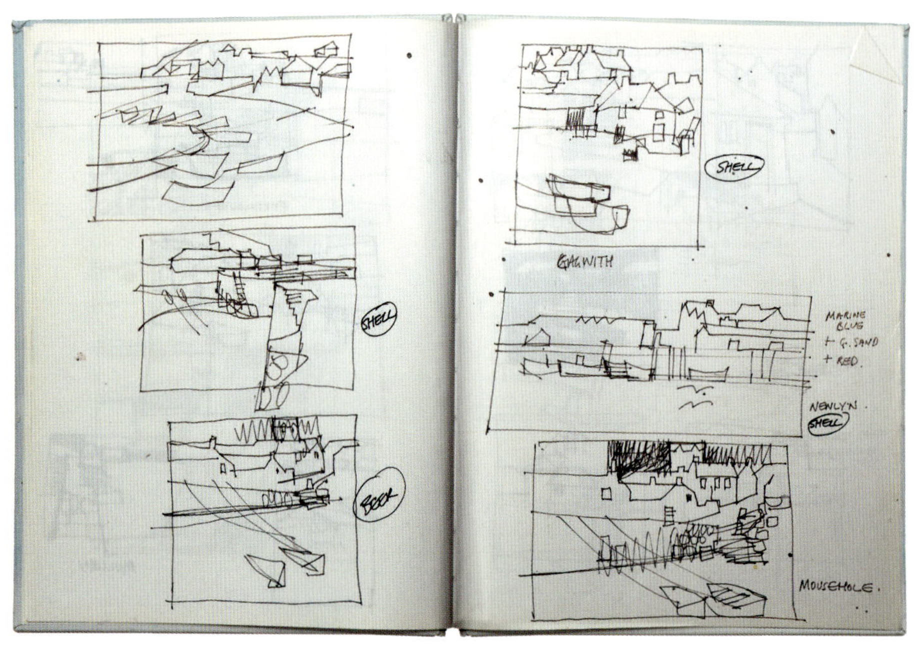

Using a sketchbook, back in the studio, I make a series of smaller sketches, simplifying what I saw even more than I did when on location.

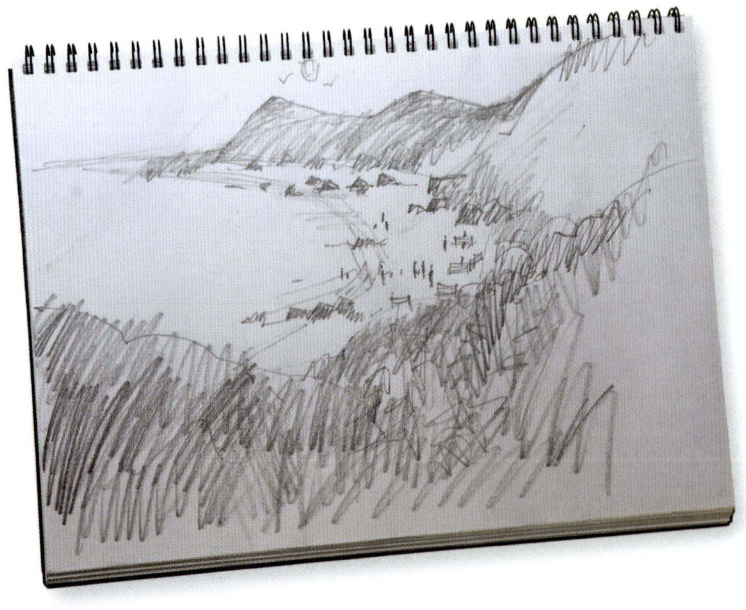

Investigation

In the studio, I use my sketches and compositional studies as preparation for my paintings. I pick out the ideas that will work in paintings. The small sketches help most in showing important areas within compositions: the main vertical and horizontal lines and shapes. In my sketches, these elements are simplified and allow me to decide where I will investigate and experiment. I only see these sketches as guides and I never start a painting by making specific drawings on my supports. You might prefer to work more carefully and to draw on your support, keeping precisely to your design, but I like to keep my options open, which is why I usually begin with a torn collage. For me, this gives me the scope to explore new ideas and keep the image fluid as I work. So I don't generally work detailed preparatory studies; they are always simplified with reduced elements in them. I prefer resolving things as necessary during the painting process.

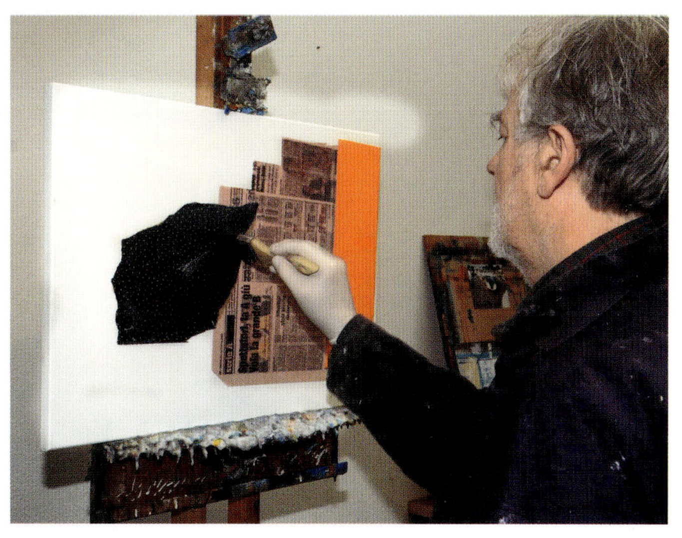

I work standing up at this point and both cut and tear paper and other collage materials. Nothing is specific, although here, buildings will go over the newsprint and the black shape will form the basis of a large rock.

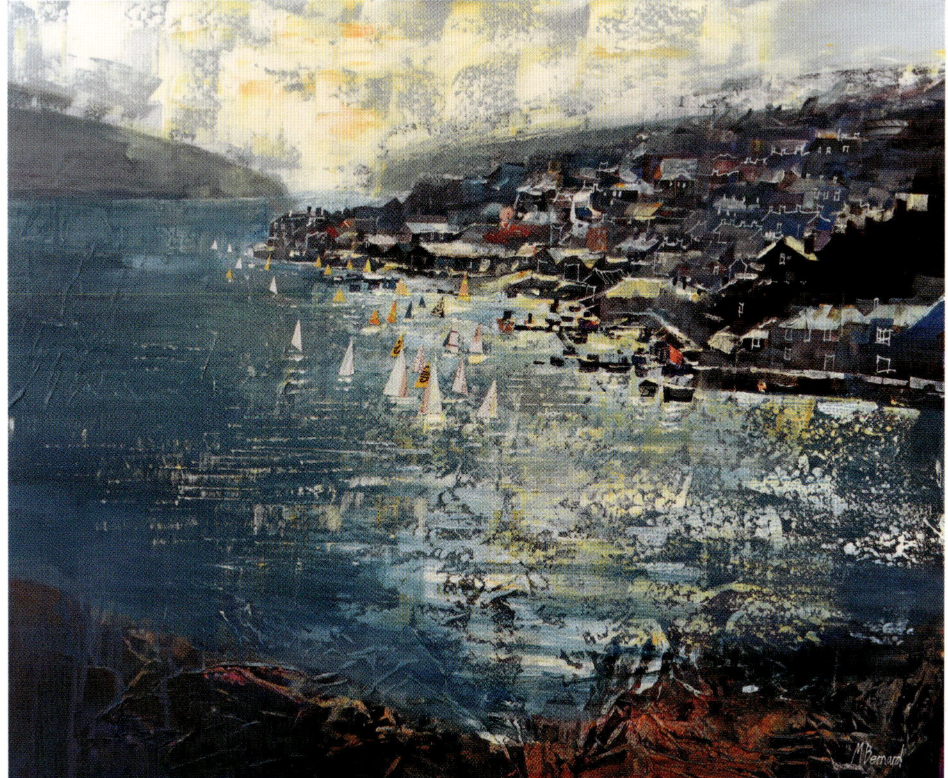

Salcombe from Snapes Point
Mixed media, 61 x 76cm (24 x 30in)
After building up the painting, I dragged thick, quite dry paint across the sky and parts of the water to create the shimmering effects of sunlight and reflections.

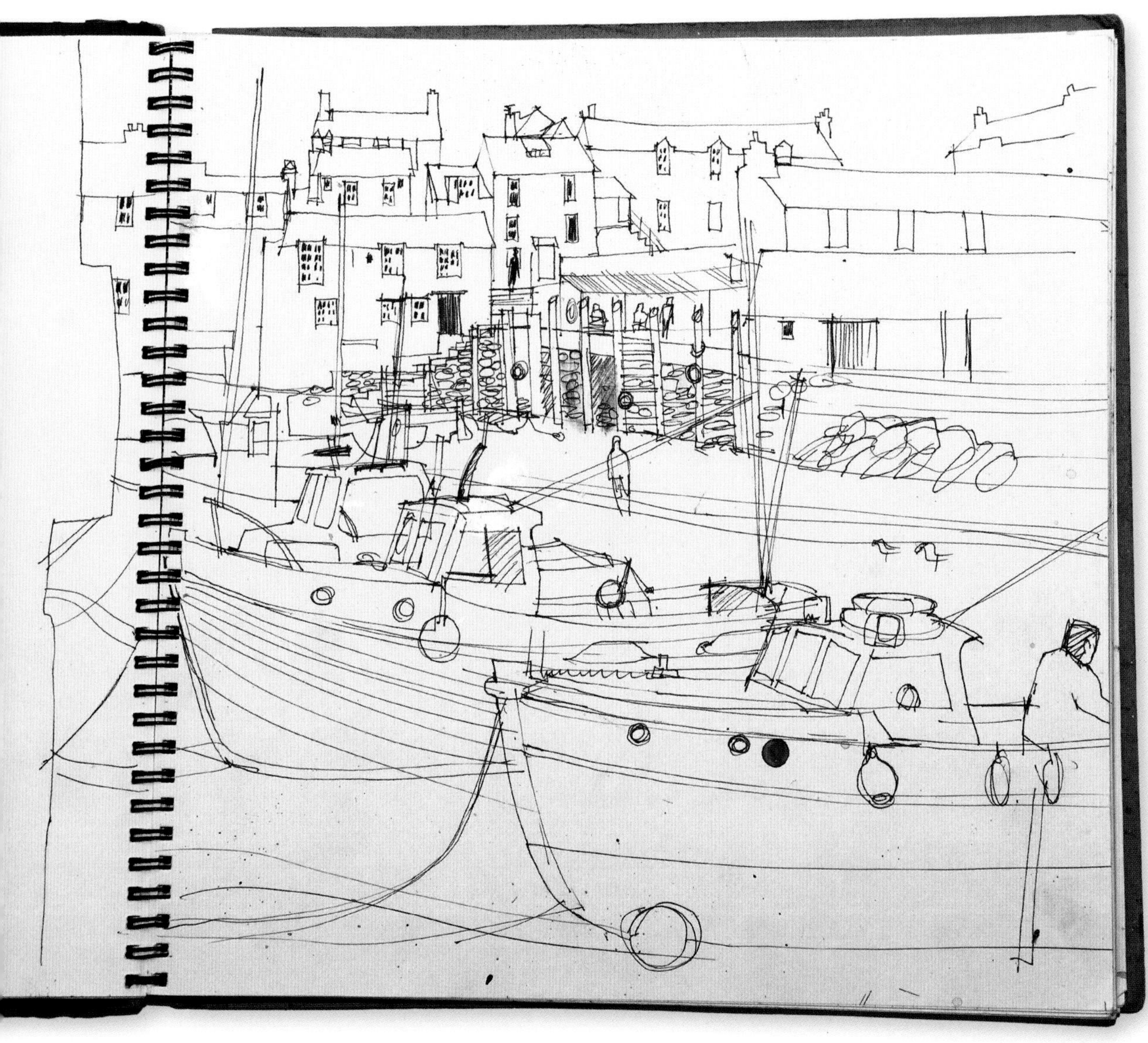

Practise drawing in front of your subject; that is, on location. In this way you will see what is important to you. I've simplified this image, making the boats in the foreground extra large for drama and omitting a bank of houses in the background. Everything is simplified, from the figures to the windows. I just wanted to capture the overall look of the place.

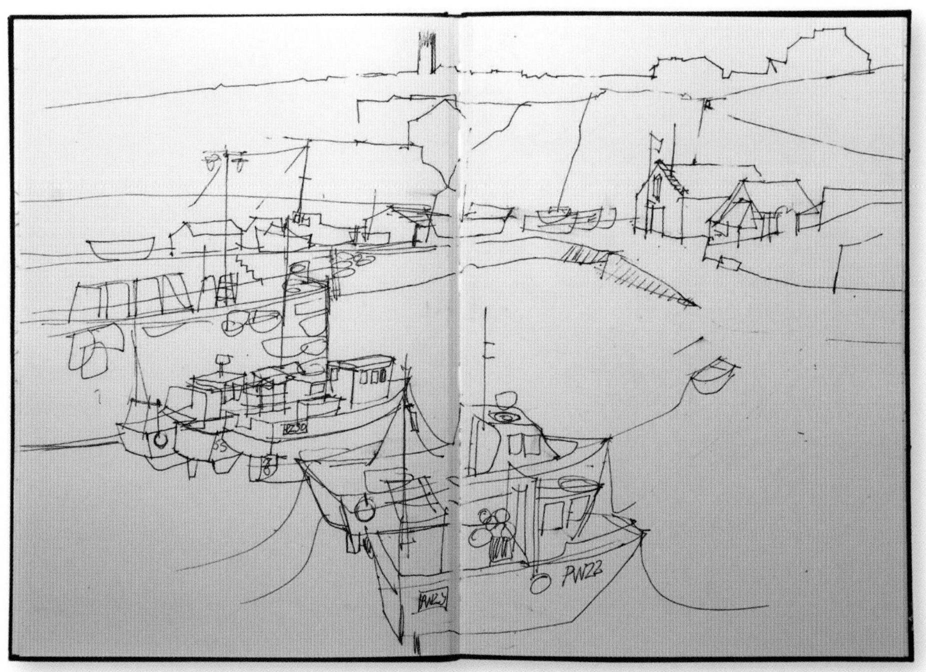

In this drawing, I used the continuous-line approach with a roller pen that was smooth and enabled me to flow across the page, linking each element. If you look closely, you will see how I've linked the rope to a boat, then the line links straight with another boat and so on. It honed my attention, ensuring that I would only include what was really important and omit what was less significant. Ultimately, it will make for a stronger painting.

In the small thumbnails, the lines refer to actual objects but they become more simplified, geometric and less about the real world, more about suggestions to evoke the idea of a place rather than rendering every nuance and detail.

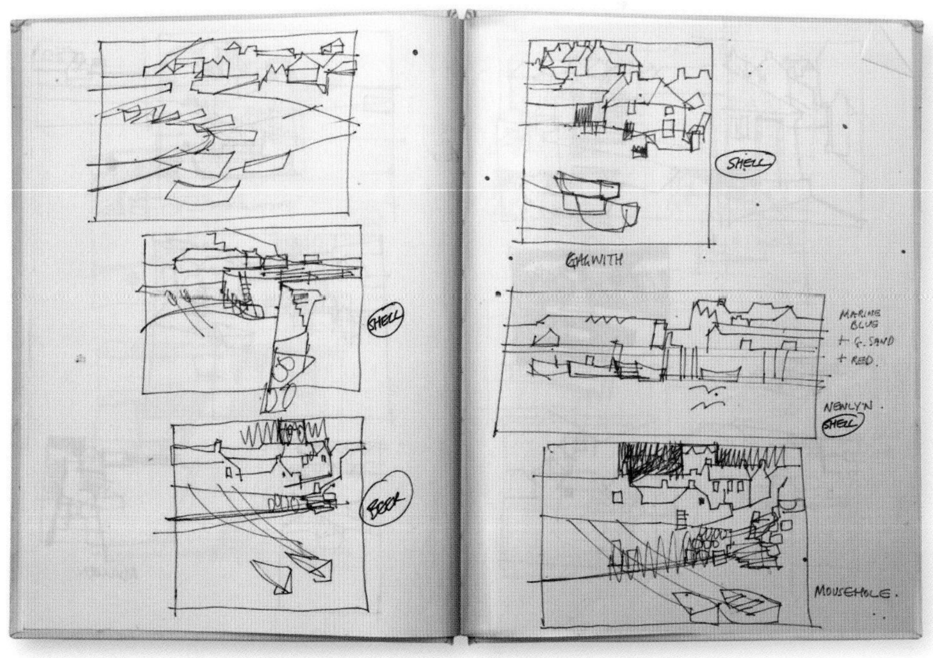

Experimental exercises (2)

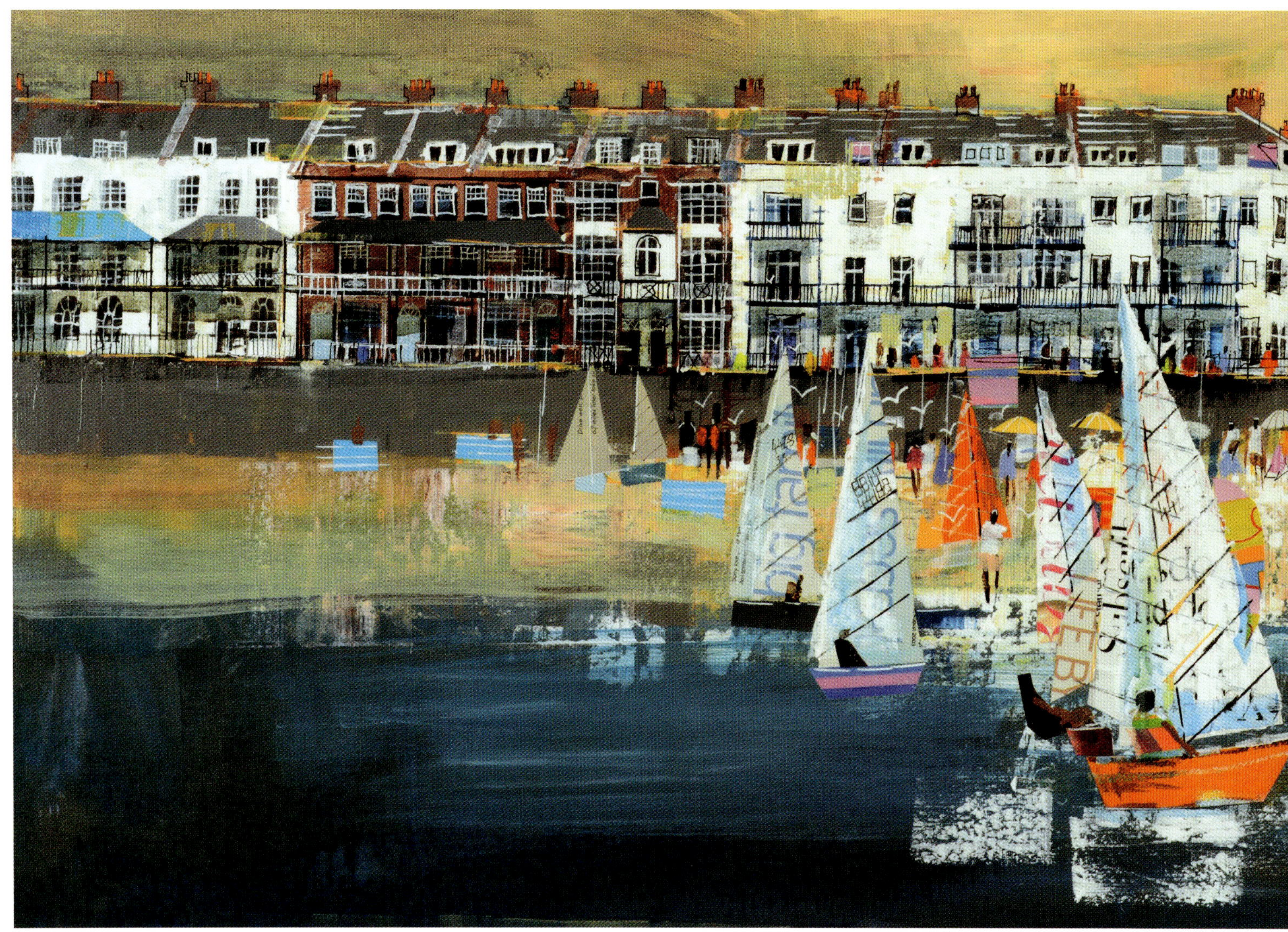

I use pieces of card like a brush. You can see in this painting where I've used the edge of a piece of card and the flat of it. The thin, straight lines are where I've used the edge and smoother slabs are where I've used the flat of it. You should practise this as you will hopefully find it as liberating as I do. It forces you to simplify the image and to move away from including too many details. Also, the angular shapes you can achieve pleasingly echo some of the ideas you see in Cubist paintings.

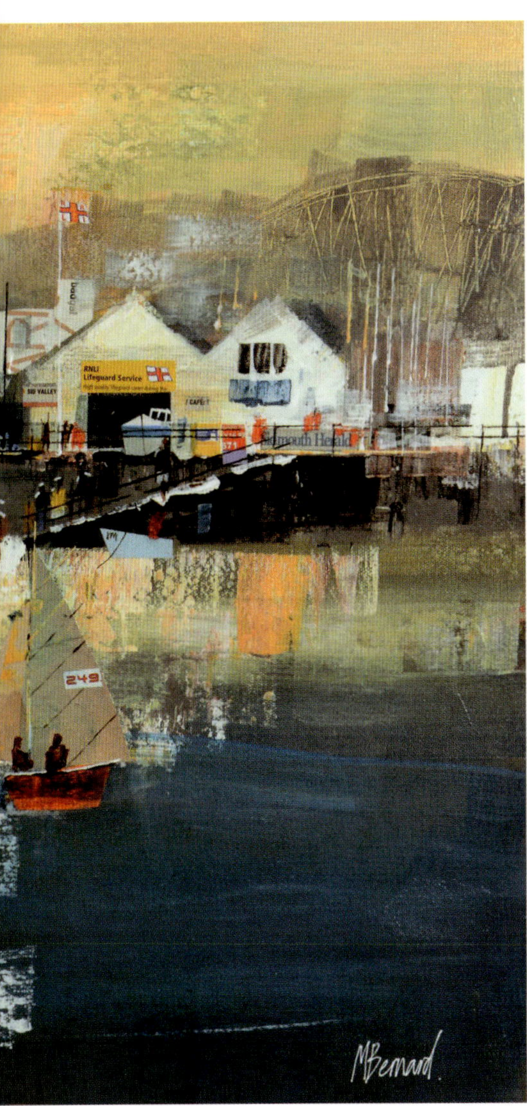

Sail boats, Sidmouth

Mixed media, 51 x 102cm (20 x 40in)
Printing and scraping paint with card
produces lavish marks that add dynamism.

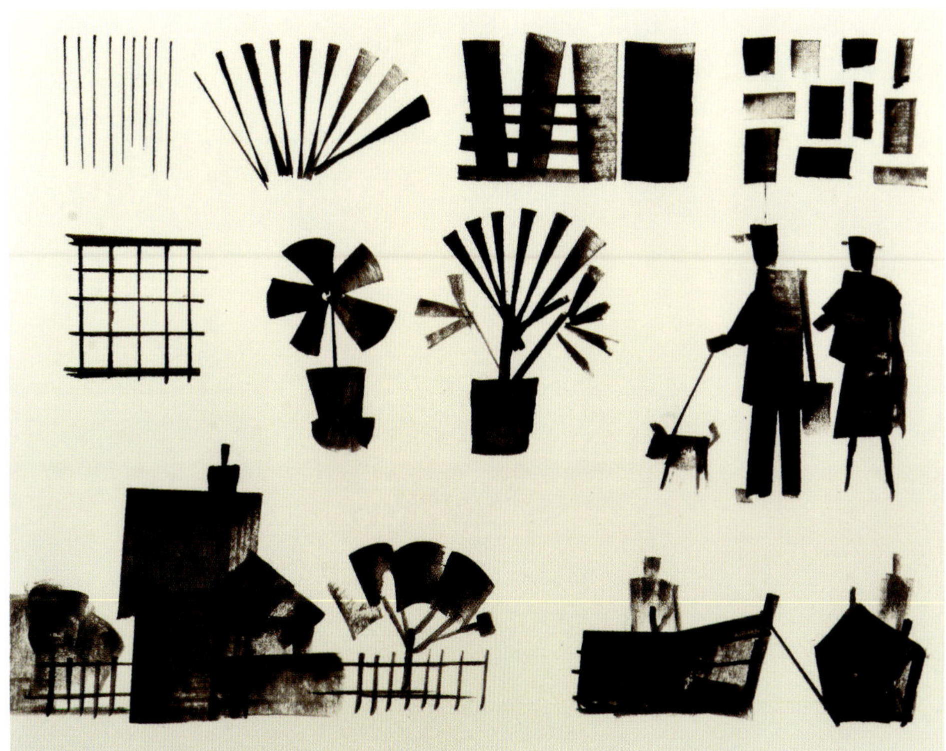

You can see on this sheet how I've applied
black ink with pieces of card and how much
expression I can achieve this way.

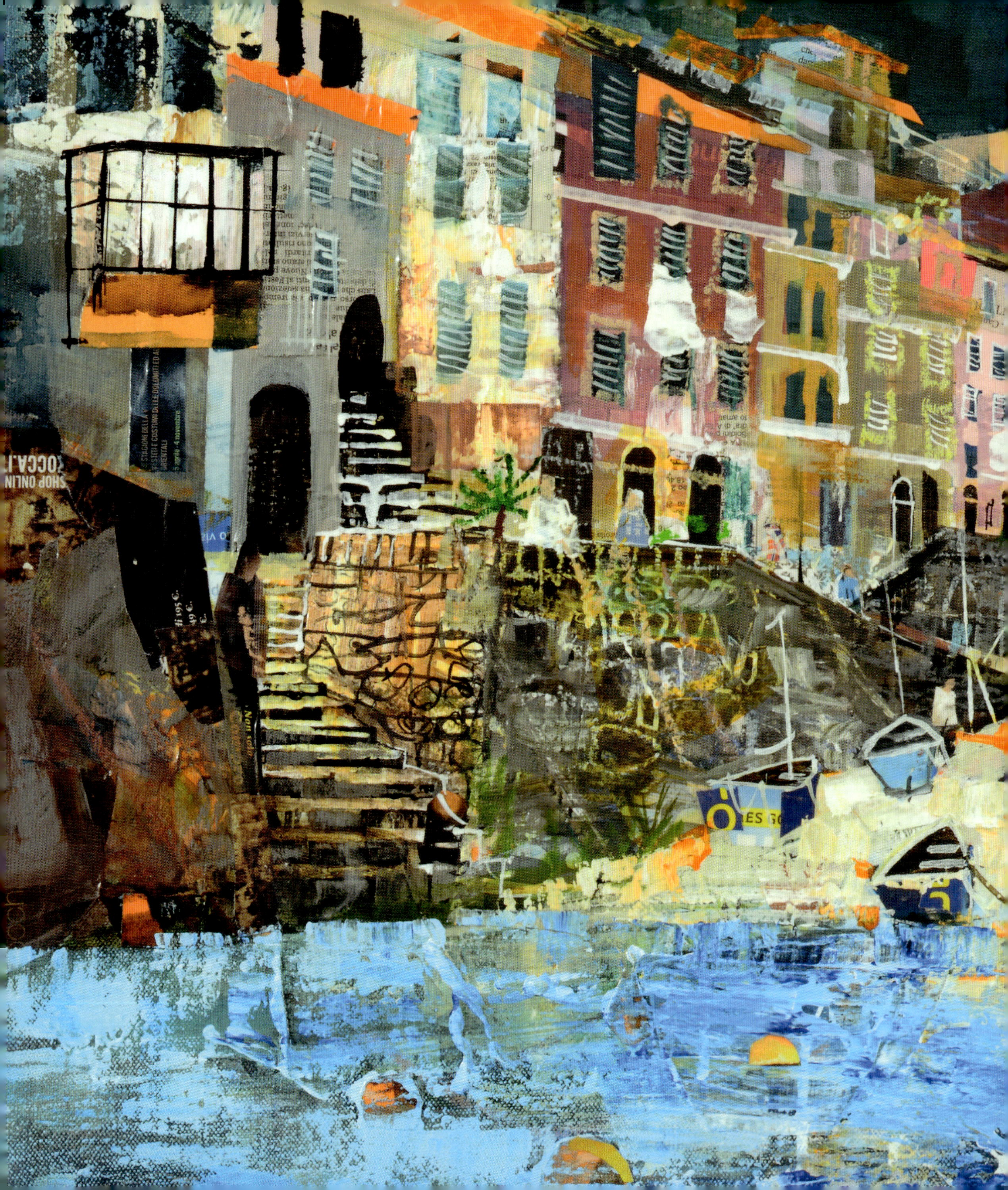

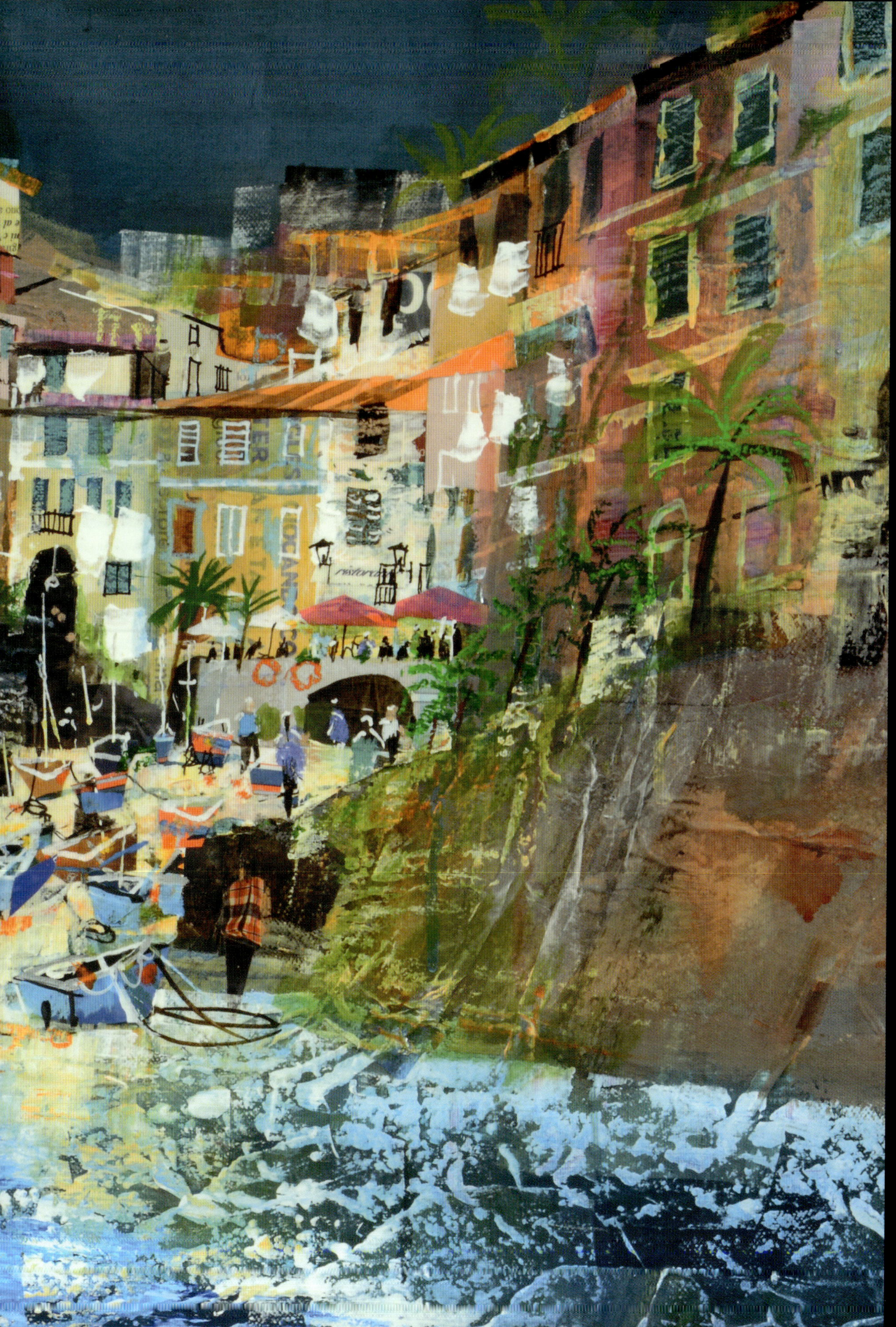

2

Palette: Materials and Combining Media

All my paintings are representations of places, but with my own personal interpretations of those locations. My belief is that the best paintings convey both the atmosphere of their subject and the artist's individual response to them. I try to ensure that each painting has impact for the viewer, that it attracts interest and provides something thought-provoking and stimulating to look at. To do this in a fresh way with each painting, new ideas should be introduced. For instance, a different combination of materials in a work can keep everything fresh by creating texture and different points of interest. Sometimes I work quickly, selecting my materials instinctively, while at other times, my approach is slower and more considered.

Working with mixed media has many advantages. Being able to create interesting colour and textural effects keeps everything exciting for me and – hopefully and even more importantly – for viewers. Using different materials allows me to interpret the various surface qualities in direct ways. I understand that a beginner to this approach might feel a bit daunted by the wide range of options using different materials and techniques, but there is no need to be. Many students I have introduced

to this way of working have found it quickly becomes invigorating and motivating. I have never had any difficulties with mixed media and I always encourage artists to try it for themselves. Of course, it takes time to develop confidence and ways of working using this approach, but the more you experiment, the sooner you will become proficient in the method and develop your own style and preferences.

Two main approaches always work for me. Along with collage, I either use water-based or oil-based media, not both together, although I do use oil pastels over acrylics. I usually work with acrylic paint, acrylic inks and/or oil pastel. You may have your own preferred mix of materials, but if not, try starting with pen and wash, diluting the ink well and building up broad areas of colour in this way. Watercolour and gouache are also good to start with, but acrylic might be too quick-drying if you want flexibility. The best way to understand how different paints work is to experiment with them so you become familiar with their strengths and weaknesses and also discover what you like and dislike about them. Before you do anything, take time to play around with different media, trying them out in your own time without giving yourself the added pressure of having to create an image.

Previous page: **Riomaggiore, Cinque Terre**
Mixed media, 51 x 76cm (20 x 30in)
Layers of collage, paint and oil pastel create a rich and interesting image that keeps the viewer intrigued; the more you look, the more you see.

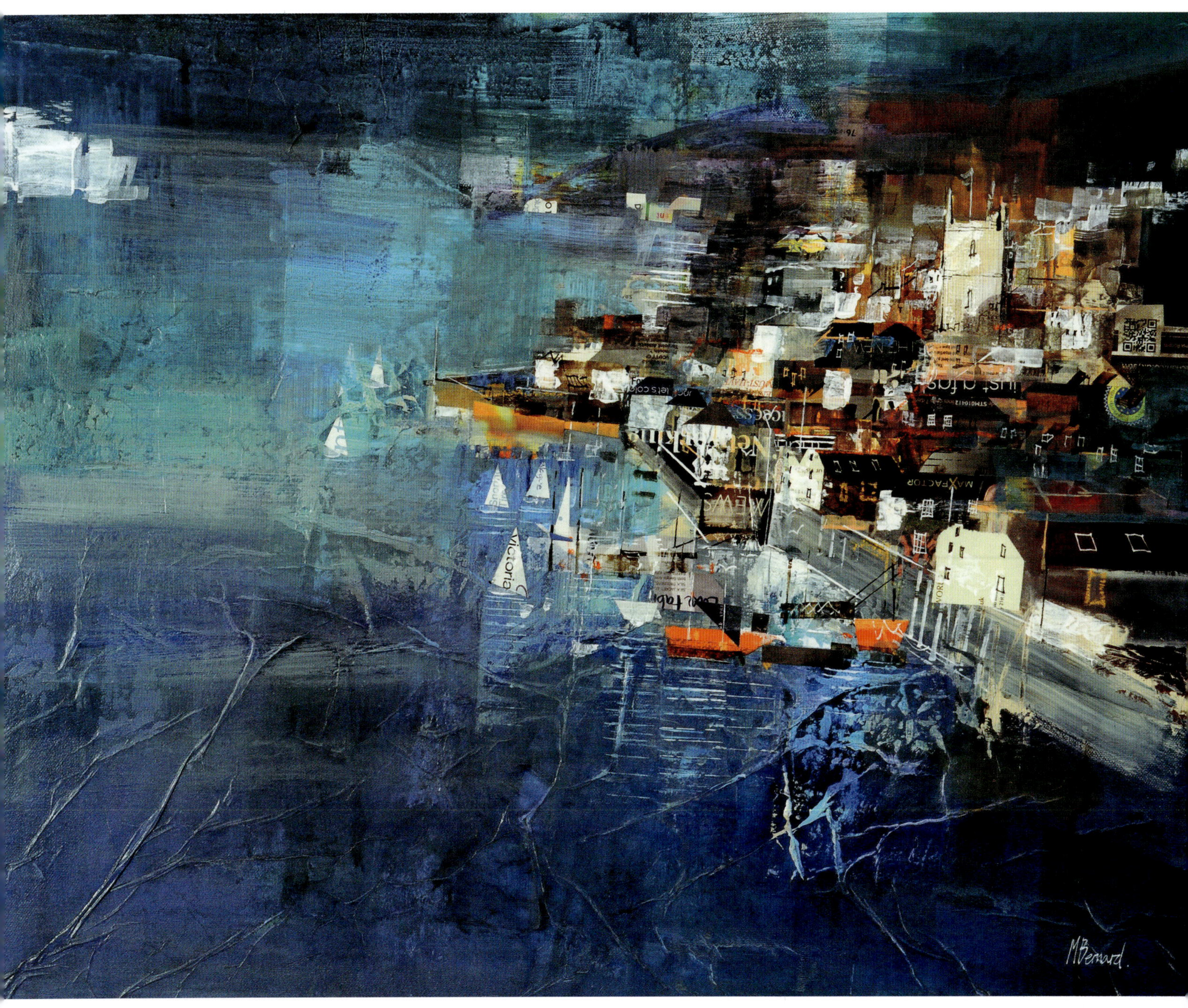

Fowey Viewed from Bodinnick

Mixed media, 61 x 76cm (24 x 30in)

Layers of mixed media create an interesting image that
suggests the location without being too descriptive.

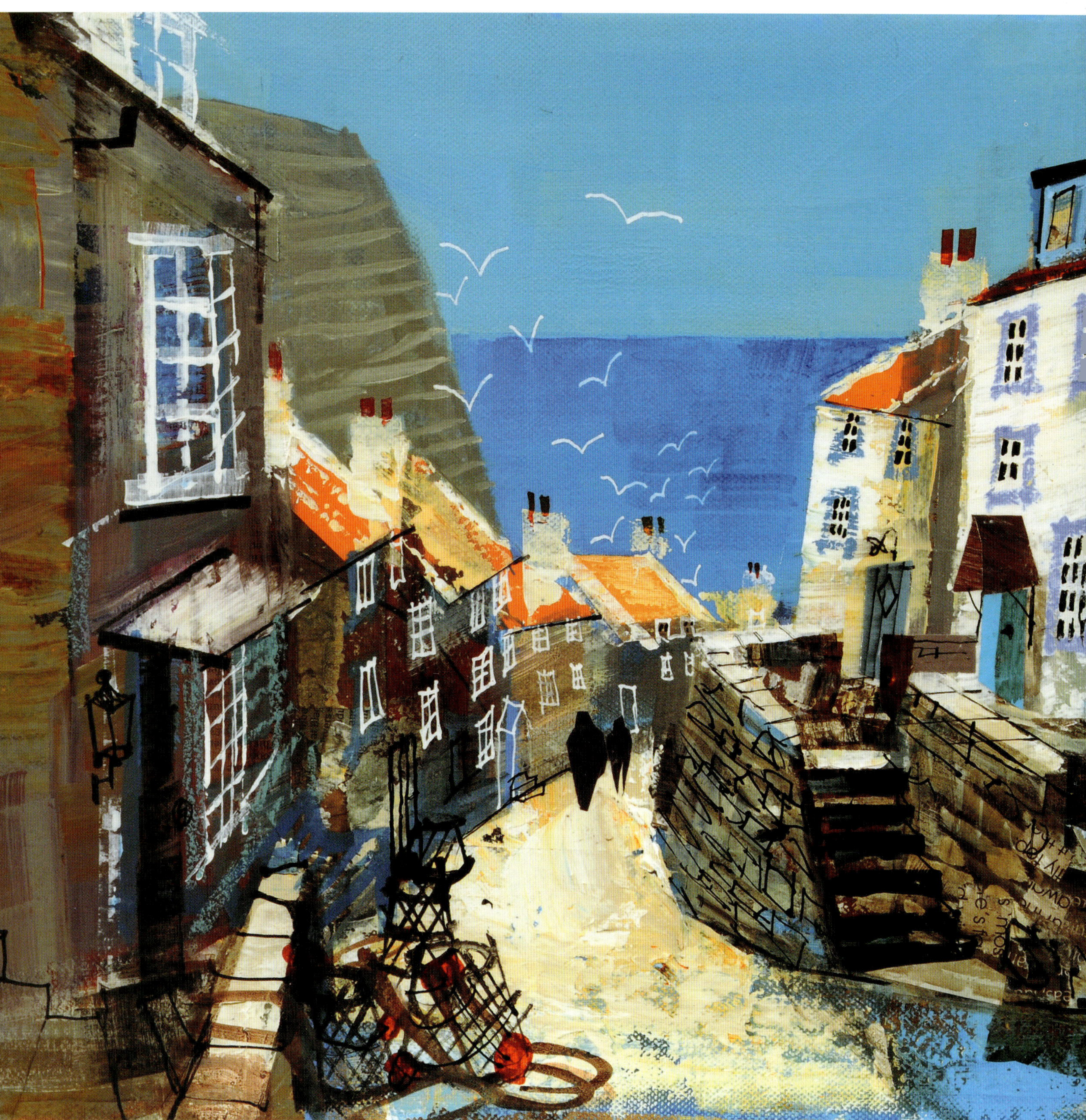

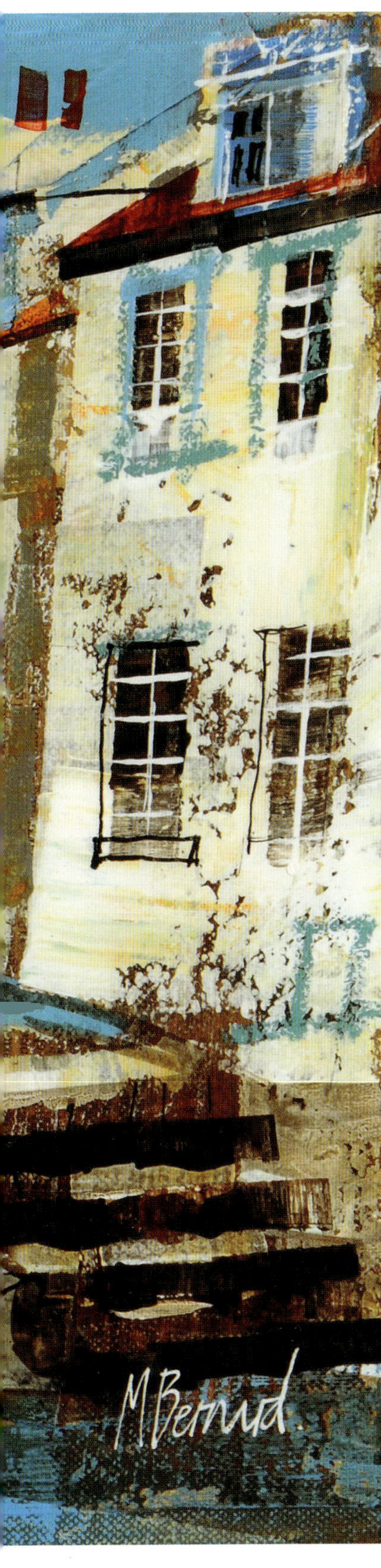

Lane to Harbour, Staithes

Mixed media, 30 x 40cm (12 x 16in)
Here the contrast of blue sea against the white houses was created by studying the negative shapes around the houses and their rooftops.

Honing things down

I always work with a reduced or limited palette, at least to begin with – because my interest in surface qualities could make the image too 'busy' if there are too many colours as well. So my overall colour palette is nearly always simplified and reduced down (see pages 44–45 for more on this). This also prevents any muddying of colours. Too many colours can become simply a range of greys and browns.

I usually use acrylic inks these days and in a variety of ways, including diluted to create subtle washes, 'neat' to create thick, textural effects, and also in layers of glazed colour, building up opaque coverings, or finely tuning transparent veils of colour, all depending on the looks I am aiming to achieve. Of course, most of this is reliant on my experience and knowledge of the properties of the paint or ink. I do similar things with other types of paint or oil pastels, for instance. By experimenting, you will soon learn the characteristics, strengths and limitations of each type of media you use.

I began using 'ordinary' inks and worked a lot in pen and ink, then started experimenting with coloured inks and then with watercolour. However, I found that watercolours often went muddy, while acrylic inks didn't. With acrylic inks, the colours tend to get brighter as you mix them. Most are semi-transparent and even when layered, instead of getting darker or muddier, they just become richer.

Looking at a scene, I see it in terms of abstract shapes. To do this, for example, when you look at a harbour, although there will be boats there, don't necessarily 'see' boats, but instead, see them as a series of shapes, perhaps a cluster of smaller shapes against larger shapes that indicate rocks, the harbour wall, the sea or the sky. Try not to be literal; if you find yourself struggling with this, remove a bit of detail.

Although I'm obviously interested in the subjects I paint, they actually become secondary. More important to me will probably be things such as negative shapes, dark and light, or contrasts, for example. I'm more interested in pattern than details, such as clutches of rooftops or windows around the harbour, or repetitions in buildings and so on.

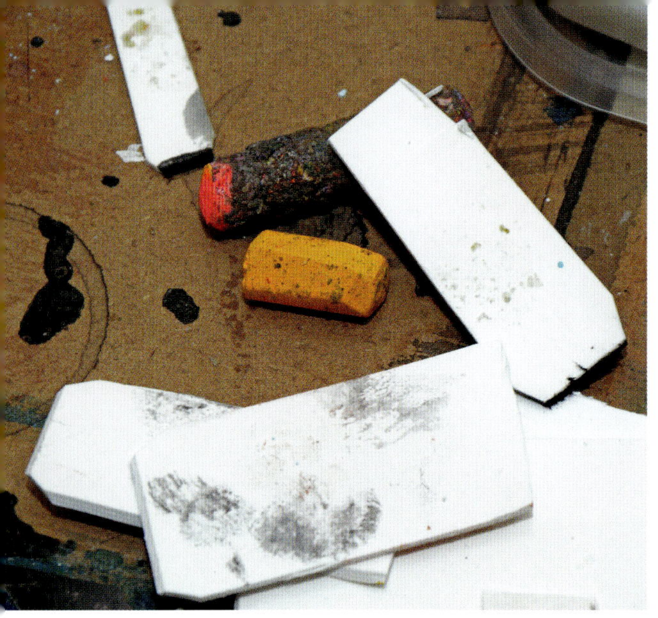
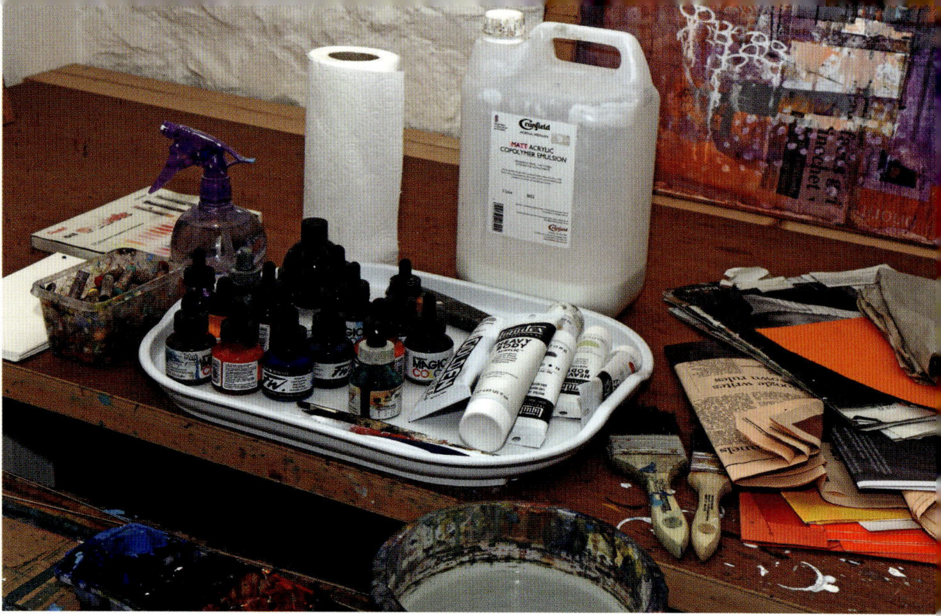
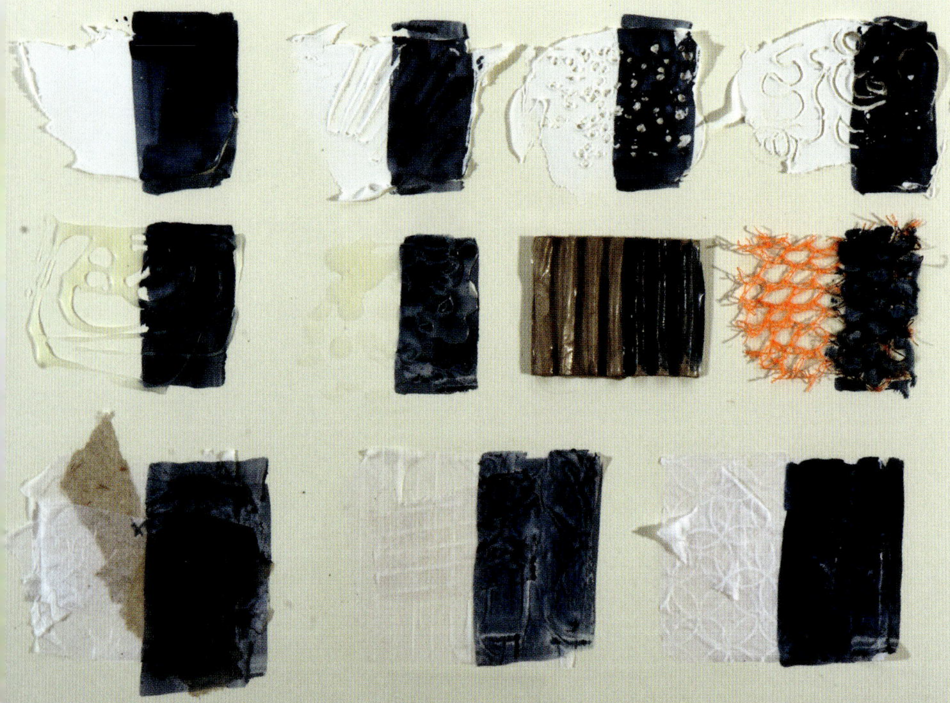
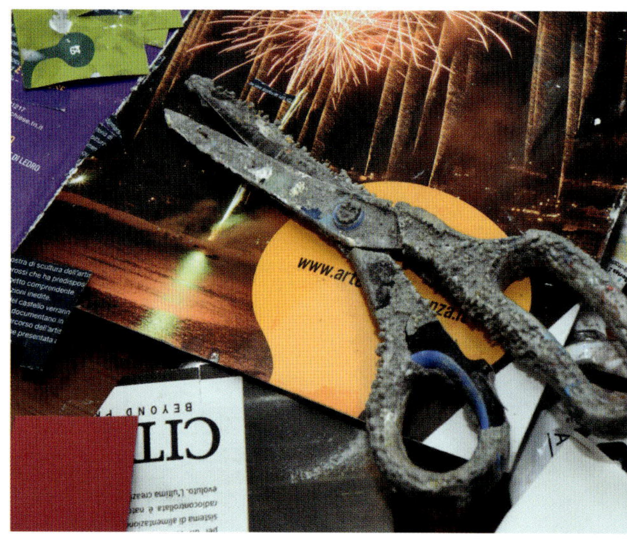
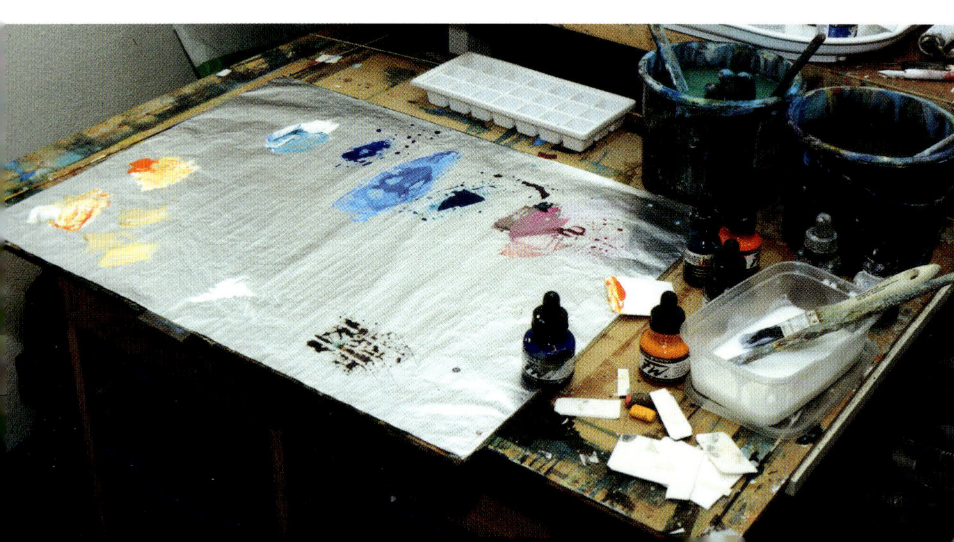
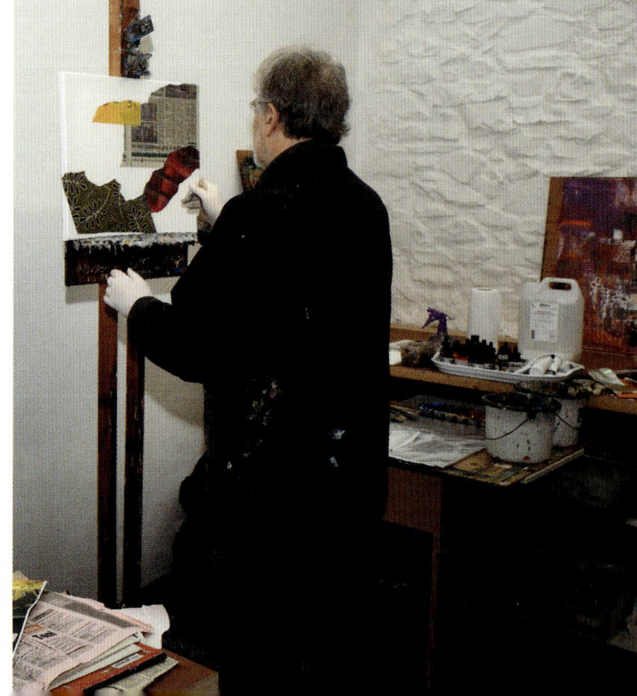

Materials and tools

On the whole, after years of experimenting, I have discovered what materials work for me and generally use these most of the time. There is enough variety and scope for me to be able to create hundreds of paintings that all look completely different, using variations of the following:

Collage materials

The range of collage materials I use is quite extensive. I work with newspaper, magazines, leaflets, tissue paper, brown paper, pastel paper, wrapping paper, wallpaper, handmade and art papers. Sometimes I might tear shapes from holiday brochures or magazines that include bright colours or visual textures. At other times, I crease, crumple or scrunch paper or use reflective, shiny or textured papers that provide different and often interesting surfaces and elements in the final painting. I usually offset these livelier collage materials with plain brown paper or something equally 'quiet'. My glue is copolymer matt emulsion.

Paints, etc

Acrylic inks are available in a wide range of colours and are incredibly versatile and adaptable. They are extra-fluid and the pigments are rich and intense. They are intermixable, and dry quickly to a water-resistant finish. I mostly use colours from the Daler-Rowney FW Artists Acrylic Ink range, the Magic Color range or Liquitex acrylic inks. These are ideal for use with a dip pen or for using in transparent or translucent washes. I also make thicker textures using Liquitex titanium white – always buy a large tube, as you'll need it – Liquitex unbleached titanium, Liquitex parchment and oil pastels. You can use the rich, intense colours of acrylic inks directly from the bottles or dilute them to achieve more subtle hues. You can create watercolour-type effects with a lot of dilution. Or you can create different effects with brushes, sponges, or by spraying, stippling or spattering. Often, I use the edge of a piece of card to create lines or drag it to create flatter marks. I also sometimes draw into the wet acrylic ink using a piece of card, fingers or a stick.

One of the advantages of oil pastel is that it will exaggerate whatever surface texture is beneath it. So it works very well over collage and paint, and if I have crumpled some collage materials, then oil pastel is one of the easiest ways to enhance that textural effect. Oil pastel is great used in stick form, on the tip or on the side.

Painting materials

I use a selection of acrylic brushes – including flat varnishing brushes, drawing pens (dip pens), offcuts of mount card (for drawing and applying paint) – plus printing rollers and toothbrushes. My palette is made of tin foil wrapped over a board.

Left: I use a range of materials and mediums in my work, including a variety of different papers, pastes, glues and acrylic inks.

Paints and palettes

In about 1992, I made a radical change from painting in oils to using mixed media and especially acrylic inks. It began for me in my attempt to get my students to experiment and simplify their work. Most people want to express every colour they see, but for me, creating a mood and atmosphere is more important. If you think about painting anything, the colours you see can have different sources: they can be actual or local – for example, the local colour of a terracotta roof is terracotta; reflected – such as a grey or blue sky or a silvery moon reflected on the sea; or shadows – such as purple or green shadows cast by some rocks. But this can become complicated, so to make your image sing, I suggest you do what I do so often myself: select any two colours to start with and make your

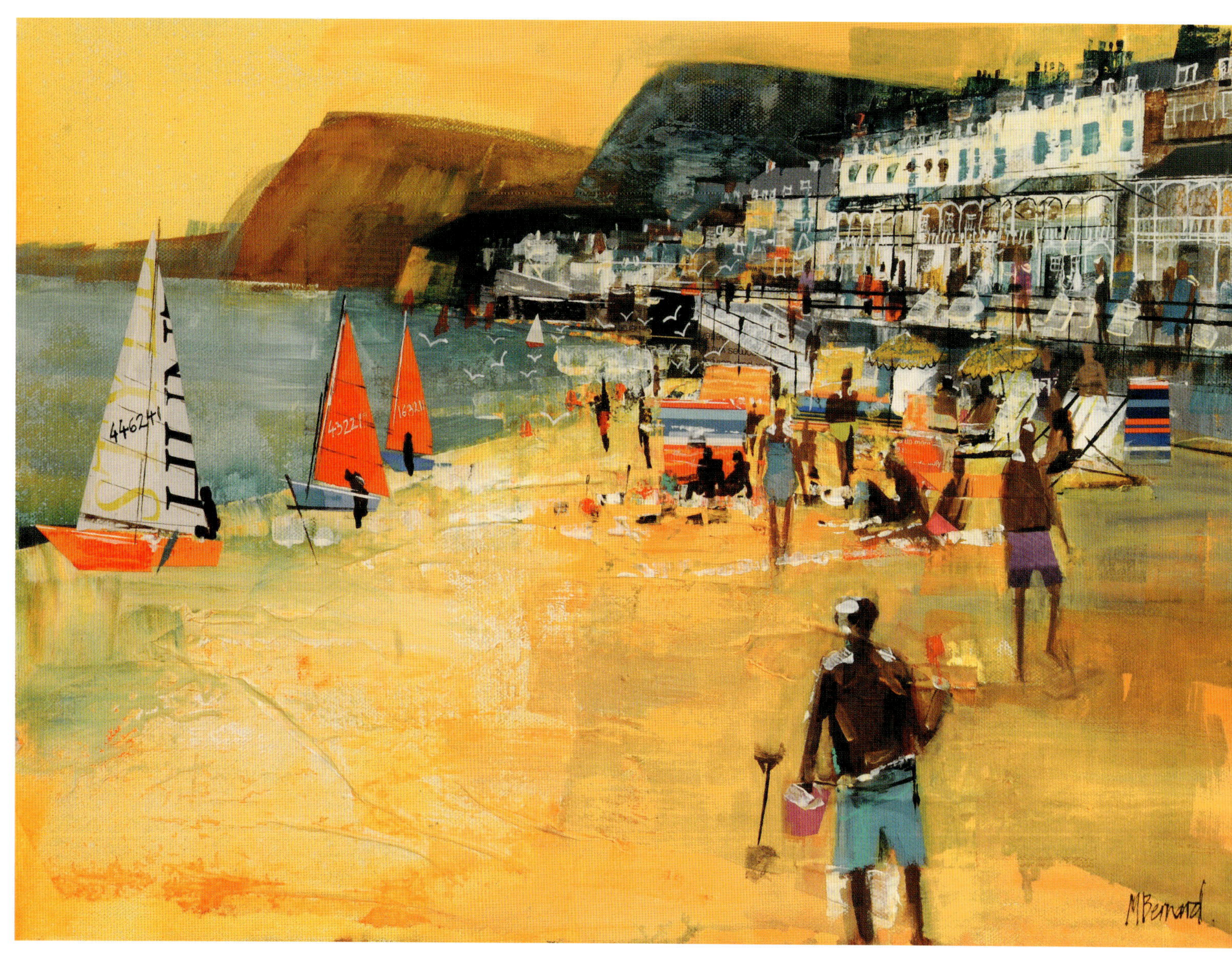

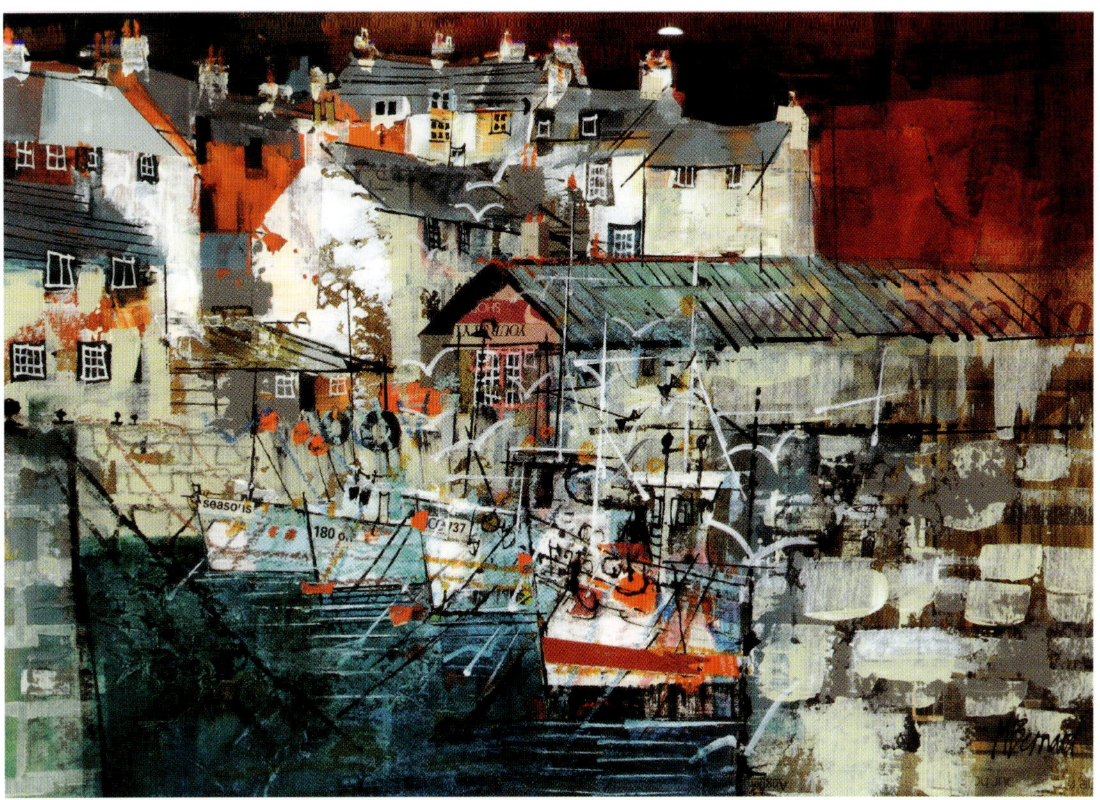

Harbour Entrance, Polperro
Mixed media,
34 x 24cm (13 x 9in)
The red sky against the grey rooftops conveys an arresting sense of drama.

painting with them. For instance, blue and orange, or blue and brown, or perhaps green and violet, or grey and red. Be ruled by these restricted colour combinations rather than literally trying to replicate what you see. This restriction will force you to become more creative and your results will be more interesting and atmospheric. When I used to give a lot of demonstrations at art societies, I always asked the audience to give me two colours and I would make my demonstration using just the two they selected for me. I made it work because it had to!

It's all about being disciplined to convey a sense of spontaneity or urgency. The two colours are made with my paints – or inks; collage, of course, allows me to add further colours and dimensions to each image. The two colours prevent anything from becoming too busy or fussy. I still work in this way for myself in my studio, beginning with any two colours. Sometimes I'll choose complementaries; that is, colours that contrast and come from opposite sides of the colour wheel, such as red and green, or violet and yellow. Then sometimes I work with harmonious colours, such as blue and green, or violet and red. Then again, sometimes I use two neutrals, such as brown and grey. It's surprising how each one turns out. Although most people love colour because it's uplifting, often the paintings that I've built up out of greys, perhaps with a spot of red, are the most popular. As I often paint the same or similar subjects from the same location, I usually try not to use the same colour scheme for a similar scene.

Bathers, Sidmouth
Mixed media, 40 x 56cm (16 x 22in)
The two main colours used here were yellow and blue with some bright spots of colour used elsewhere to enliven the composition.

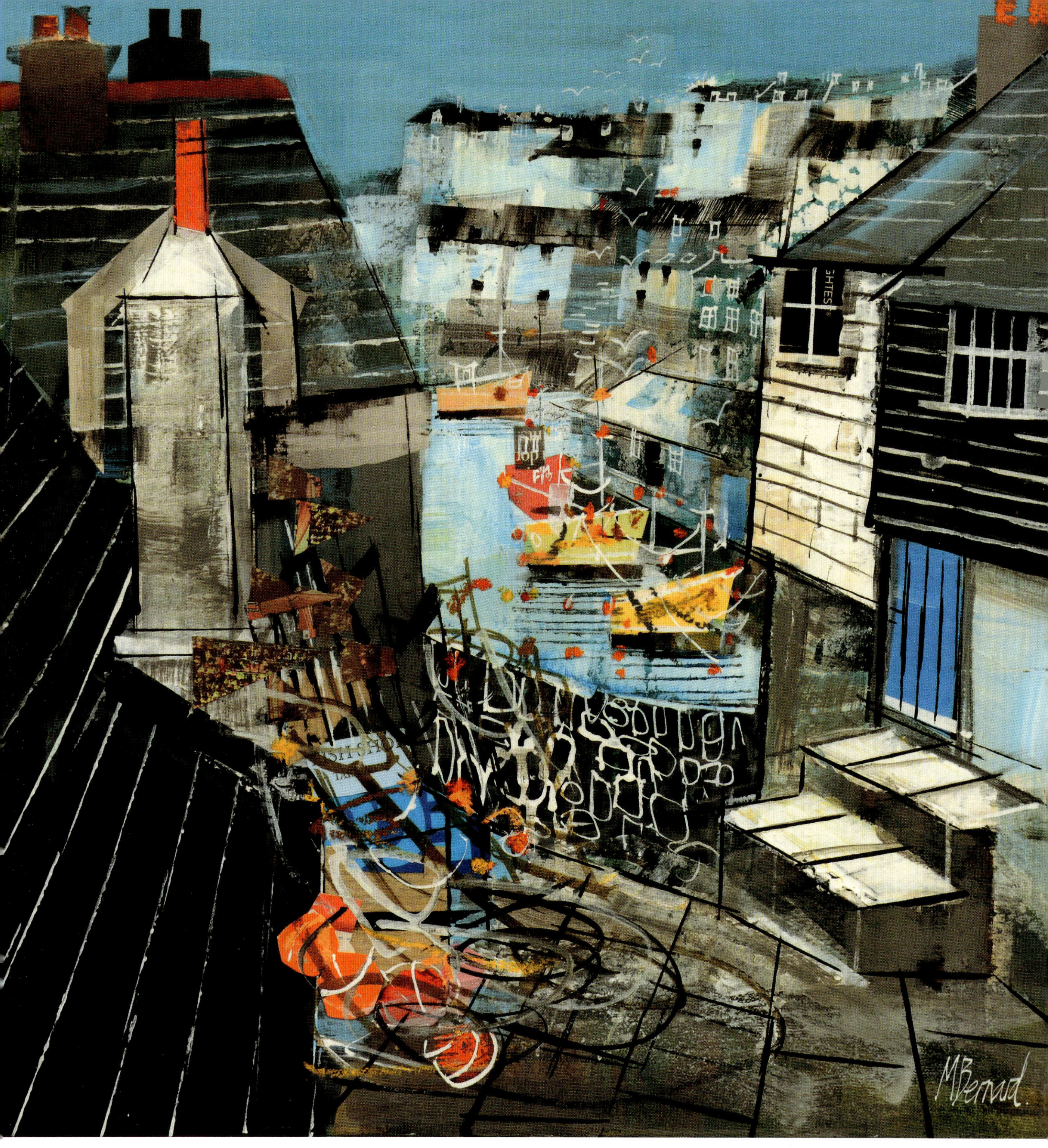

Collage

As with my two-colour system, another method that I developed from the demos I've often given at art societies is starting with a random collage. This was a deliberate move away from pencil outlines, which I find too restrictive. To get the same sort of loosening up, I often encourage beginners to work with decorating rollers or wet-in-wet watercolours to begin with – almost anything, really, to get rid of the stark white of the paper. This can be a way of replacing collage when you are starting out. Another way of working is to do a random collage – just stick down materials as you please – and then find a scene that fits it well, or that you could make work.

For some time, I had a period of painting with watercolour washes, then cutting the paper in half and using the two pieces for two entirely different paintings. On these, I would sometimes add some collage, but now I tend to use collage in the first place. I establish the main shapes with materials that work well together, such as magazines, silver foil and newsprint. The main sorts of things I base these large collage shapes on could be harbour walls or buildings and so on. At this stage, I'm looking for divisions, such as between a cliff and the sea, or the sea and a cluster of boats. I stick these general shapes down using copolymer emulsion, which is a binder for acrylic paint that works well at holding down the collage and isn't too thick. As mentioned, I make these main, inexact shapes by tearing, or less often cutting, then sticking them down. Then I let that dry and drag a big brush across the work with my two colours. It's all very instinctive and spontaneous. This method has evolved for me through my years of experience, but anyone can do it. You have to be positive about your decisions – what you will put where, how big your shapes will be on your surface, what colours and tones you will use and so on.

Working on demonstrations in front of audiences also taught me that with people watching and working to a time limit, I had to make things work! And I learned that your first, instinctive decision is usually the best. So don't dwell or dither – be definite and go for it. Give yourself a time limit to get this first stage down – and time yourself; stick to it. Try to find ways of imposing restrictions on yourself and this will bring out your natural spontaneity.

Left: **Inner Harbour, Polperro**
Mixed media, 40 x 40cm (16 x 16in)
I used lighter colours between the buildings to convey a sense of distance and allowed my collage shapes to remain on show for this image. The lighter colours have the effect of atmospheric perspective, capturing a sense of three dimensions.

Right: **St Michael's Mount (Summer)**
Mixed media, 40 x 61cm (16 x 24in)
While most of the vibrant effects in my paintings are made with acrylic inks or other paints, collage enables me to create shapes that explain the entire composition.

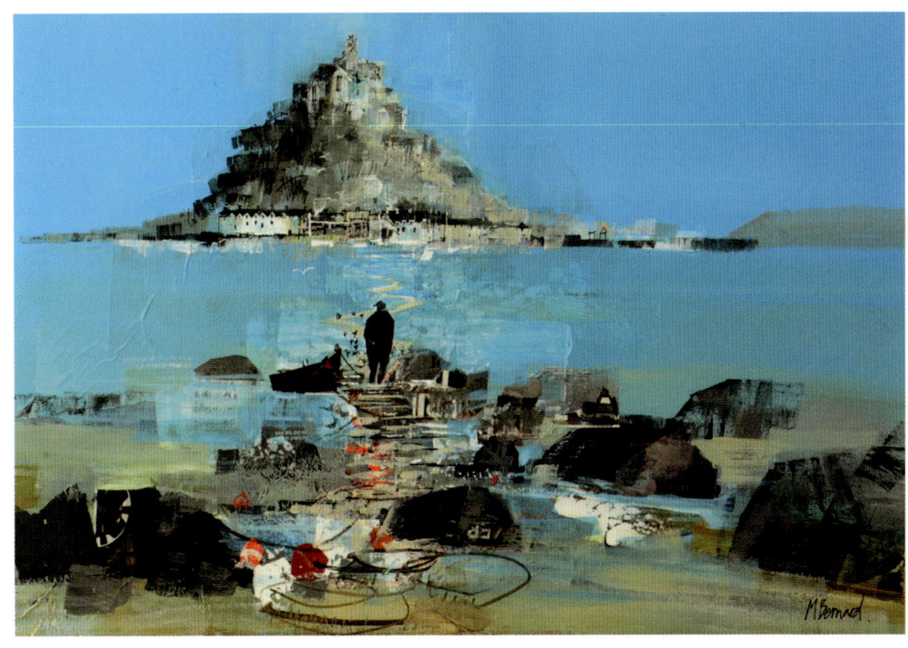

Releasing the inner child

I've found what I like and what works for me. However, sometimes I like to experiment with other things, such as different means of applying paint. Or sometimes I change my viewpoints, or I try different materials, such as netting or corrugated card. You could do the same; use things such as big brushes or pieces of card to drag your first layers of paint across your collage, for example. My studio is fairly tidy and organised so I know where things are, but a lot of my collage materials end up on the floor and sometimes, later, I find things that I dropped at an earlier time for another painting, and I use these unexpected things on impulse. However, I rarely use found objects such as shells or sticks and so on. Yes, I'm always seeking textural effects, but for me these have to be non-identifiable in my paintings.

By being organised with my collage materials in my studio, I know exactly where things are and this gives me freedom to tear or cut shapes in an instant, which suits my impatience and I find liberating. It's the most enjoyable part of the work for me, really; I work instinctively and tearing or cutting shapes and textures gives me the opportunity to play like a child. Then I go through the next, more soothing, process of sticking all the pieces down.

The collage must be dry before starting on the next stage, but then I will often wet it by spraying it with water to allow the ensuing paint to blend and merge. I apply acrylic ink using bold, loose marks, loosely and intuitively in order to attain what you might call 'happy accidents', which create a semi-abstract, soft-focus appearance, encouraging the viewer to engage his or her imagination and see beyond the subject. I dilute the acrylic medium with water for use with thin papers, but apply it undiluted for gluing materials such as corrugated card, mountboard and fabric.

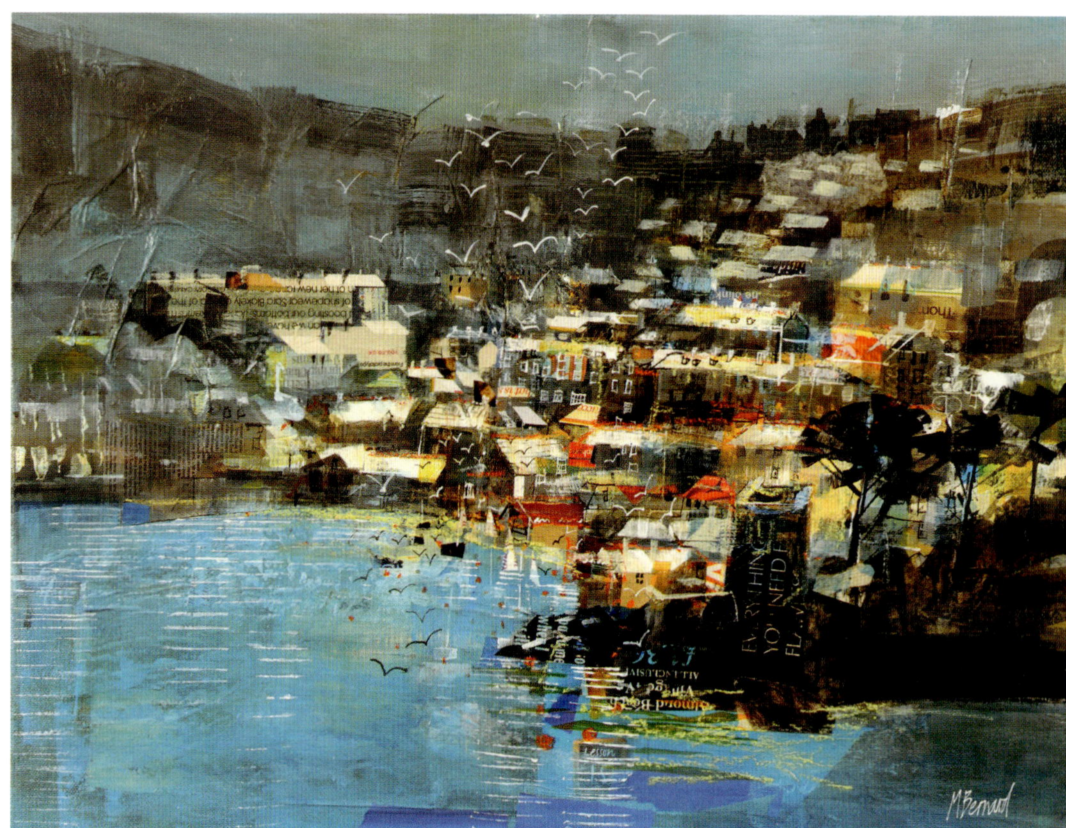

Summer Light, Polruan
Mixed media,
46 x 61cm (18 x 24in)
You can see here how I often use the words on bits of magazine or newsprint in my collage. By placing the lettering upside down it isn't used to be read, but to add a further dimension and sense of texture.

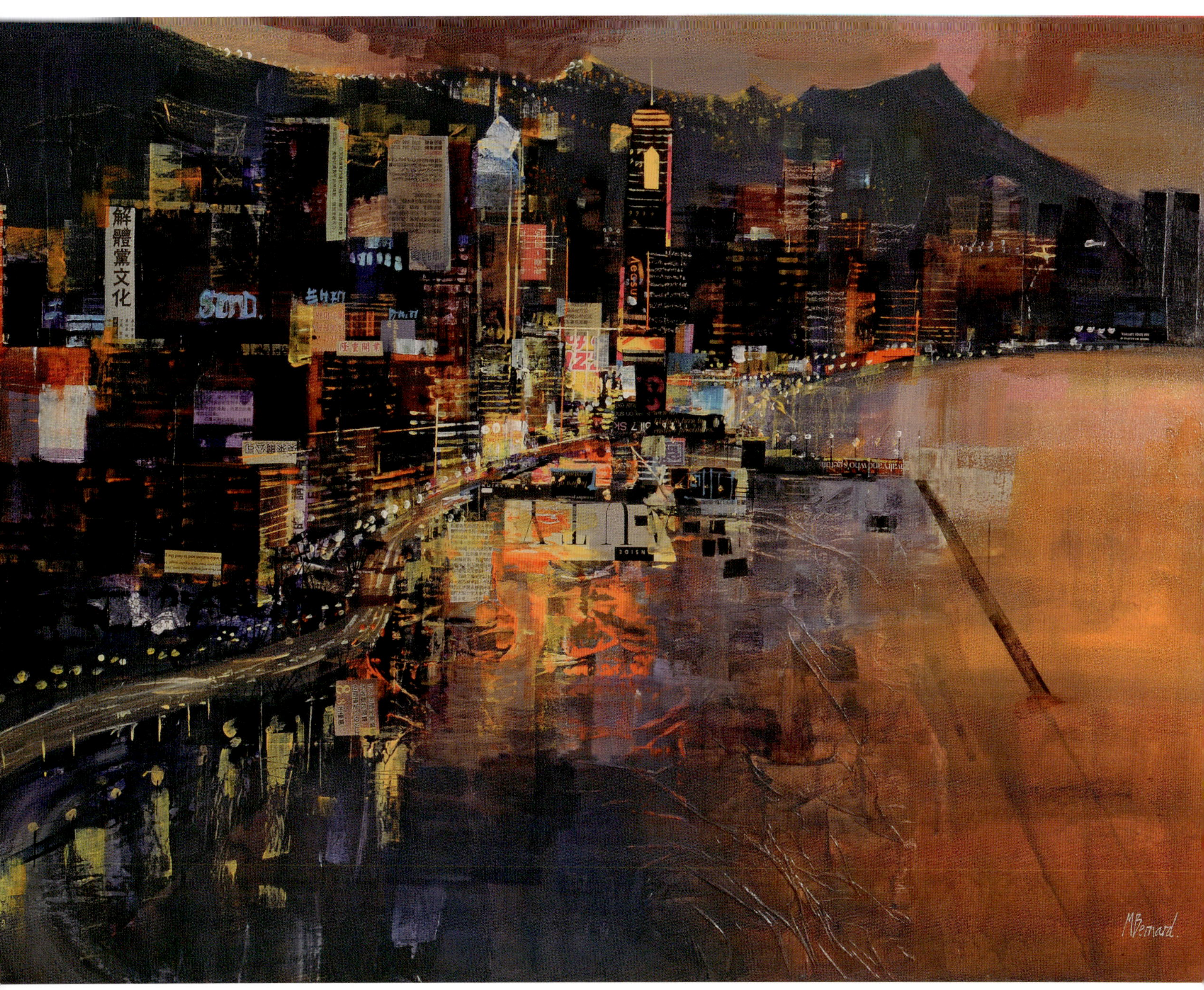

Sometimes I use a plant spray filled with water that makes everything run and drip into and over the collage, creating unrehearsed, unexpected, interesting effects. Most of the inks are semi-transparent and can be built up with richly coloured layers. I also use thick white acrylic paint directly from the tube to create impasto effects. An alternative method, which I sometimes use, is to impress a paper shape into an area of wet acrylic paint.

Hong Kong Harbour
Mixed media, 76 x 102cm (30 x 40in)
A mixture of words and cut and torn pieces of paper, plus lines drawn with the edge of a piece of card, create this atmospheric view of Hong Kong Harbour.

Trialling and investigation

It's good practice to experiment a bit before you embark on
a larger work. Before you start, you could try making fairly
small collages using only magazines rather than a range of
collage materials (see page 52). These small collages can
effectively be thumbnail designs. Don't draw anything, just
make shapes with torn paper. Then look at them, turn them
around, hold them up, pin them on a wall and look at them.
What jumps out at you? Which bits do you like or dislike? Is
there anything that reminds you of a particular location?

Another idea is to make patterns from looking at a
scene and reproducing a simple version in just black and
white in order to find the best balance and format for your
final composition. I used to do some of these things, but no
longer always do, as these days I prefer to be an explorer
in the new territory of the painting. Sometimes, initially, I
create a three-tone collage as I look for likely shapes and
try to work out what proportions will work.

Another good idea, and something I have always
done, is to use an A3 or A4 sketchbook and experiment
with materials, colours and other ideas. Use alternative
materials or tools, such as large housepainters' brushes
or rollers, sponges or a comb. Try all these different ideas,
filling the pages of your sketchbook, enjoying the feel of the
materials, the textures you make and the variety of things
you can produce. As you work, keep thinking how these
ideas can create atmosphere, patterns or a sense of place.

The essence of my approach now is to develop my
design or composition during the painting, and the main
way I do that is to put down interesting outlines and blocks
of colour on to my paper or (more usually) board. Once I
have put down the first shape, I try to repeat it elsewhere
on the painting, but in a different size, in a different context,
in a different colour or from a different angle. This helps to
pull the composition together, to lead the viewer's eye into
and around the work, but it needs experimentation to
get it right.

Sailing on the Dart
Mixed media,
81 x 114cm (32 x 45in)
Here I have kept to
an extremely limited
palette to enhance the
sense of harmony and to
allow me to concentrate
on the repeated shapes
and angles.

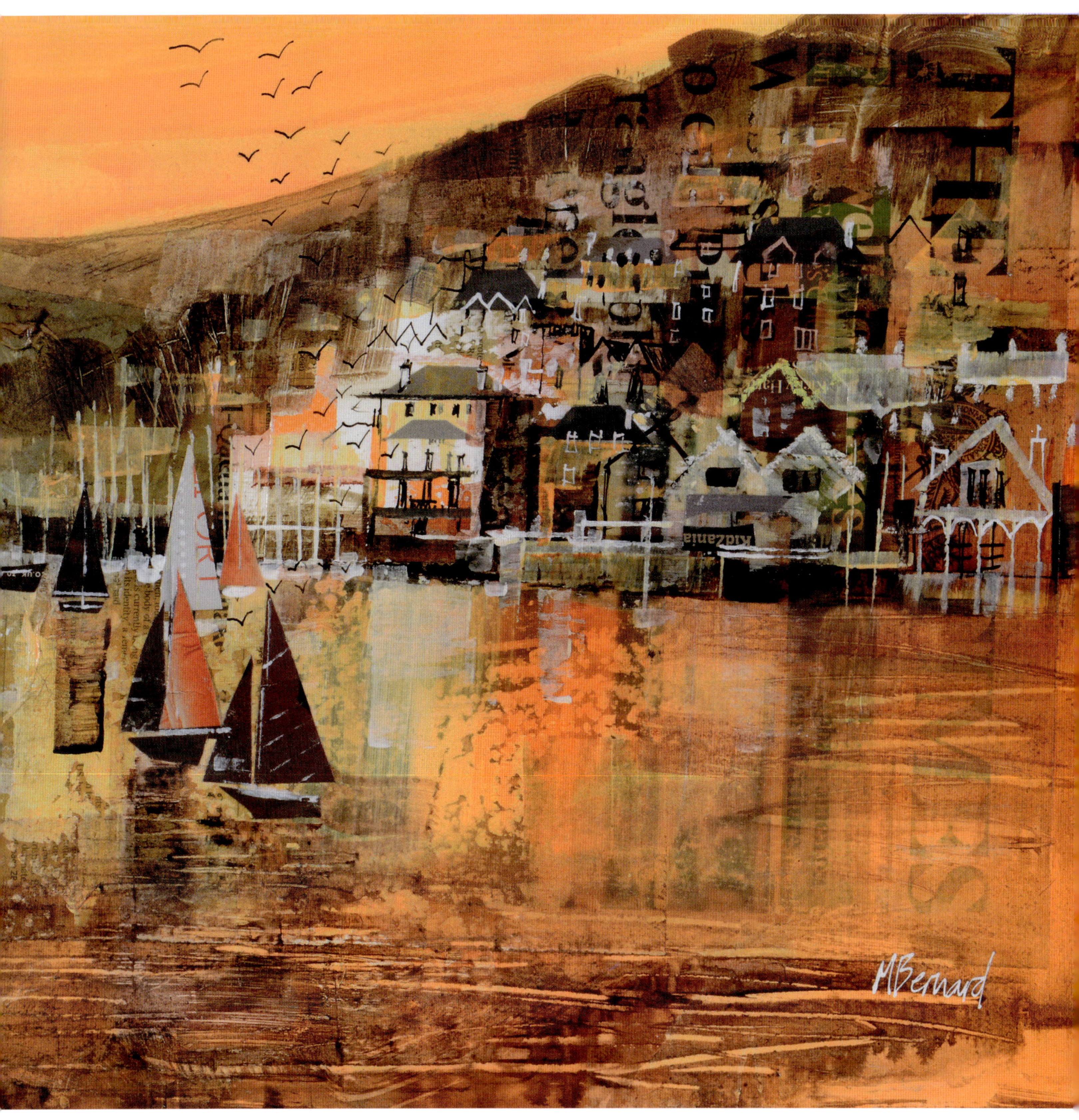

Experimental exercise

Take a magazine and use the colours you find as if they were paint. Here in these thumbnails, you can see how I've cut or torn simple shapes to build up abridged images. You can do the same and it will help you to focus on the basic shapes you need in a painting as well as how you will use the collage. I've done this with coloured magazines here, but you could also do it with newspapers as you explore tone. If you keep practising using torn or cut pieces of paper as here, you will soon find that you can instinctively seek the type of paper that will make the most impact for whatever it is you are portraying. Of course, this is slightly different from my technique of using collage randomly under a painting, but it gets you into the frame of mind and the way of working that will ultimately enhance your larger work. It's a kind of collage doodle that you can do almost anywhere, any time, and it will hone your skills and eye rapidly.

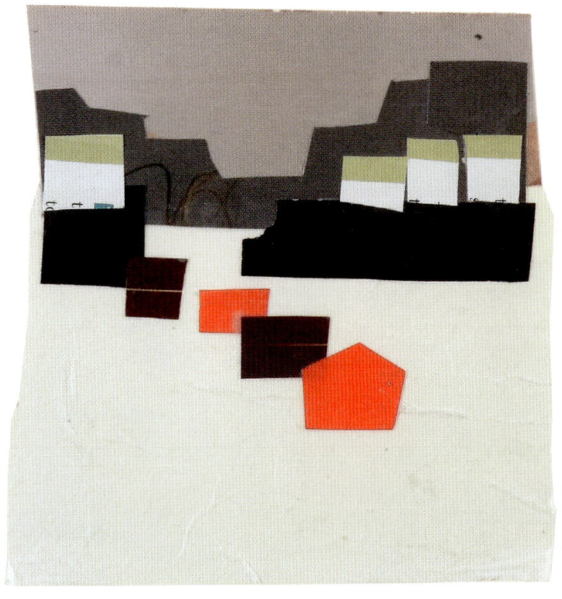

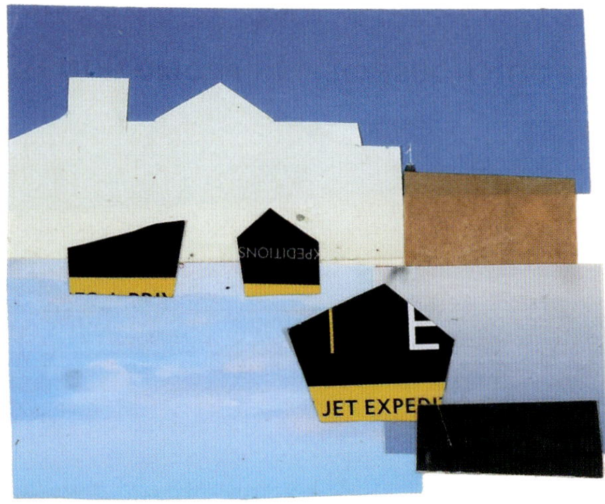

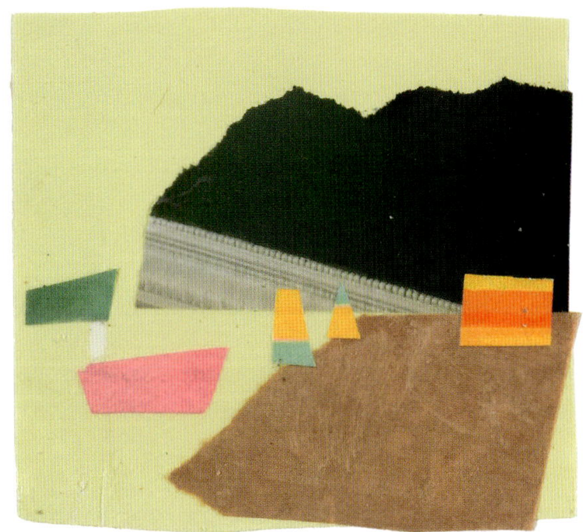

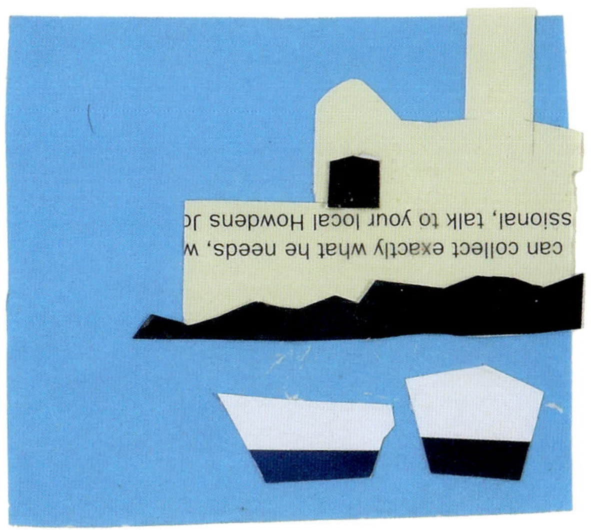
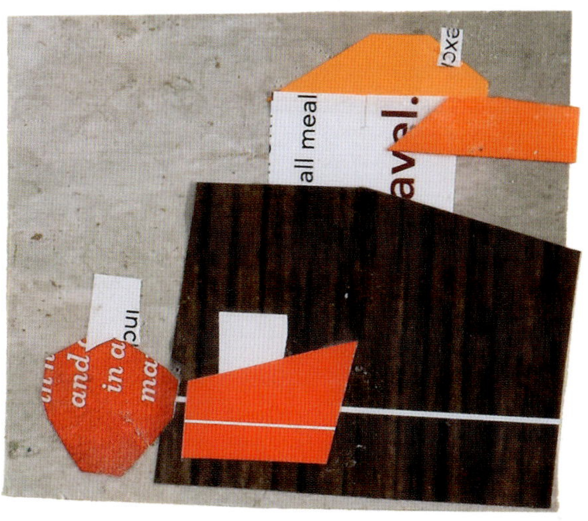
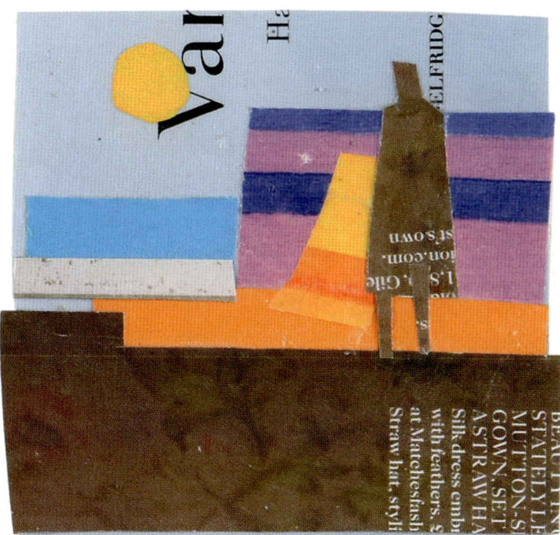

Modification

Right from the start, I tweak, adjust and modify my paintings, and do this right through the creative process. Beginners tend to see everything in detail. We're taught from an early age to draw carefully all that we see, but for my style I prefer a looser, freer approach. Some people have a process to do this, but I find the best way is trial and error. That's why mixed media helps this because, especially with collage, a lot of the method is about taking away; it's a process of elimination. John Blockley was an early inspiration for me. His innovative watercolour paintings defied all 'rules', resulting in a unique visual language. His work was full of atmosphere, interesting colours and textures that expanded the characterisation of watercolour painting. But more specifically, I was particularly inspired by one of his drawings of Port Isaac; when I visited the location, I was surprised to see that he had left out a whole bank of houses. At that point, I realised that artists are allowed to leave things out of their paintings. You shouldn't have a guilt complex if you omit aspects of a view; give yourself permission to leave things out or move them. This is your painting, so make it yours; reduce any complications and create overall effects rather than precise details.

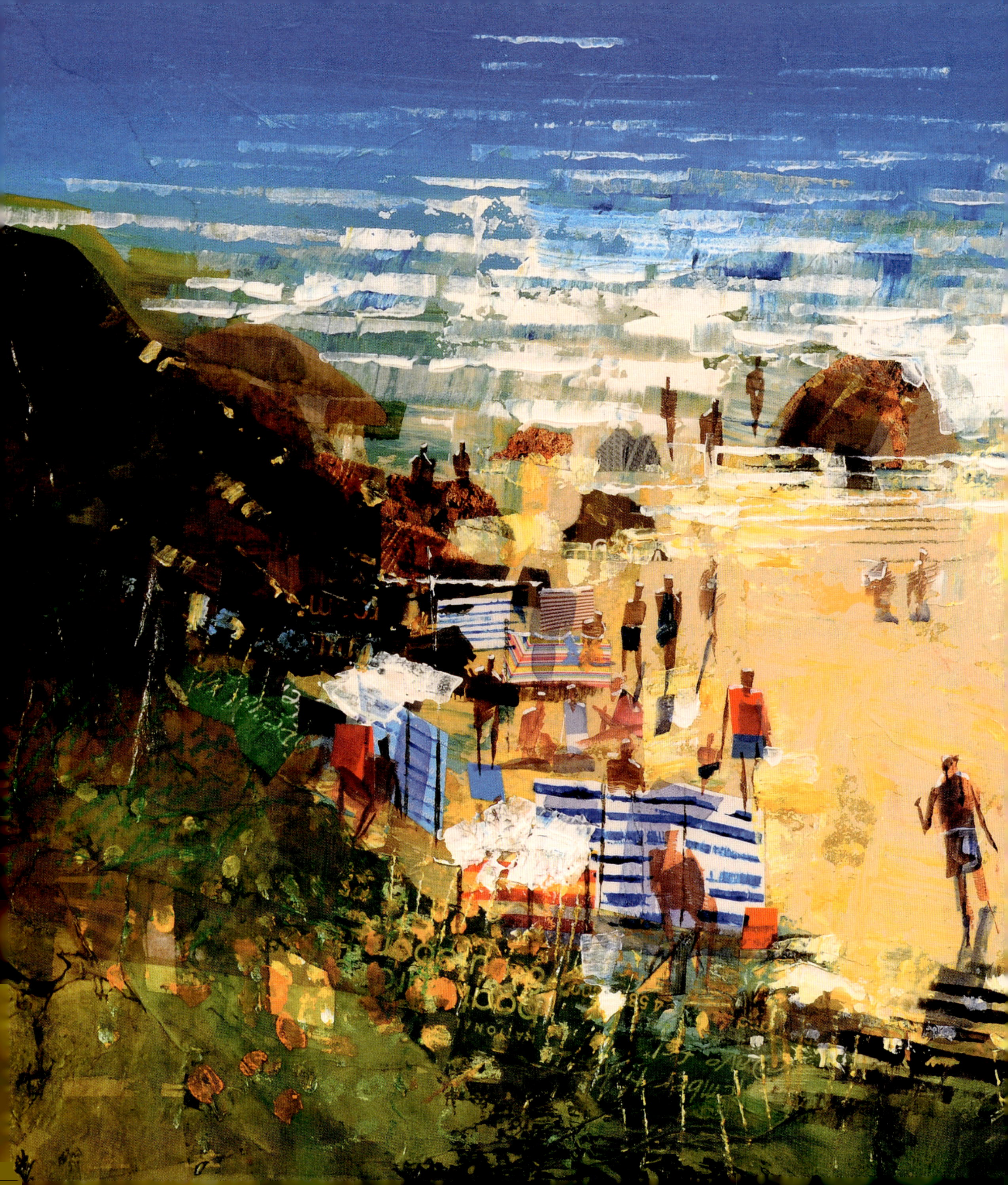

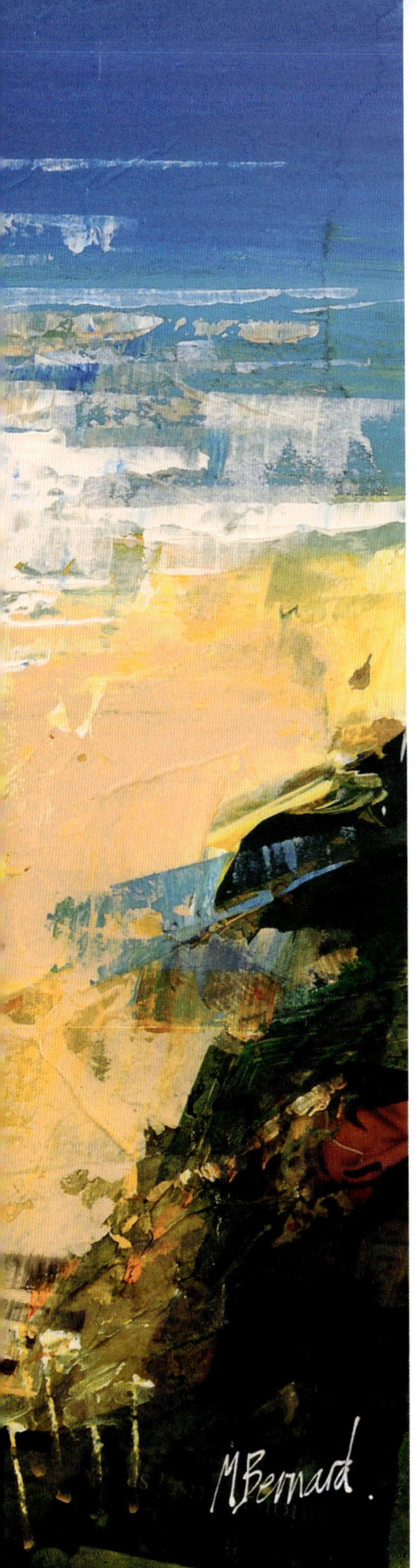

Pattern

As mentioned, pattern is important to me when creating a composition. While I look for light and shade where these will contribute to the overall pattern, I sometimes invent or move patches of light or shade in order to help create an interesting design. The repetition of patches of colour forms an important part of the overall pattern and helps to keep the viewer's eye moving around the picture, taking in all the elements of the image.

In order to create patterns, I use a variety of tools and techniques – for example, acrylic ink applied with broad and fine pen or brush, acrylic paint spread on with pieces of mountboard, cut to small or large sizes, and oil or soft pastel sticks used on the side. Sometimes my use of bold colour in different areas across the image also creates overall abstract patterns.

It does not invariably produce a satisfying painting, of course. No matter how much I have looked at the subject though a viewfinder, trying to find the best viewpoint, trying to cut some of the objects so that only a part of them appears in the picture (for this helps to increase their abstract quality), sometimes I find that the resulting picture lacks impact.

It is then that I most value the practice of cropping – using two L-shaped pieces of mountboard to see whether a selected part of the painting will make a better composition. Sometimes this can have a dramatic effect, turning a horizontal format into a vertical one, focusing attention on to the main subject more forcefully, increasing the degree of abstraction, creating a better balance and so on. Before framing any painting I now adopt the practice of seeing whether cropping would improve it, and it has become an essential part of my procedure. *Late Summer Swimmers* has been cropped in this way.

Late Summer Swimmers
Mixed media, 35.5 x 40cm (14 x 16in)
The overall impression of this is a busy beach scene in joyous colours, but I built it up completely with pattern; looking at the patterns on the grass, the patterns created by the windbreaks, the patterns formed by the figures. It's all pulled together by the composition.

Project – Riomaggiore

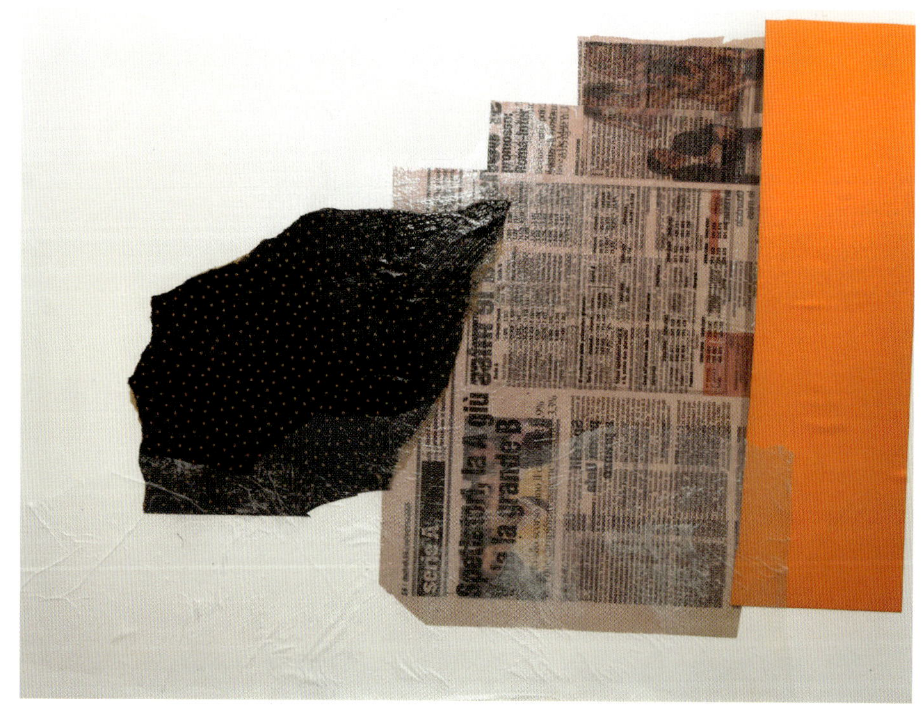

1 I started here by building up a collage using a variety of papers, establishing an overall composition for the painting. There are dark shapes in the centre, which suggests the rock formations beneath the houses that cluster around the bay. Newspaper above this suggests some of the buildings, and crinkled tissue paper in the foreground indicates where the sea will be.

2 I am also considering how different shapes work together and how the entire composition will interrelate. If you look across the work, you will see that I generally balance what I stick down across the entire composition. Similarly, I am thinking about textures and how I will use them to create interest in the painting later.

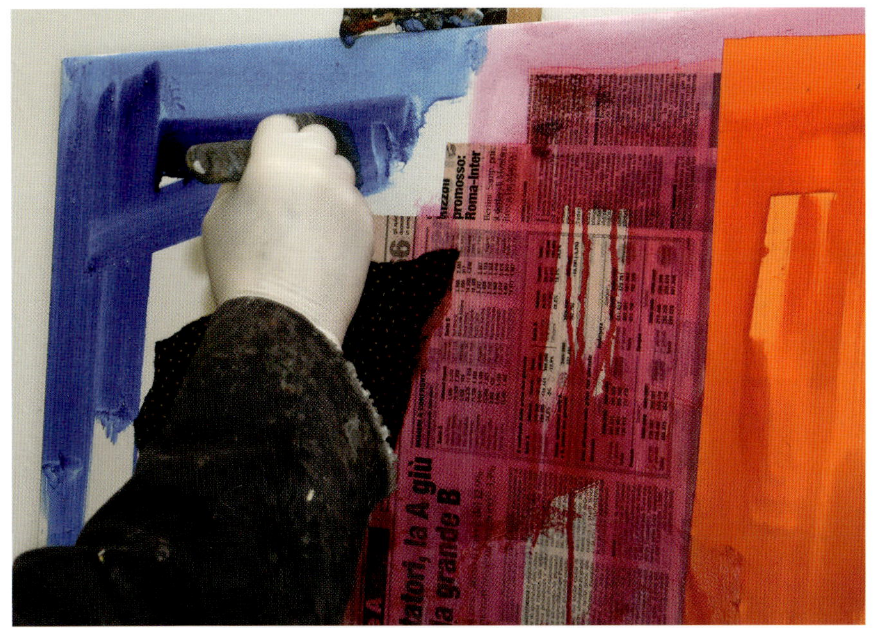

3 I develop the collage further before starting to apply the two main colours that I have chosen for the subject, which are FW Rowney blue and Liquitex quinacridone magenta. I apply these with a soft-haired 5cm (2in) varnishing brush. The collage must be dry before starting on this stage. With the painting held vertically at an easel, I apply the colours randomly, allowing them to create haphazard effects.

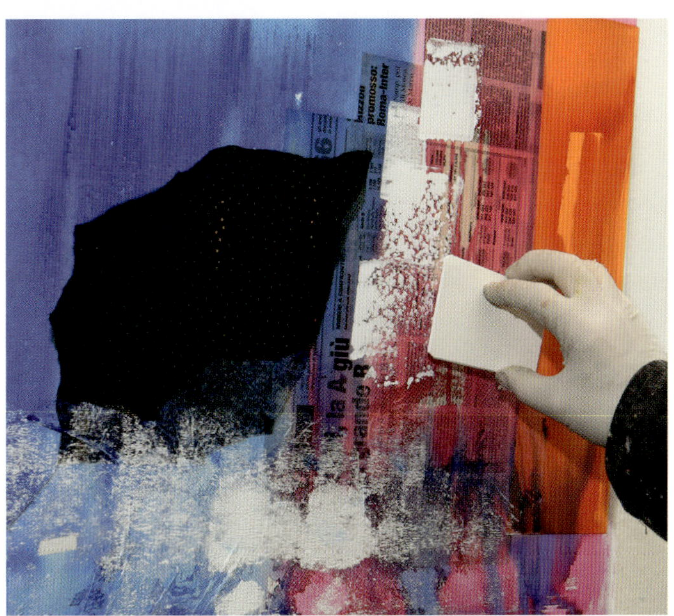

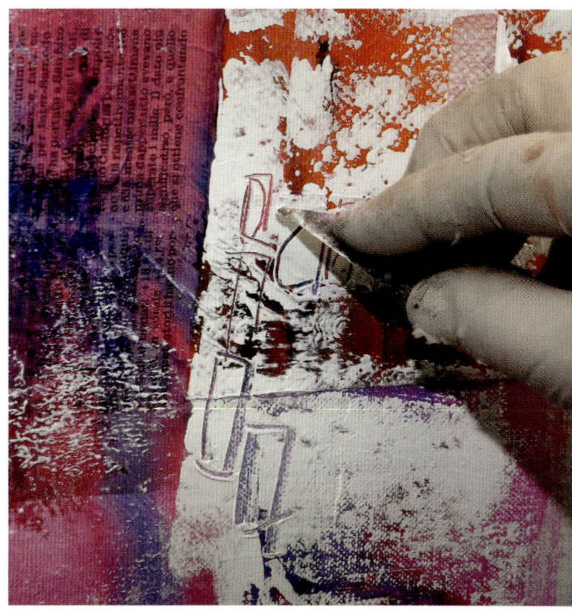

4 With the entire painting surface now covered in some way, either with collage or colour, I begin to think more particularly about textures. For this I use Liquitex unbleached titanium and Liquitex titanium white. I aim to create a sense of unity by repeating the texture in different areas, but I avoid the areas of the initial blue or magenta, which will relate to specific parts of the subject matter. As well as adding texture, the white acrylic imparts a luminosity to the painting later on, when coloured glazes made from diluted acrylic inks are applied over it.

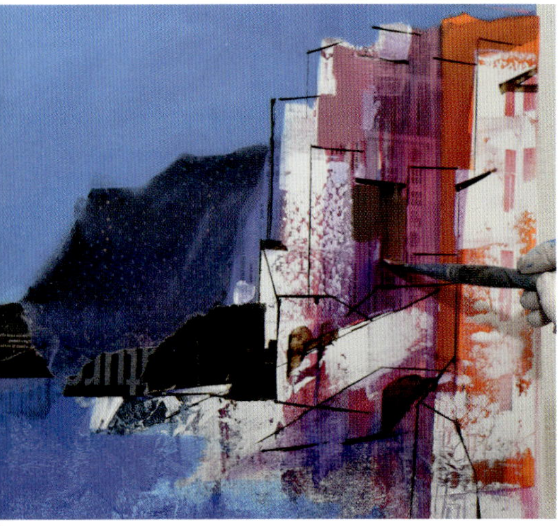
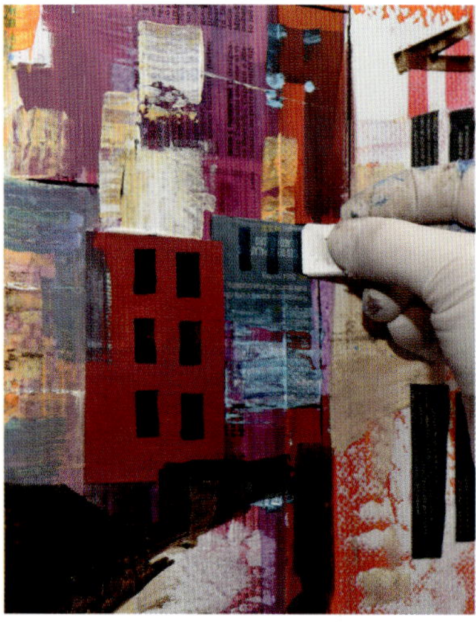
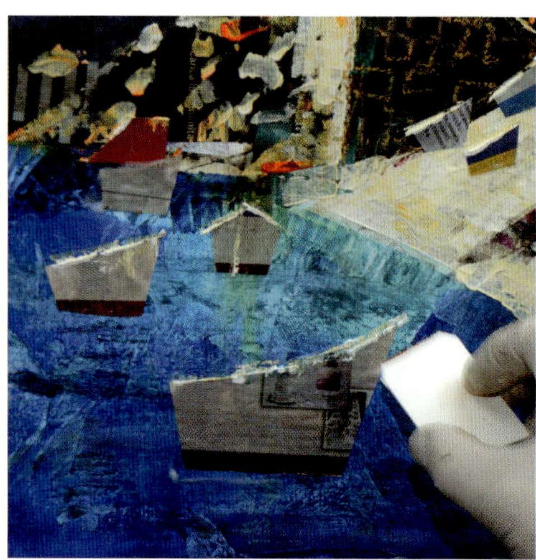

5 Checking back at my drawings of the location, I start to create some recognisable elements. I begin to define the houses clustered around the bay. The challenge now is to balance abstract areas with realistic aspects and the textural with the smooth passages.

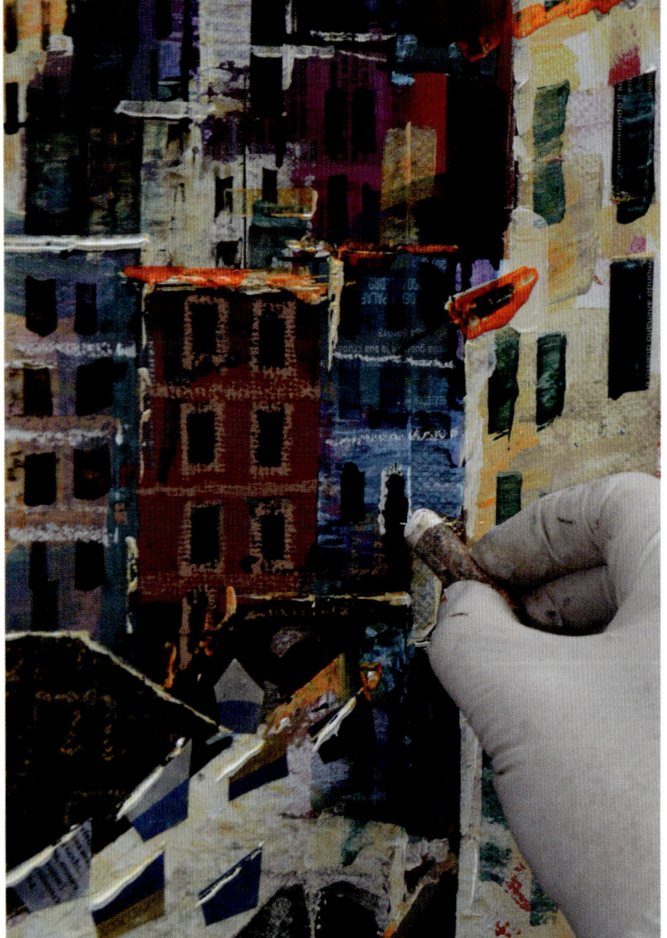

6 This is a really fun part of the painting! I add some finishing details with oil pastels (as you can see around the windows and on the bridge) and with dip pen (on the balconies). I don't fuss too much, these are just a few general indications.

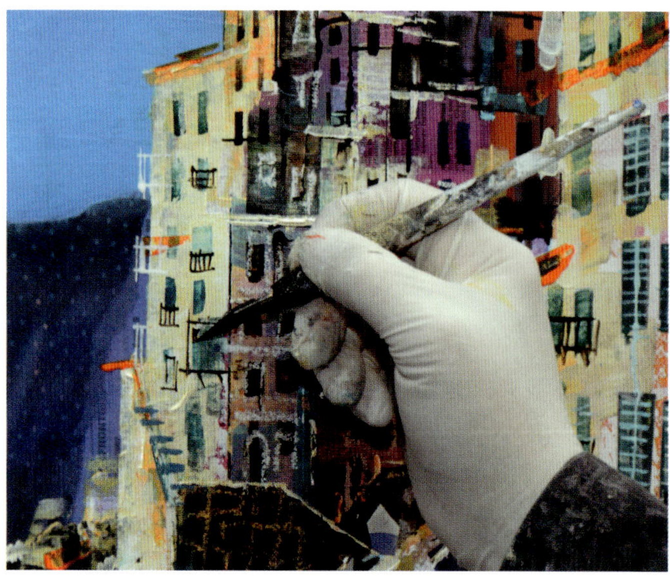

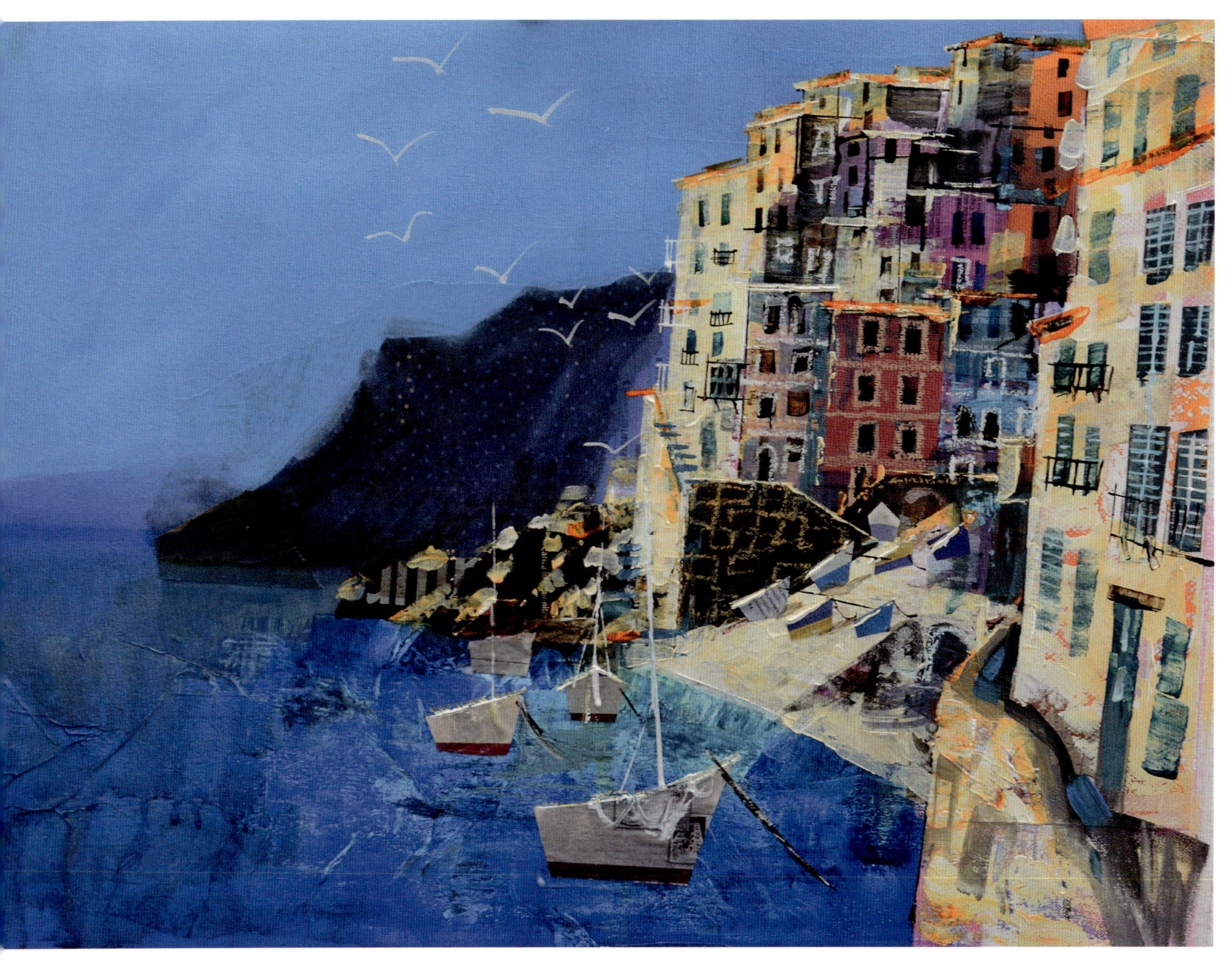

Riomaggiore

Mixed media, 51 x 76cm (20 x 30in)
This small fishing village in the Liguria
region of Italy is one of the colourful
locations I never tire of depicting. Here
you can see the result of all my layers
of materials.

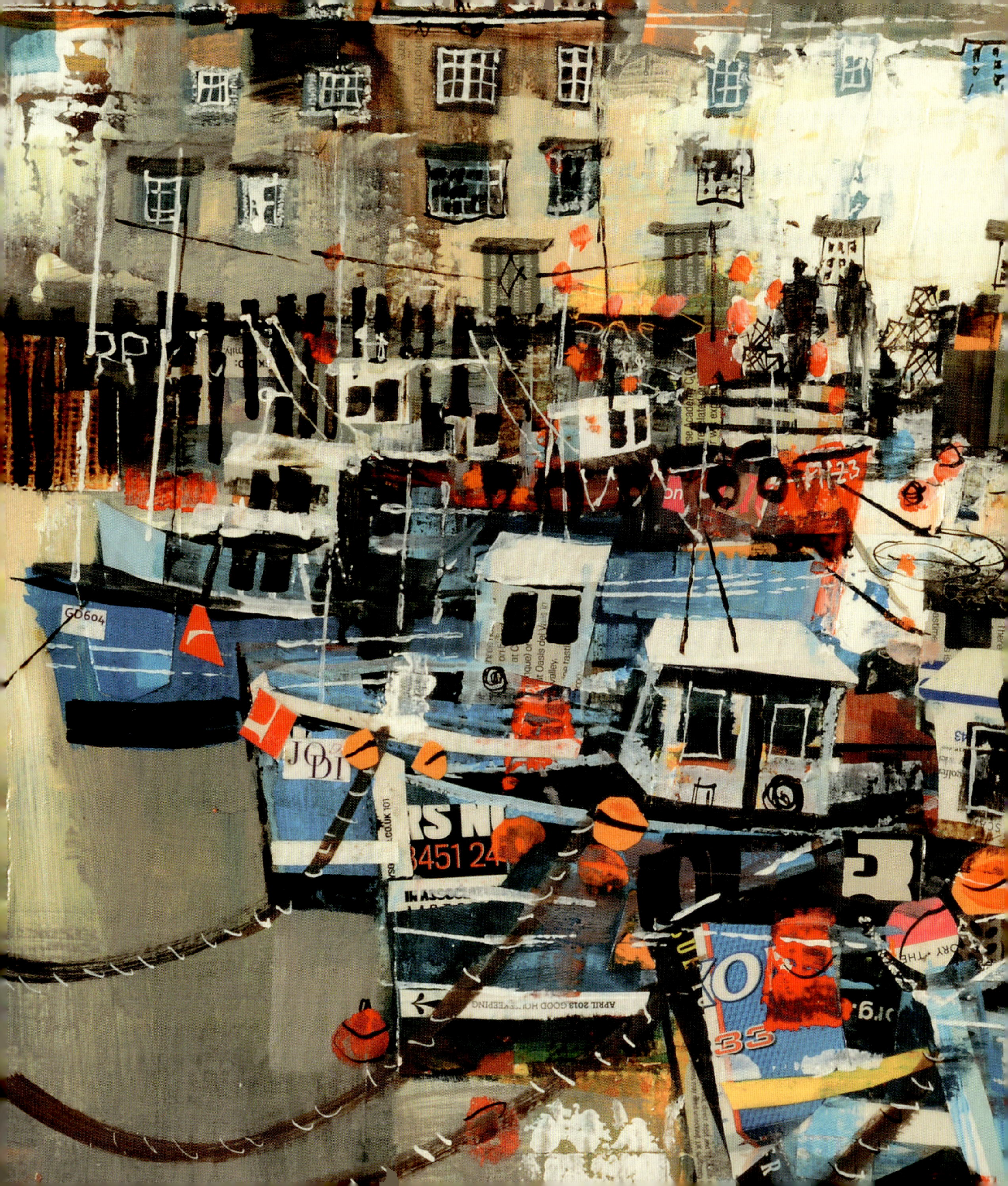

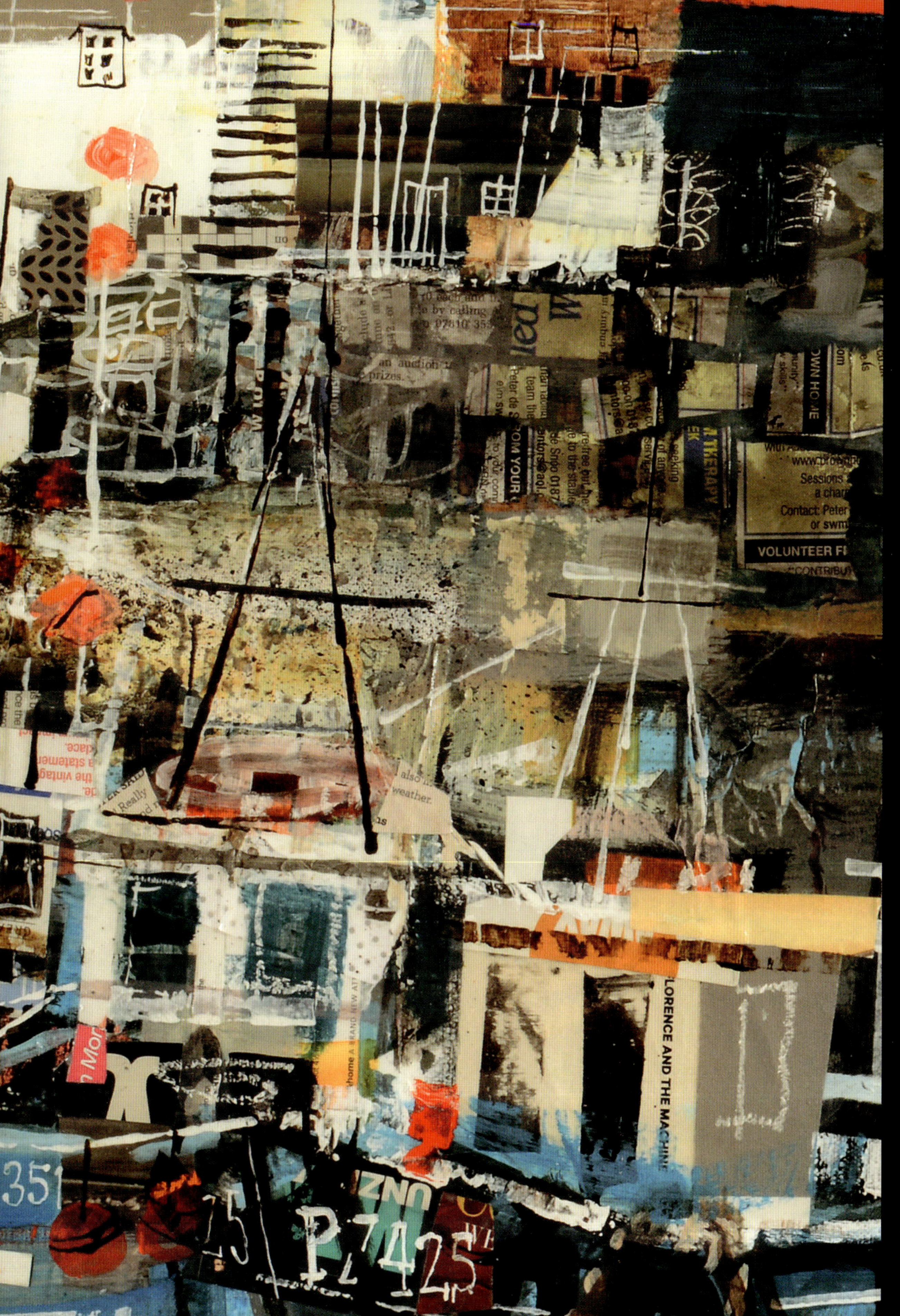

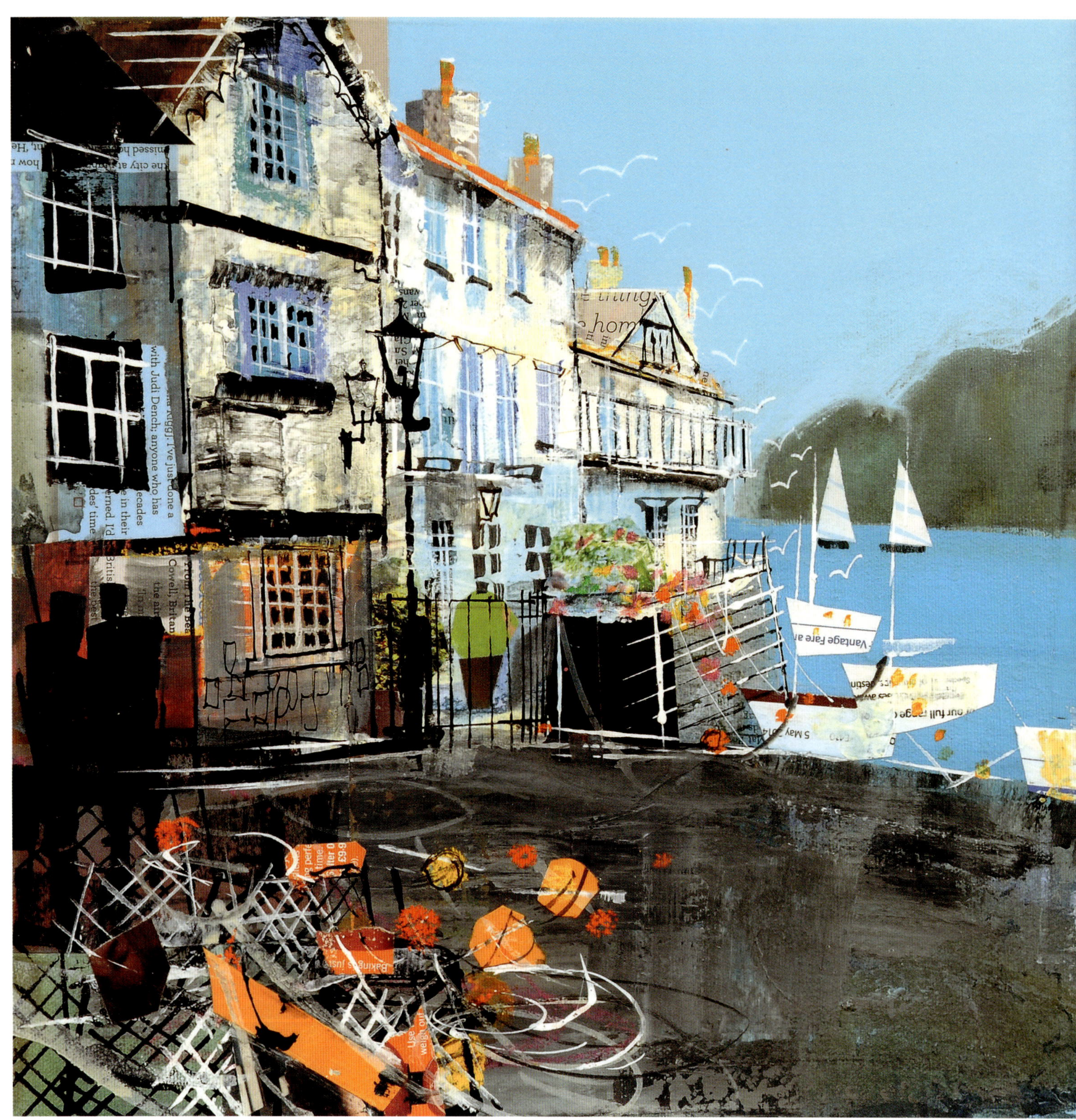

3

Creative Techniques

Although my paintings are based on real places that I see and observe directly to begin with, they all have strong abstract qualities, which I encourage any aspiring artist to try to emulate. I strive to create a balance between objective depiction and subjective ideas. This gives more freedom to explore ideas and techniques and to reflect inner thoughts and feelings.

While drawing is my starting point, I draw what I see as initial sketches, and I learned gradually that quick sketches hone my thoughts, force me to make decisions about what to include and what to omit, and shape what I will ultimately do in a painting. There is a natural inclination in us all to draw as realistically as possible, but, with experience, you can become more focused and selective. For me, the most important aspects in my initial drawings are qualities such as the spaces between shapes, tonal values, relative scales of things in a scene and the most important elements that caught my eye in the first place. Then, once I have made my quickly drawn sketches, I have most of the material I need to create a composition. Rather than copy this closely, I usually start a work with loose, abstract shapes made out of collage. So really, the process begins without details and becomes even looser, with even fewer details as I progress.

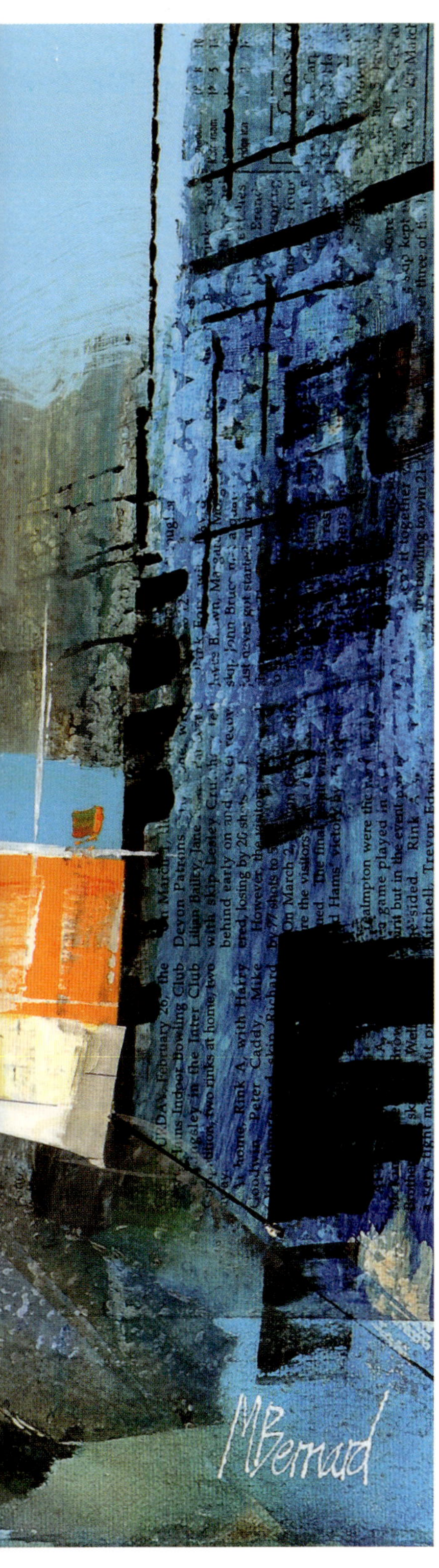

Glimpse of the Dart

Mixed media, 30 x 40cm (12 x 16in)
Building up the layers in order is fairly crucial to creating a finished work that compels the viewer to look closer. So collage was applied under and over some of the painting.

Previous page: **Harbour Fishing Boats, Polperro**

Mixed media, 61 x 61cm (24 x 24in)
A busy scene needs careful handling. I reduced many elements, but also incorporated some fine lines to create a sense of reality.

Sketching and photography

As with the two-colour composition idea, if you restrict yourself timewise when you are making your initial sketches of a place, you will find that you only draw what is essential to you. A time limit makes you self-selecting, ensuring that you only capture the essence of a scene. You might be attracted to tonal qualities or light. I'm particularly attracted to contrasts of larger shapes against smaller, such as the foreground against the background – you will notice that there are bigger shapes in the foreground and smaller shapes further behind. This is a natural phenomenon caused by the way we see and it will add to the sense of perspective in your paintings. When deciding on a composition, I often frame things; so, for example, I might look through buildings or rocks or masts and out to sea – these naturally occurring viewing frames frequently make for interesting images (see *Italian Fishing Village*,

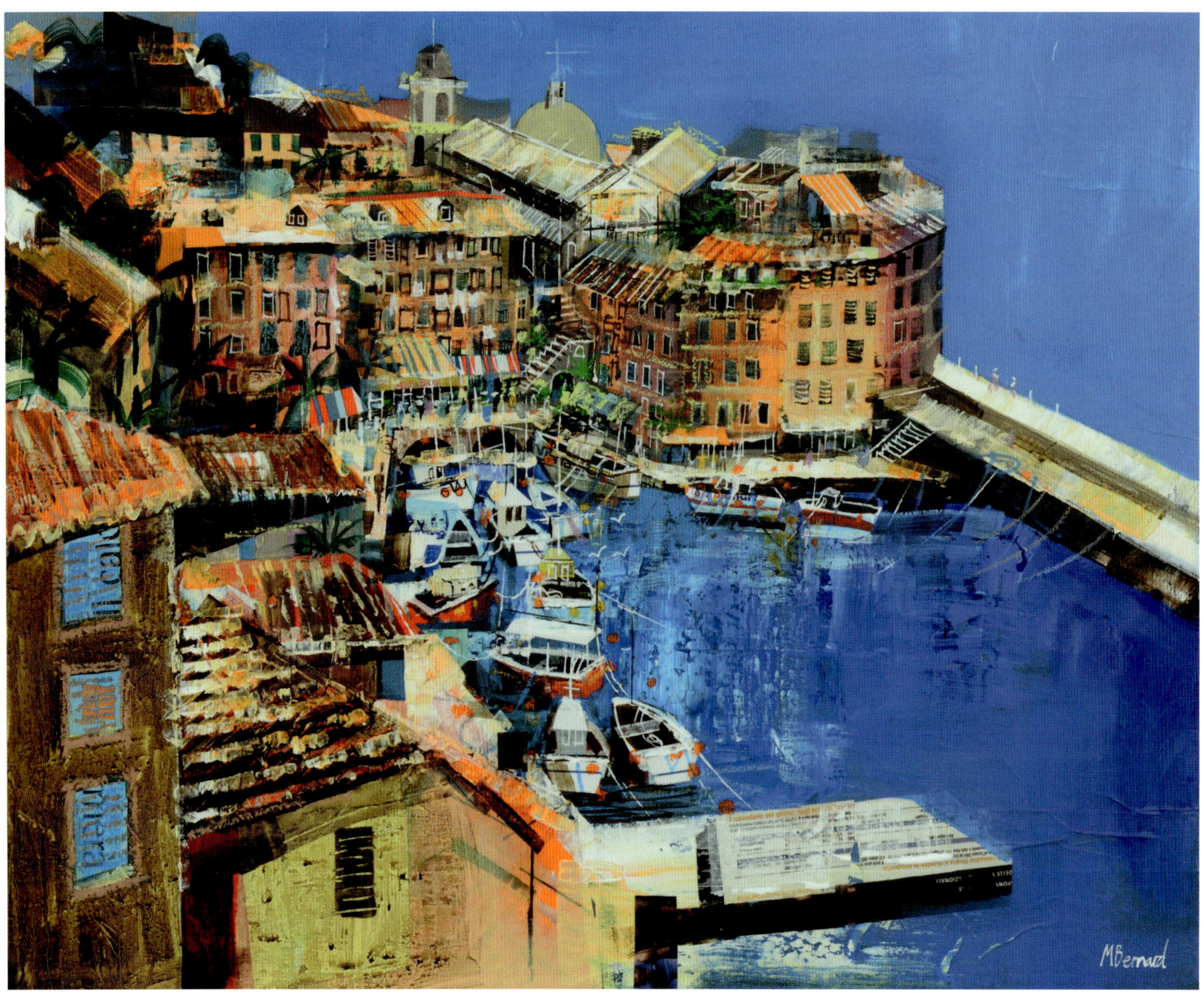

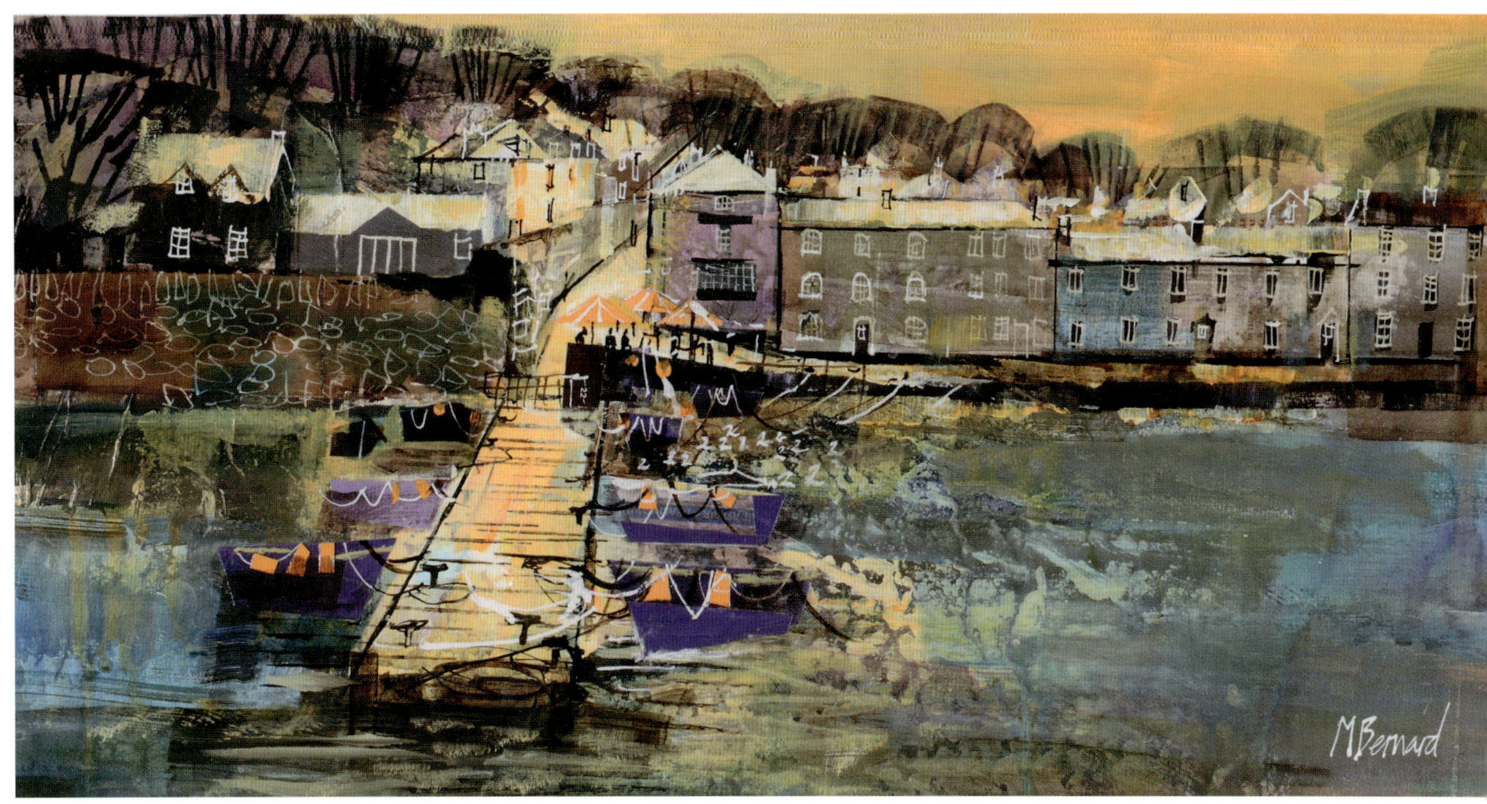

Dittisham, Devon

Mixed media, 25 x 48cm (10 x 19in)
Here, the boat shapes reduce in size to
give a sense of depth and distance. I also
repeated similar colours from the boat
hulls in the tree line.

Camogli, Italian Riviera

Mixed media, 61 x 76cm (24 x 30in)
After several sketches, I worked on this
complex composition, filling the image with
rectangles and lines. The high viewpoint
adds a sense of drama.

page 6). For these sketches, you can either take a small
sketchbook, or take an A3 or A4 book.

Drawing is an essential skill for all artists and I tend to
use lots of pencil or roller pen. Drawing and observing are
two of the earliest and most important aspects of a work
of art. By drawing from observation, you will learn to look
closely, analyse and build up a visual knowledge of the scene
you are about to make a painting of. Drawing also helps you
to develop your observational skills. The more you draw,
the more you will refine your skills in looking; you will notice
shapes, tones, textures and colours more than you did.

I also often take photographs, as these can be useful
for elements such as perspective, or something interesting
in the background or foreground that you forgot to add.
However, while photos can be useful, don't copy them! They
should never be used literally, only as aids. The moment
you start following photographs closely, your freedom and
individual creativity will be lost. Try taking black-and-white
photos or turning your coloured images into monochrome;
in this way you will be able to differentiate between tones
more easily – tonal qualities are extremely useful for
creating a harmonious or dramatic image.

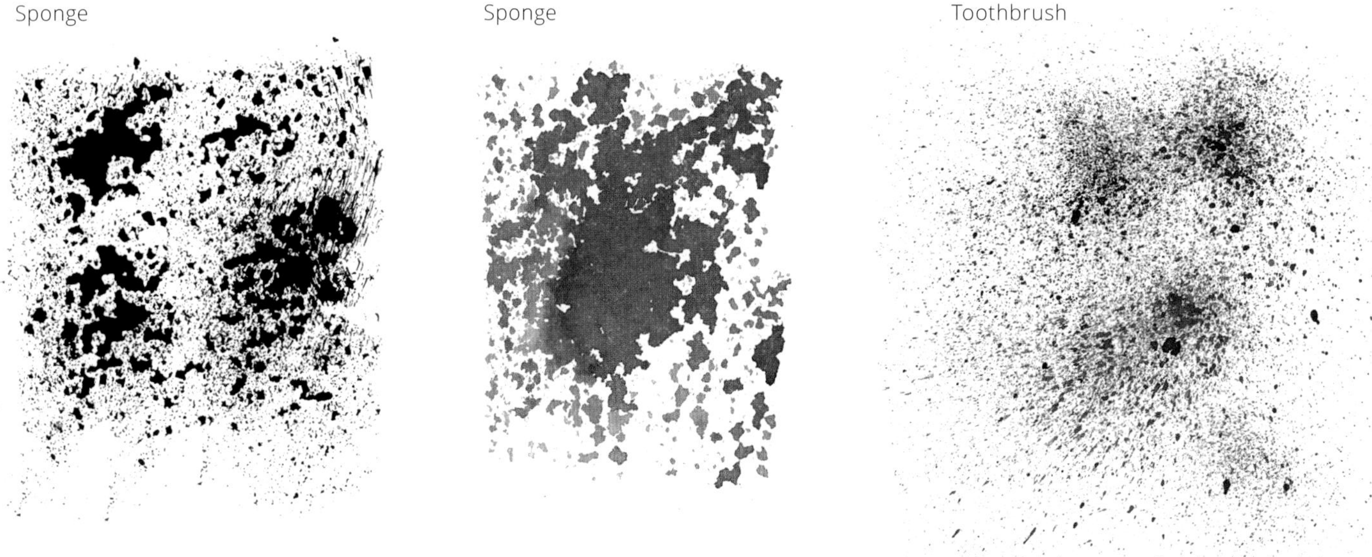

Experimental exercise

Consider different ways of creating texture. You can make actual textures by crumpling tissue paper, using corrugated card or other already textured materials, or you can create a sense of texture such as I have here with ink and different implements and tools. A sponge can create varied marks; a lino roller is less flexible, but can still make different effects; spattering with a toothbrush can be great for creating the look of sea spray or rain or simply a textural effect over grass or rocks. Then, here, I've also tried bubble wrap and used my finger to make all sorts of marks that imply various textures.

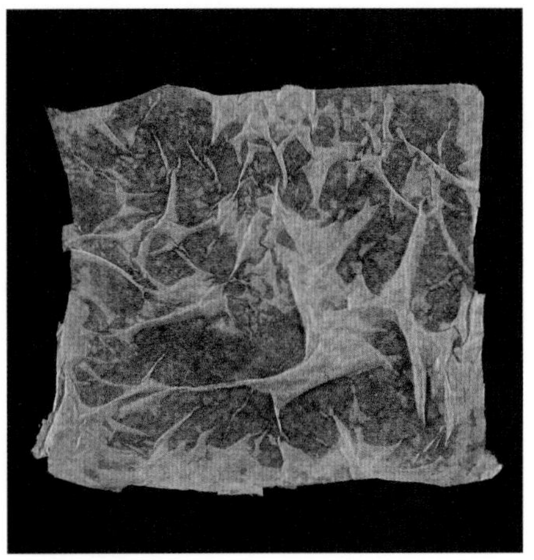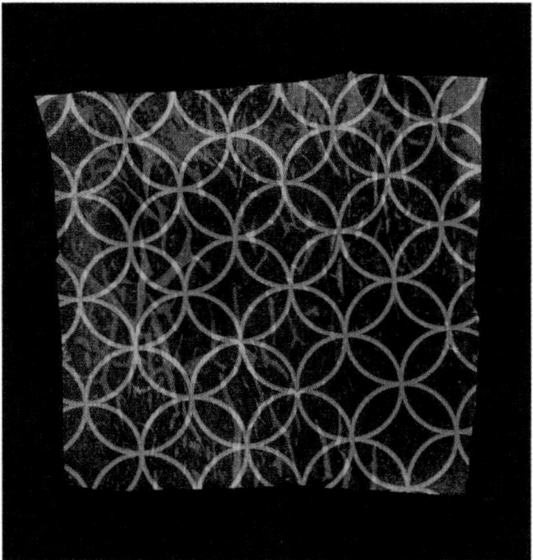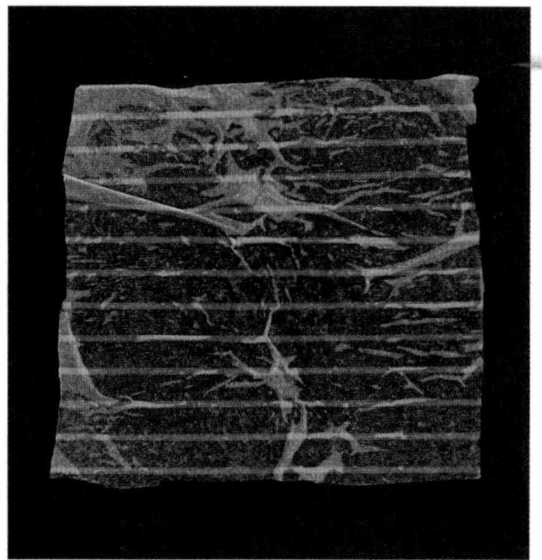

Crumpled tissue papers

Intuition and confidence

Experiment with even more different materials: try sprinkling sand into your paint while it is still wet, crumpling paper, or spreading thick paint with a sponge or your fingers. Be open-minded about what these textures might convey, as they can be used imaginatively in all kinds of images.

Trust your own instincts. Fight against the natural tendency that most people have to work precisely and literally. Part of this way of working, of loosening up, is to use alternative materials as I've discussed here, and part of it is to be conscious of allowing yourself to relax and let things flow. This can be a leap of faith if you're not used to working in this way, but you have to believe in yourself and in what you're doing; develop your own confidence to use your intuition. At first, this may mean that you have to fake it to make it! This is something that will come more naturally to you the more you practise. Your picture must have a bit of oomph about it and it won't if you labour over the details. If you start feeling timid or tentative, your work will always appear overly cautious, but start boldly and with confidence and this will shine through. Daring can be created through something quite simple, such as a bit of bright colour somewhere in the composition. Look at the entire composition and imagine it carved into thirds, then in one of the thirds add a bit of colour using your intuition. This might end up as your focal point, or it might simply be a bright spark in your image. Either way, it will add interest and will enliven the work.

Finger

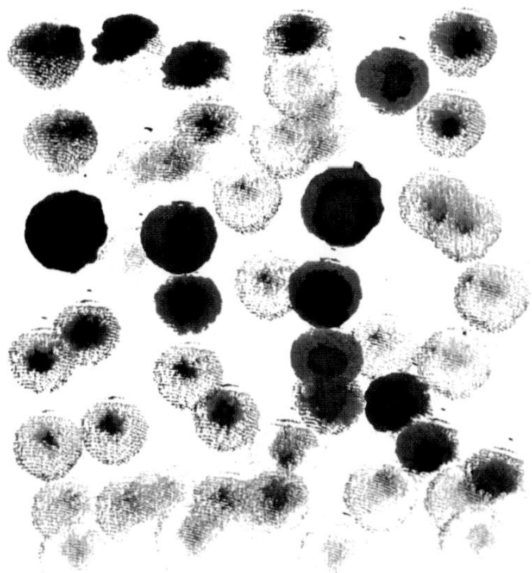

Repetition

Shapes and patterns that repeat each other will naturally draw the viewer's eye around the picture, and I strive to repeat shapes across my compositions, although I also purposefully create differences in this repetition, rather as a composer will introduce variations on a theme. Such variations tend to stimulate interest and make the picture appear dynamic rather than static. Diagonals have a similar effect; they keep the eye moving around an image. Masts of boats are particularly useful in this way, as they not only keep the eye moving, but they also serve to link different parts of the picture, for example, the foreground to the sky, the water to the buildings, the sea to the rocks. Consequently, I may repeat the shape of a boat several times, but from a different angle each time. I may deliberately lean a mast over to create a diagonal or to link two areas. Never ignore your own underlying sense of what might work, of what might make your scene appear lively and dynamic.

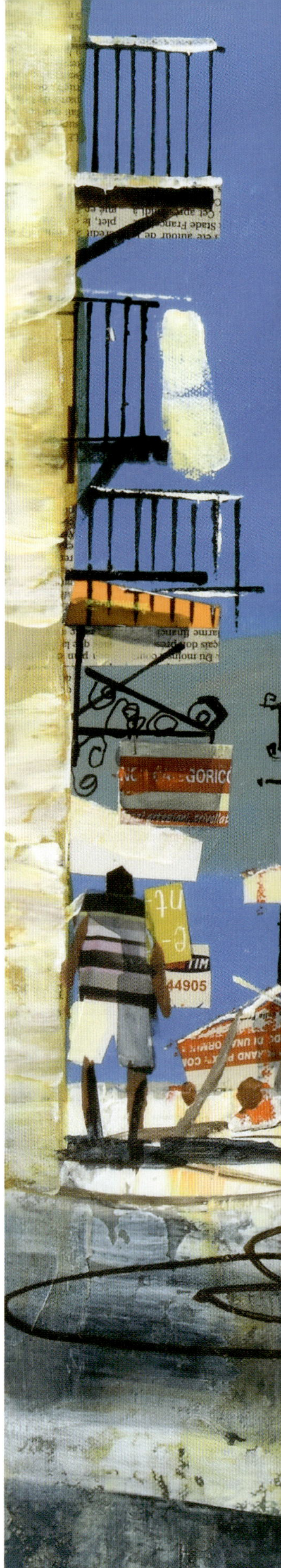

Fishing Village, Tuscany
Mixed media,
51 x 51cm (20 x 20in)
Swirling lines of shadow in the foreground pull you into this scene, and the repeating balconies keep your eyes roving to take in everything.

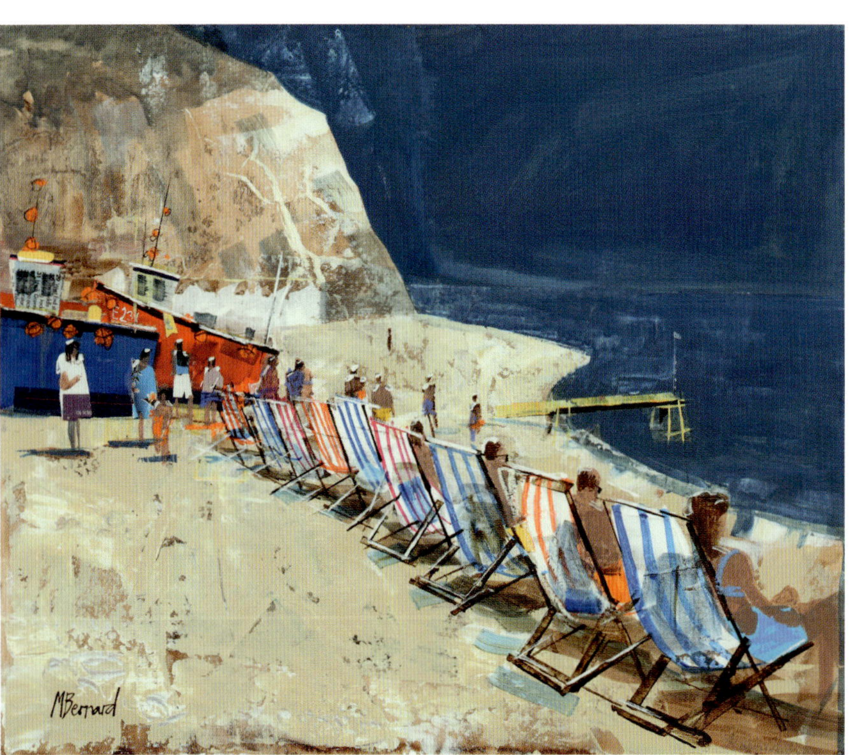

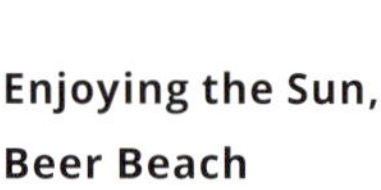

Enjoying the Sun, Beer Beach
Mixed media,
46 x 38cm (18 x 15in)
The diagonal line of deckchairs and the repetition of their stripes and wooden legs help to draw the viewer's eye deeper into the composition.

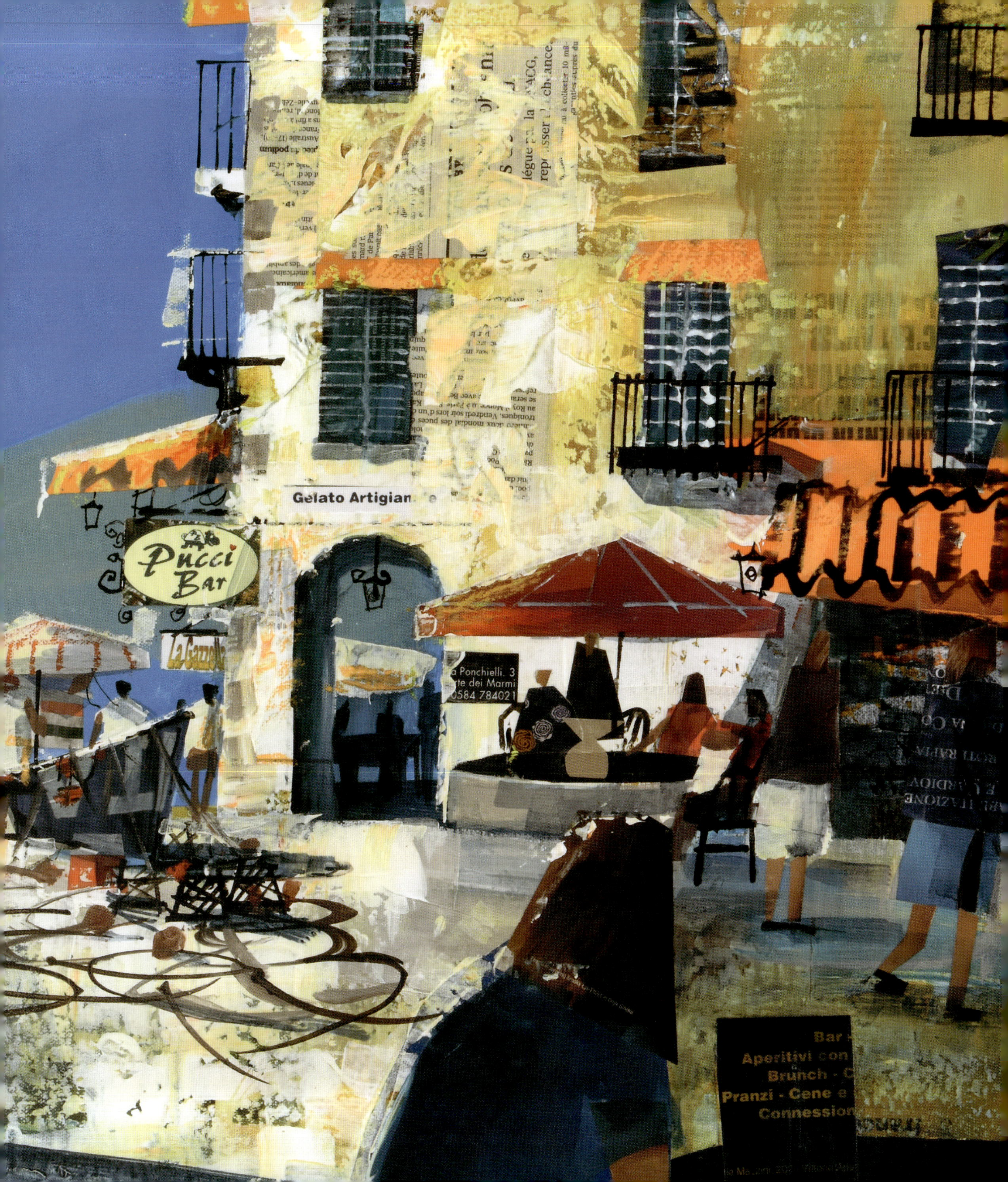

Gelato Artigianale
Pucci Bar
La Jeannette
Ponchielli. 3
rte dei Marmi
0584 784021
Bar
Aperitivi con
Brunch - C
Pranzi - Cene e
Connession

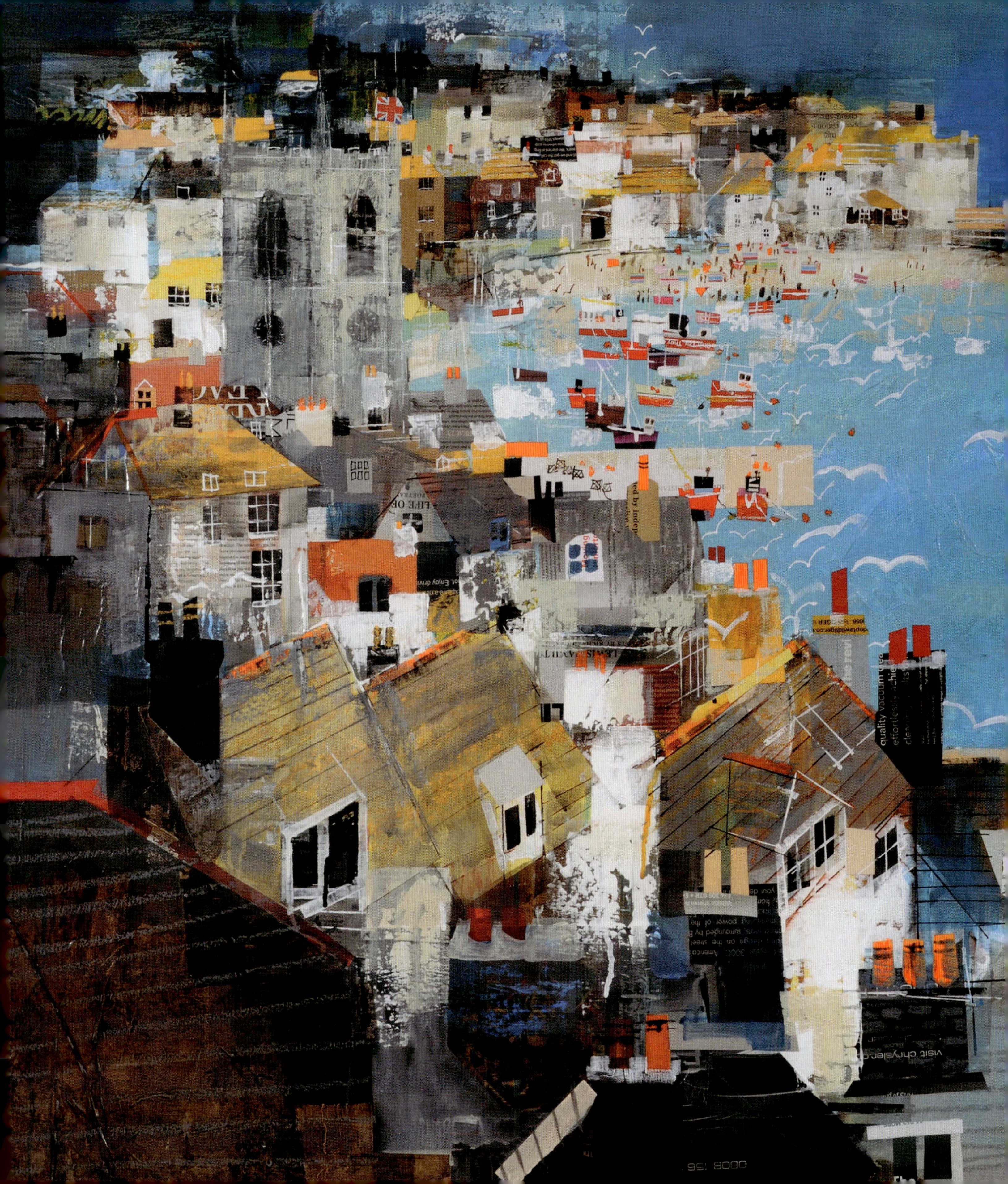

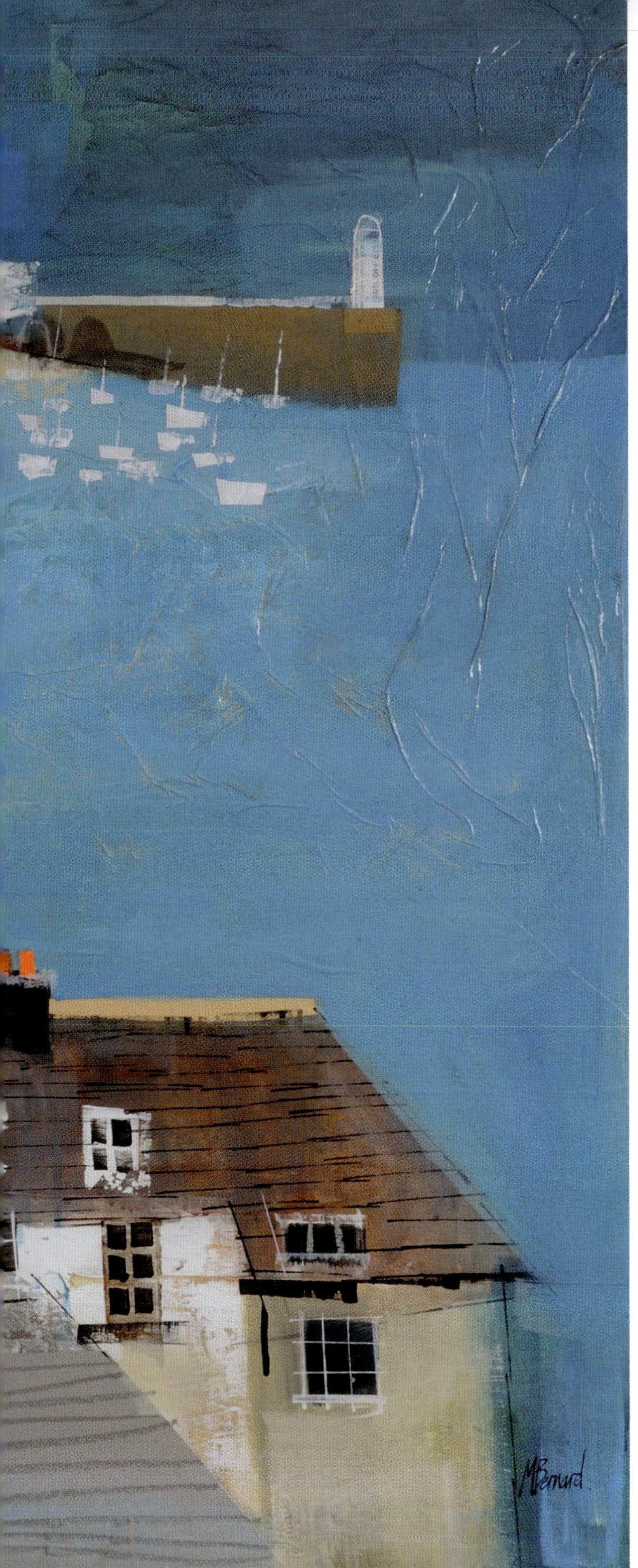

Starting with collage

After gathering information through sketches and photos, back in the studio, I begin working on paper, board or canvas. I prefer working on board as I might adjust the size later, which is not so easy to do with a canvas! Then I begin tearing my collage materials. This isn't an exact process; I might overlap some of the paper shapes, and I try to avoid placing them exactly parallel to the edges of the painting paper. Rather than having lots of right angles and parallel lines, I prefer more subtle angles and diagonals as these create a more dynamic quality in the design.

My collage materials are used to create shapes which relate to the structure of my subject: for instance, rough square and rectangular shapes for buildings. When the glue is dry, I apply acrylic ink in bold random strokes, which encourages wonderful colour and textural 'accidents'. From this state of chaos, I endeavour to define the subject through various drawing techniques, building up to a stage where the subject has recognisable passages, but at the same time retains a semi-abstract, impressionistic feel, so hopefully engaging the viewer's imagination.

Some artists like to position all the torn and cut paper shapes on the backing sheet of paper or card before gluing them in place. This allows them to consider the relationship between the different shapes and make alterations if necessary, before committing to a particular arrangement. However, I prefer a more intuitive, direct approach. I start with one shape and fix that in position, and then I add other shapes in relation to the first one and so on.

Harbour View, St Ives
Mixed media, 86 x 112cm (34 x 44in)
In many places across this painting you can see the collage that lies beneath the ink and paint. The vantage point I have taken is a high one, giving me a panoramic view of the scene.

Achieving spontaneity

However you work, my advice is to try to remain mindful throughout the process. Stop to look at the overall image every now and then, and work both instinctively and deliberately, as the painting may move in slightly unexpected directions. You might find it helpful to work as I do, never trying to force a work in progress to remain as you initially perceived or imagined it, nor to overwork any area or areas. Make use of things that you happen upon: for instance, part of a coloured photograph from a magazine may resemble a piece of rock, sea or a building. I tend to utilise these things, and place them where they will be the most descriptive. Or I might apply strokes of ink or oil pastel over the top of collage or marks later when I am looking back at a painting I have been working on, in order to give that area a slight lift. At this stage, I often look back at my original location drawing and notice where divisions, marks, shapes and surface effects are needed to bring the painting back to reality – while still trying to attain a lively, spontaneous and colourful view that is not too static, lifelike or prescriptive, but nonetheless recognisable. I start to resolve the essential elements. The challenge is to balance areas that give meaning and definition with those that are left as textural, abstract qualities. Finally, I draw with a dip pen and some black or brown acrylic ink to add any further outlines and details that I think are necessary.

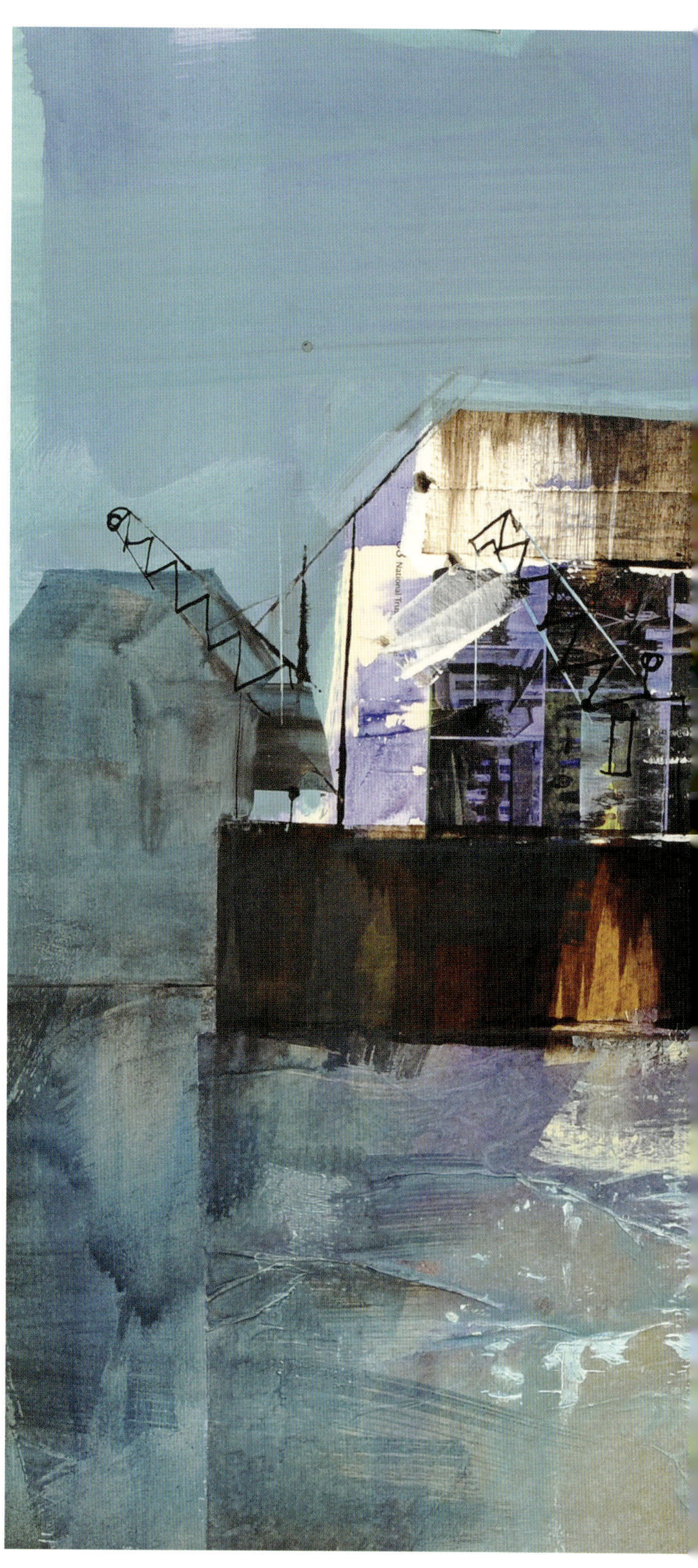

Boatyard, Fowey

Mixed media, 40 x 61cm (16 x 24in)
Most of my compositions can be roughly divided into thirds. Here you can see some edges where I have cut the collage materials and some where they have been torn.

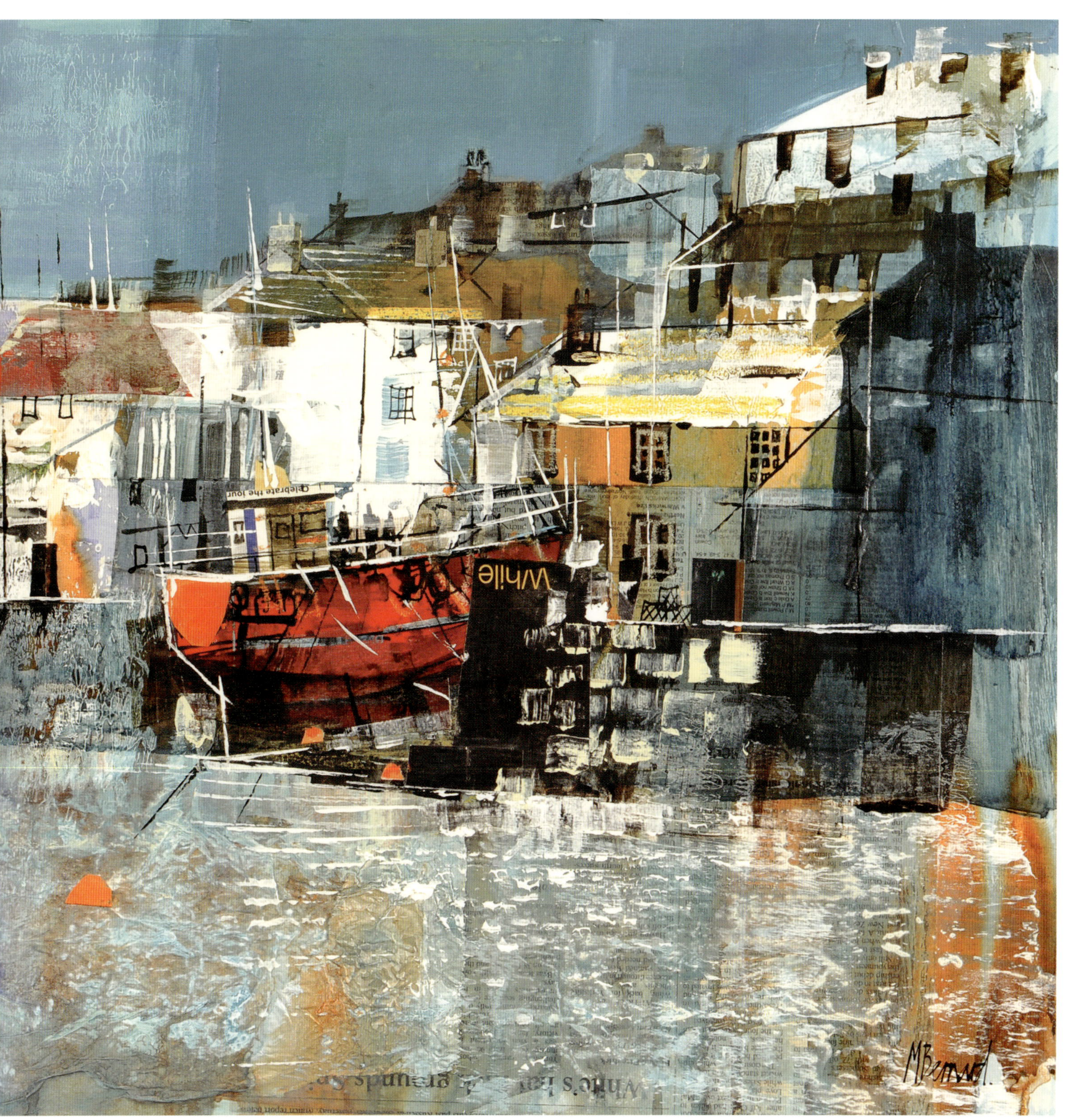

Celebrate the jour
While

Using collage effectively

When working on a painting, I usually try to include some papers that are particularly relevant to the subject matter. For example, for a painting inspired by a Cornish harbour, I might tear shapes from an appropriate holiday brochure. In other paintings, I sometimes use printed papers from newspapers or magazines to suggest different textures – perhaps the brickwork on the side of a building – although I am very aware that this should be kept within reason, otherwise the painting becomes too busy. In any event, I think contrast is important, so I like to offset the more exciting textural surfaces with plain papers, such as brown wrapping paper, pastel papers or white tissue paper.

I can't emphasise enough how light-handed and open-minded you should be with this approach to creating paintings. Be on the lookout for interesting papers and try not to restrict yourself. Having said I occasionally use words or images from travel brochures, I don't let myself become bogged down with or tied to this approach. It would be easy to become prescriptive with the papers you use; to try to emulate things you see with collage materials – for instance, photos of walls from a magazine used for brick walls in your painting – but aim not to do this: constantly move yourself away from any rigidity.

My way of working is to be bold. Take your first shape and stick it down, then build up from there. If you continue in this way, your final painting will be fresh and a bit unusual; not careful and exact. Too much planning can remove any sense of intuitiveness and dull the overall effect. If you're really not happy with a shape, position or a particular paper, simply stick another over it. I might overlap some of the paper shapes, and I try to avoid placing them exactly parallel to the edges of the painting paper. Rather than having lots of right angles and parallel lines, I prefer more subtle angles and diagonals. These create a more dynamic quality in the design. Once I have decided on a shape and glued it in place, I cannot alter it. But ironically, by adopting this approach, I am able to keep the initial stages of the painting fairly undefined –

so allowing me different options in terms of the way to proceed. Generally, I start with just four or five shapes: these, as I have explained, will indicate the key divisions within the composition – for example, where a telegraph pole intersects a field, or the top of a harbour wall abuts a building. I often emphasise such divisions and extend them right across the image.

To secure the collage shapes in place, I use a matt acrylic medium – usually Spectrum Copolymer Emulsion. Essentially, this is the same medium that is used in the manufacture of acrylic paint. An advantage of this medium is that it is waterproof, whereas PVA, which is equally suitable as an adhesive, is water-soluble. I dilute the acrylic medium with water for use with thin papers, but apply it undiluted for gluing materials such as corrugated card, mountboard and fabric. An alternative method, which I sometimes use, is to impress a paper shape into an area of wet acrylic paint.

Collage can be used at any stage during the process. As long as you wait for each area to dry before applying either more paint or further areas of collage, you will be fine. So for instance, an extra prominent rock, a boat or a figure, can all be added with either cut or torn paper after your painting is finished and dry. Then you can add a few judicious details with more paint or ink. Or you can add the tiniest of pieces of paper to create a focus of interest almost anywhere, such as for windows or highlights on the hull of a boat.

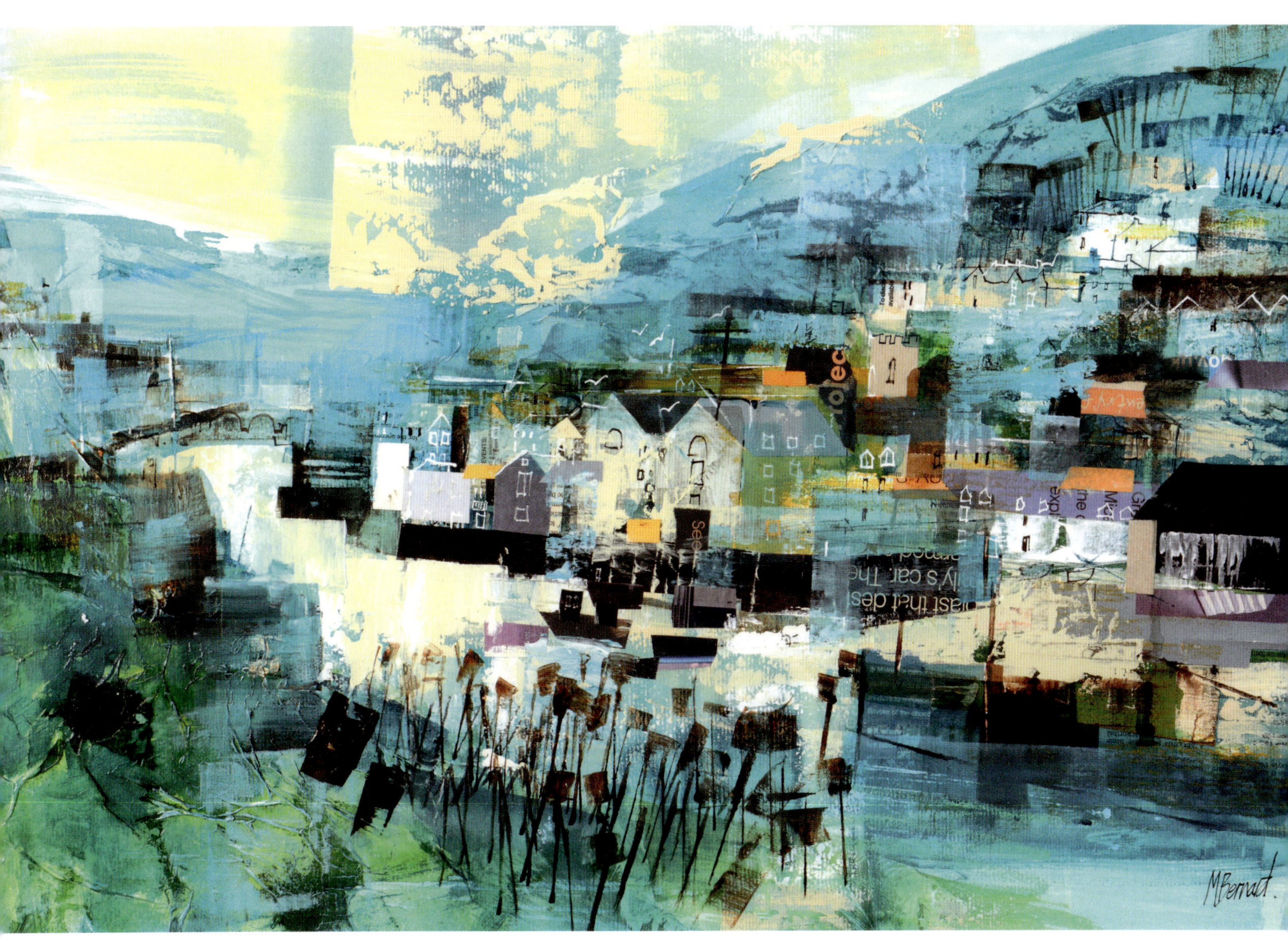

East Looe, Cornwall

Mixed media, 40 x 61cm (16 x 24in)
Here, I used one colour overall, plus some
brown for the darker tones and outlines.
You can see where I have pressed opaque
cream paint shapes into the image.

Interaction of collage materials

By experimenting with varied materials, you are giving
yourself a broad range of possibilities, but be aware
of each material's advantages and limitations and how
they interact with each other. This comes with practice.
Another thing to become familiar with is how to look at a
scene, to see overall patterns rather than shapes. What
attracts me most are patterns within scenes, whether
these are of buildings, boats, gondolas or rock formations.
Each artwork is built through initial blocks of colour that
develop patterns that I see in front of me and that are
also pleasing to my eye, that interact and imply a sense
of spontaneity, freshness and freedom.

While ordinary paper and magazines are effective,
try experimenting as well with different types of paper,
such as Japanese rice paper, handmade or art paper,
old maps or sheet music, or even any old, experimental
watercolours that you may have abandoned or discarded.
These all interact beautifully with each other, whether by
their marked contrasts or their similarities. In my studio
I now have an extensive stock of these various materials,
stored in separate boxes for each type. I can put my
hand on almost any of them, almost instantly, so my
process is not interrupted. So for example, if I am shaping
something to emphasise what might be, perhaps rocks
on a craggy cliff or a flat bank of buildings, I can grasp an
appropriately textured or patterned paper without thinking
too much about it. In this way, my painting remains fresh,
spontaneous-looking and hopefully not too contrived. For
example, tissue paper might be randomly scrunched (a
little) for the sea, a thick, handmade paper used for rocks,
and flat, smooth wrapping paper for a manmade structure

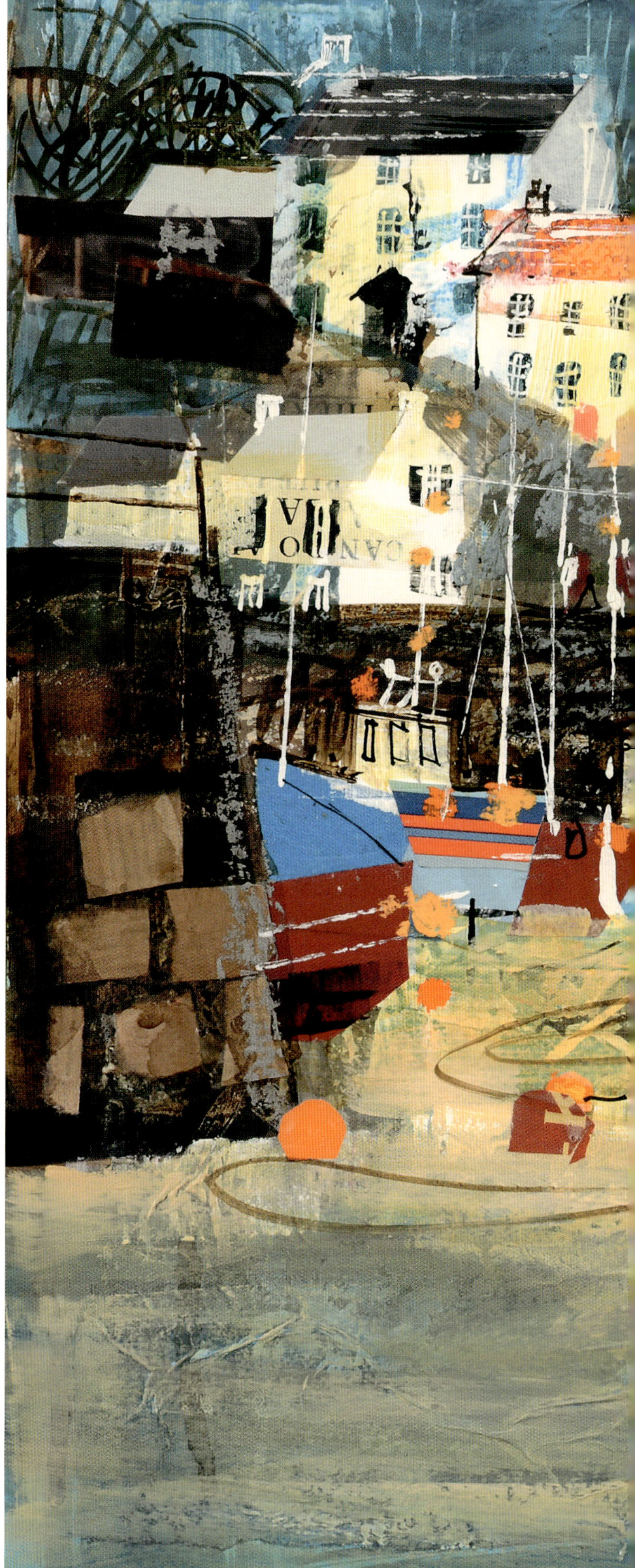

Lynmouth

Mixed media, 38 x 30cm (15 x 12in)
Because this is composed with a
low viewpoint, most of my larger
pieces of collage are in the centre
of the composition and above.

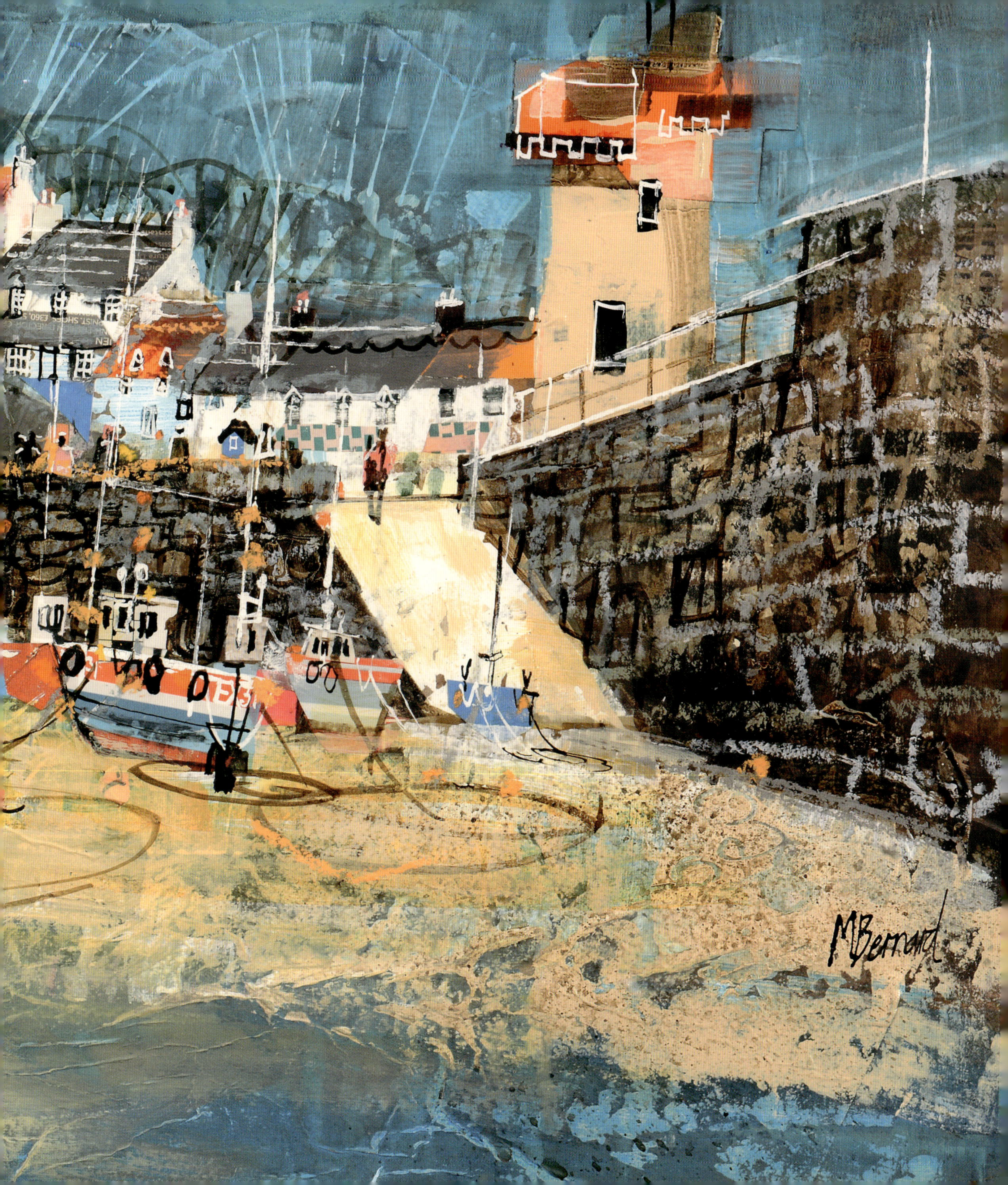

MBernard

such as a wall or a boat. I build each collage to establish a sense of the basic design for the painting and I continue considering the textures and how I will portray them through my collage materials. I keep looking and thinking, working quite rhythmically. Mainly, I work quite rapidly at this stage, creating a flow, but sometimes I'll pause and take more time to consider what I need, or hunt for that perfect paper to use. I keep tearing or cutting and sticking. The whole surface does not have to be covered and the layers should not be too thick. You can always add more later. The demonstration on pages 101–103 is a good example of how I often apply collage in the initial stage. Other collage elements, such as sails, boat hulls, signs and lobster pots are added later, as required.

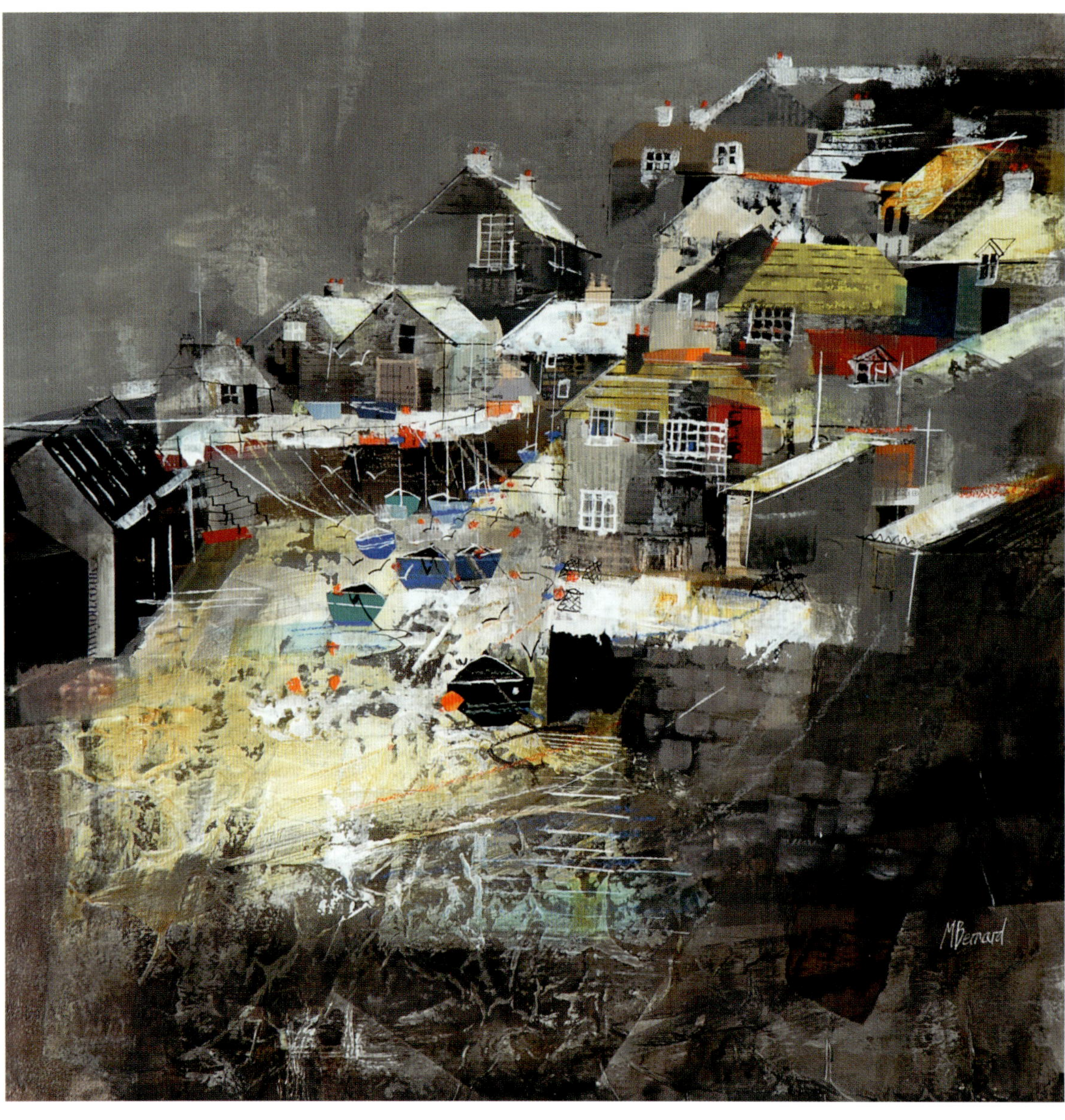

Winter Light, Port Looe
Mixed media, 61 x 61cm (24 x 24in)
Various vertical lines from the buildings are repeated across the painting, making key divisions that lead the viewer's eye along and around the scene.

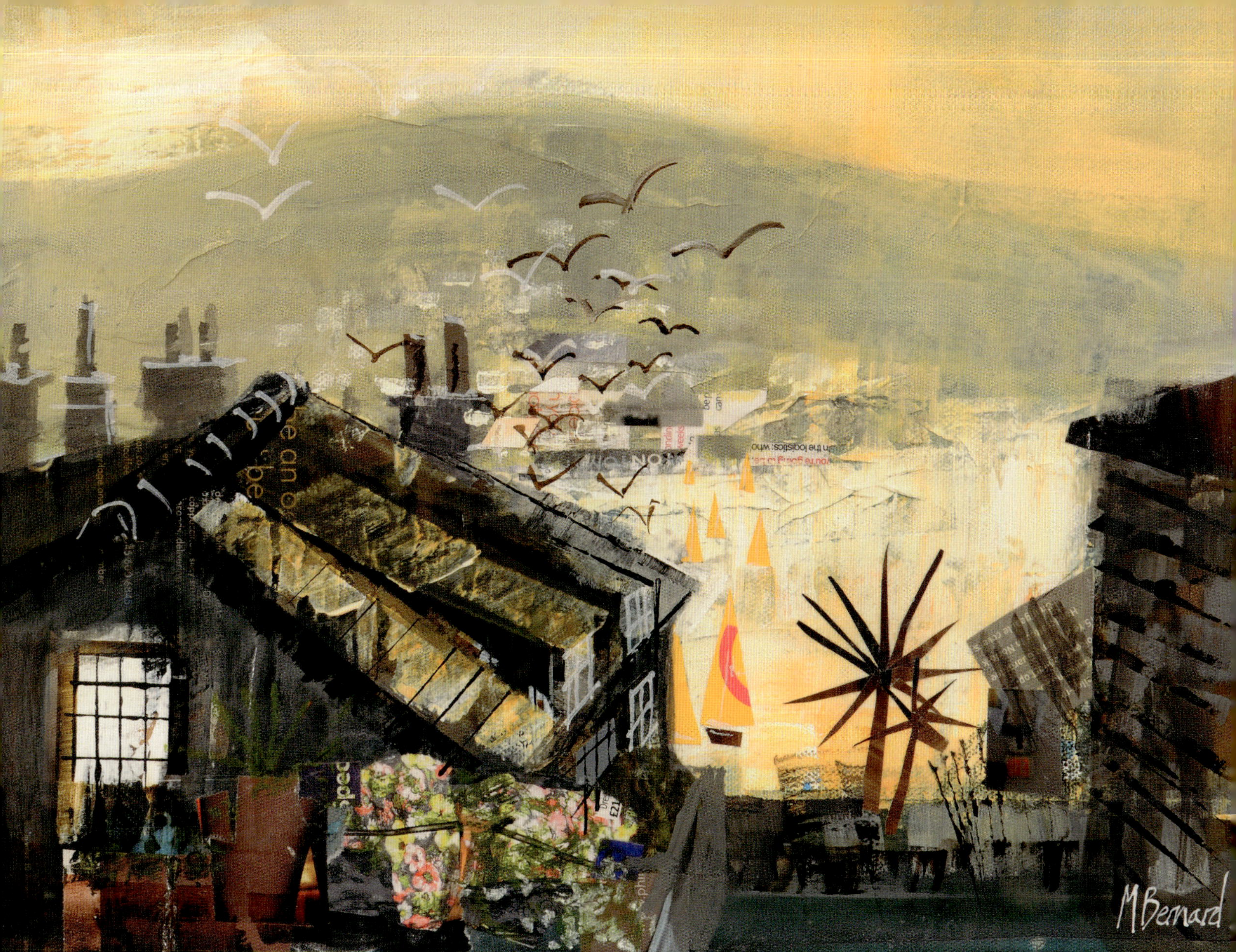

Being adventurous

Have you ever tried working without lines, or taking risks with materials? Well, now is the time I suggest you do! There are great advantages in being adventurous as you work. By trying to do something out of your comfort zone, that is more ambitious than you would usually do, or more experimental, you might discover a new style, a completely different 'look' – or at least find what you do not like! For me, mixed media enables me to stretch myself all the time. It allows me to be more expressive and individual. Accept that by pushing yourself in this way, you

Evening Rooftops, Dartmouth
Mixed media, 30 x 40cm (12 x 16in)
Here, I've been adventurous with the trees, the flowers on the rooftop and the birds in the sky. The only really defined aspects of this painting are the edges and the suggestions of the window frames and glazing bars.

will be taking risks that you might find uncomfortable, but that you will ultimately find rewarding. Remember that there is no set way of working. Work as intuitively and as freely as you can. Do not let the subject matter overtake your creative process. Once you overcome the need for outlines and that initial, overly defined start, you will find the painting process becomes far more inspiring and in turn will motivate you to be even more adventurous. This might not happen overnight. You may need to work at this but, for me, I found making detailed, realistic drawings and paintings inhibiting; being freer and more adventurous gives me far more scope and reduces limitations. By starting with a few collage shapes, torn and placed on your paper or card, you are immediately giving yourself the opportunity to grow and expand on your chosen scene. Alternatively, by drawing and trying to follow exactly what you see you will check your development and expansion and confine your creativity.

I used to tell my students to begin with anything other than a detailed drawing. As discussed already, a loose, free collage, rollers with paint or wet-in-wet watercolour washes are exciting ways to blot out the daunting prospect of white paper in front of you, to inspire rather than inhibit you as you begin. Although I usually encourage artists to use one or more reference to a particular place, occasionally I begin a work with no set subject in mind, purely using my memory and imagination.

A free technique

Many of my works simply happen. They are the result of my being free and open to intuition, to chance and happy accidents, and of my experiments such as playing with materials, with lost and found edges (see below) and with ratios and dimensions to create different effects.

At the start of a painting, when I am applying collage, although I usually know what the subject matter will be, I also generally have no clear sense of direction. I might decide to emphasise or define an area or object, or I might suppress something else in another area by painting over it with opaque paint, adding more collage or glazing it with a semi-transparent ink. Usually, I use large brushes, pieces of card or lino-printing rollers, continuing the broad treatment that I started with. Most of the time, I don't apply paint with brushes, and certainly rarely with small brushes. Instead I prefer to use anything but, such as palette knives, rollers, bits of card or toothbrushes and so on. Or I spray my paint surface while it is on my upright easel and allow the dribbles and runs to become part of the image. Then, surface effects can be left as interesting textures for themselves, rather than becoming used for anything specific. In these ways, gradually, a painting takes on a more abstracted air; it becomes less realistic, more individual and more conceptual.

Lost and found edges
The balance of lost and found edges is important for adding feeling and intrigue to your painting. Basically, lost edges are those that blend into each other, such as an object blending into its shadow. Found edges are those where you can see the outline of an object.

Project – Devon Beach

Before starting this painting, I made a quick drawing of the location in pencil to capture the main shapes and tones. Back in the studio, the painting went through the following stages:

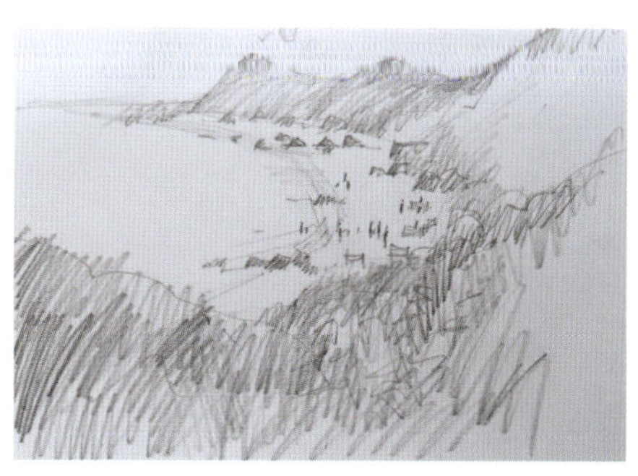

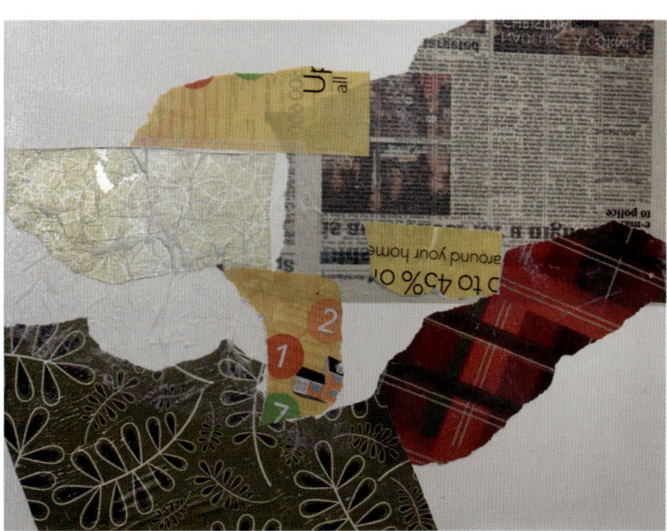

1 I build up the collage base, using a variety of papers, including newspaper, wrapping paper and shiny paper. The contrasts are random and the sizes different. Most of the pieces of paper are torn. Using tissue paper, I tear some large shapes to create the rocks and cliffs, plus some parts of the water in the foreground. At this stage, nothing looks like my observational drawing; it's not meant to. However, I aim to make the waterway snake from the foreground to the background to lead the viewer's eye through the composition. Where I've used magazines for the collage, I've deliberately placed the words upside down and where possible back to front, as I want the lettering to create interest, but not be a distraction.

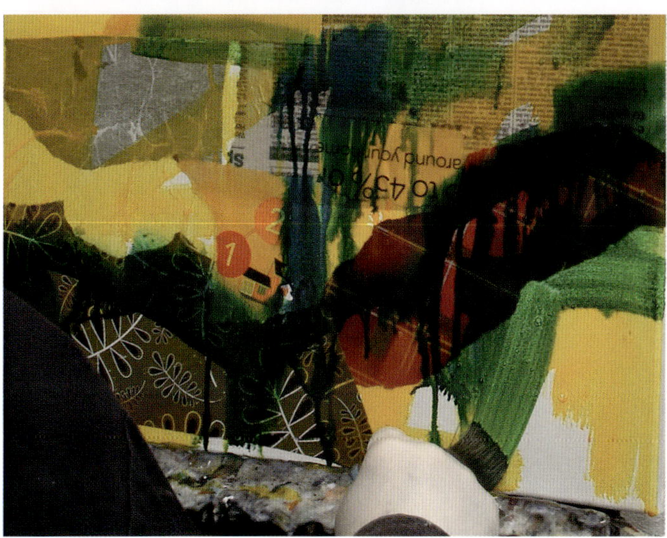

2 Now I soak the collage in mainly FW acrylic ink in Indian yellow, but I let some Liquitex turquoise run down the board randomly.

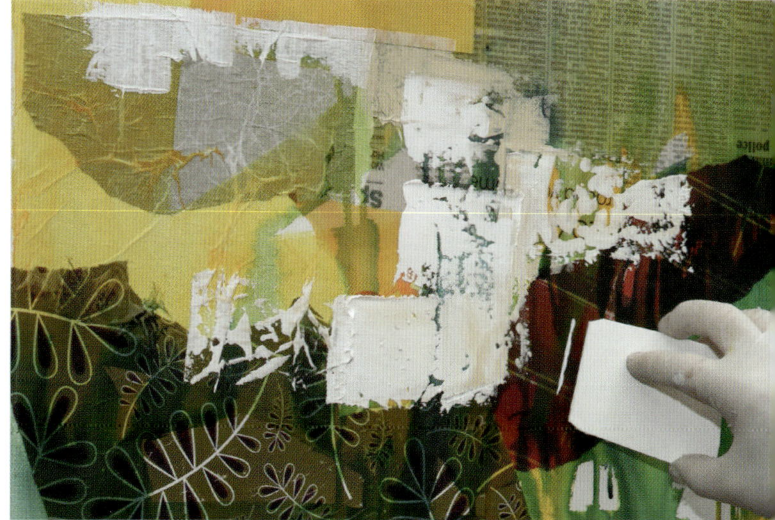

3 Using a piece of card, I block on some Liquitex titanium white that is completely opaque. Sometimes I use the flat side of the card, at other times I drag the edge over the painting.

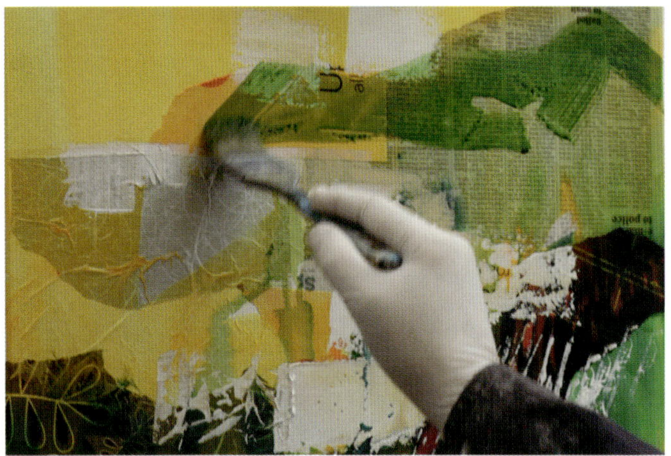

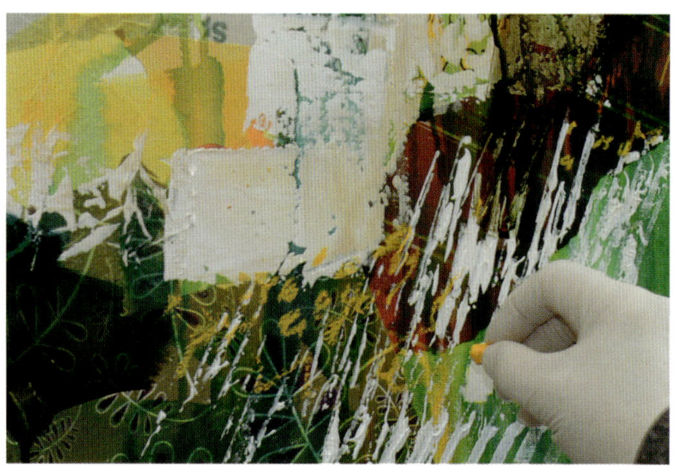

4 With a decorator's brush and some diluted Liquitex turquoise, I create certain areas of contrast with transparent washes.

5 With yellow oil pastel, I stipple on some colour and add more transparent turquoise over the yellow, which becomes green where the two colours mix together.

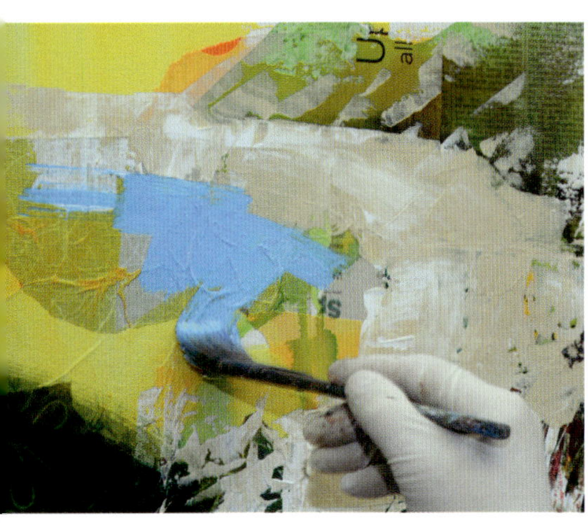

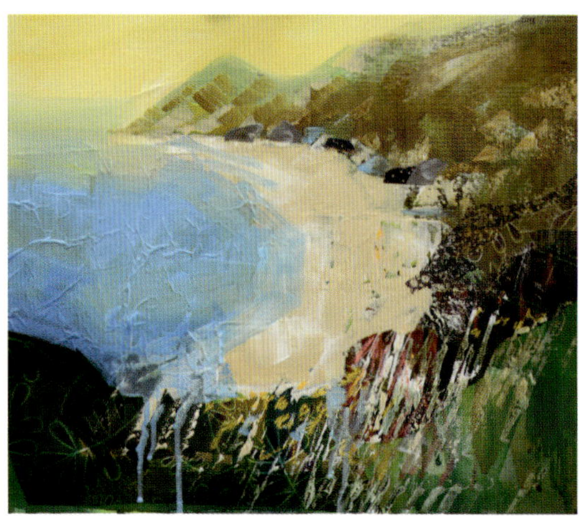

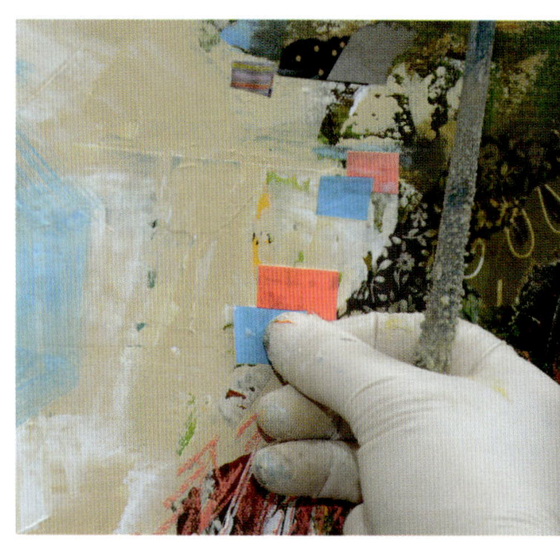

6 Using a brush, I apply the turquoise blended with white – which has now become fairly thick and opaque.

7 I gradually build up the shape of the beach and sea in the cove as I saw it from my vantage point high above.

8 I add more collage – smaller pieces this time, and more opaque white.

9 Using my piece of card, I create certain details and marks that suggest shapes, patterns and textures. The windbreaks and figures on the beach are all implied with the side of my card.

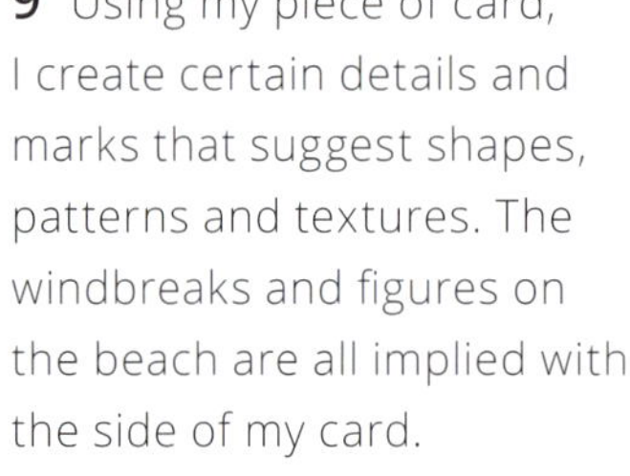

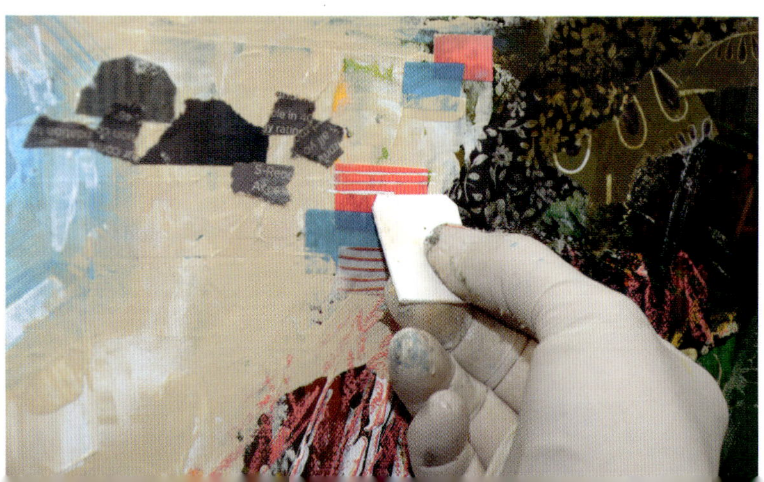

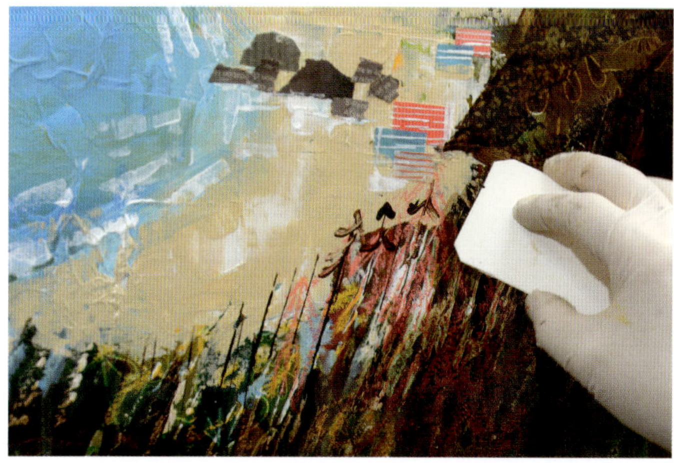 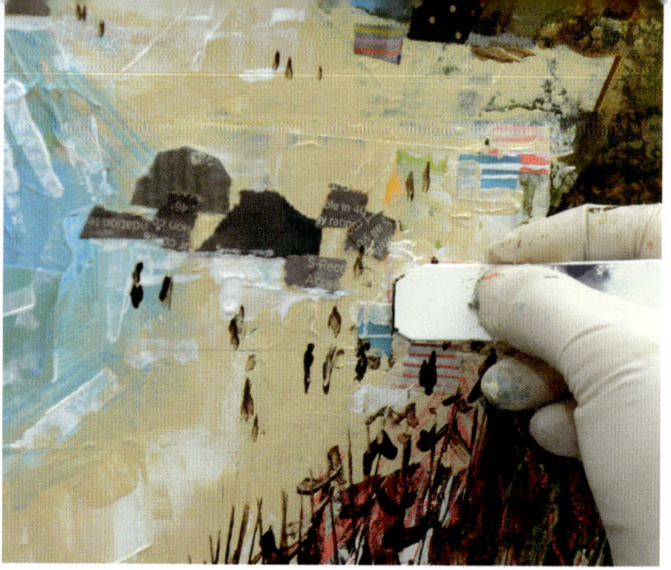

10 Working across the image, I create shapes that suggest depth and distance, figures and rocks, keeping things as balanced and as free as possible.

11 To complete the painting, I add some details, but I make sure that I stop before the image becomes too realistic.

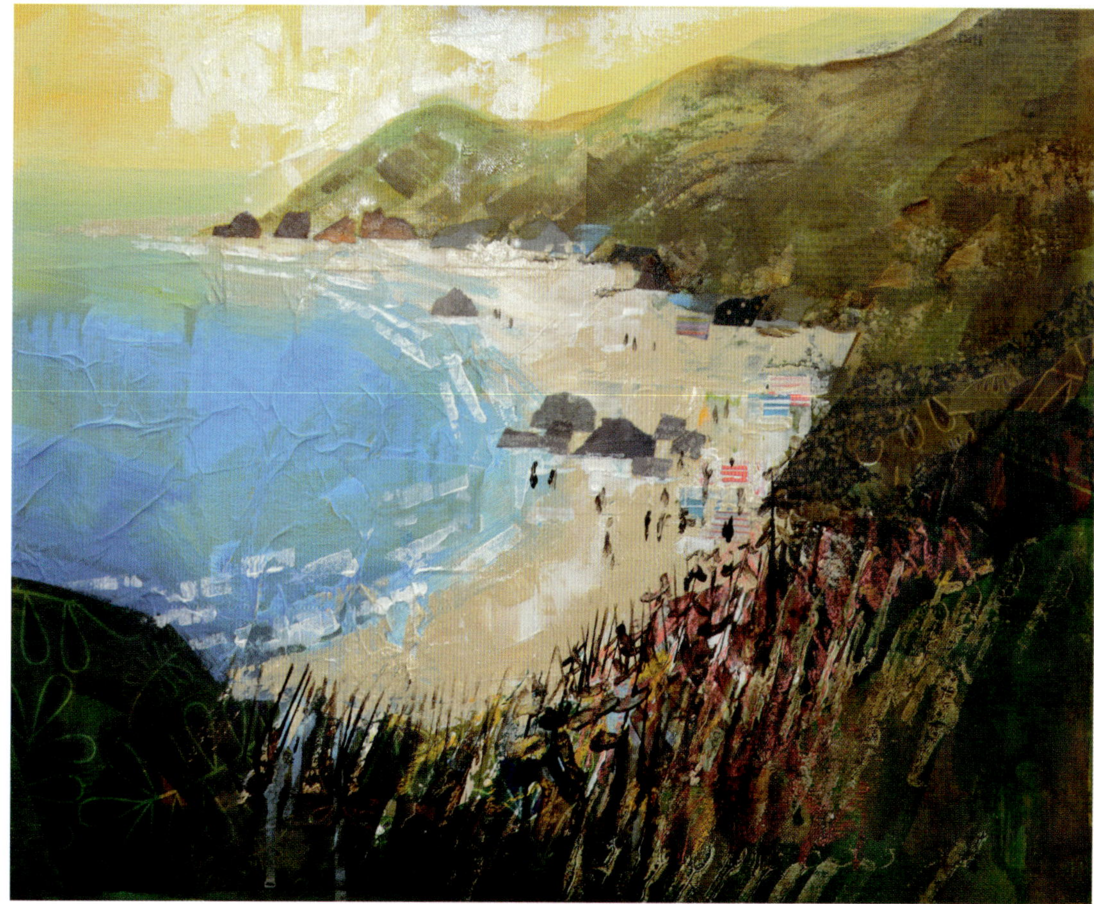

Devon Beach

Mixed media,

40 x 51cm (16 x 20in)

To create a sense of aerial or atmospheric perspective, in the distance are soft, pale colours and no sharply-defined edges, with deeper colours and textures in the foreground.

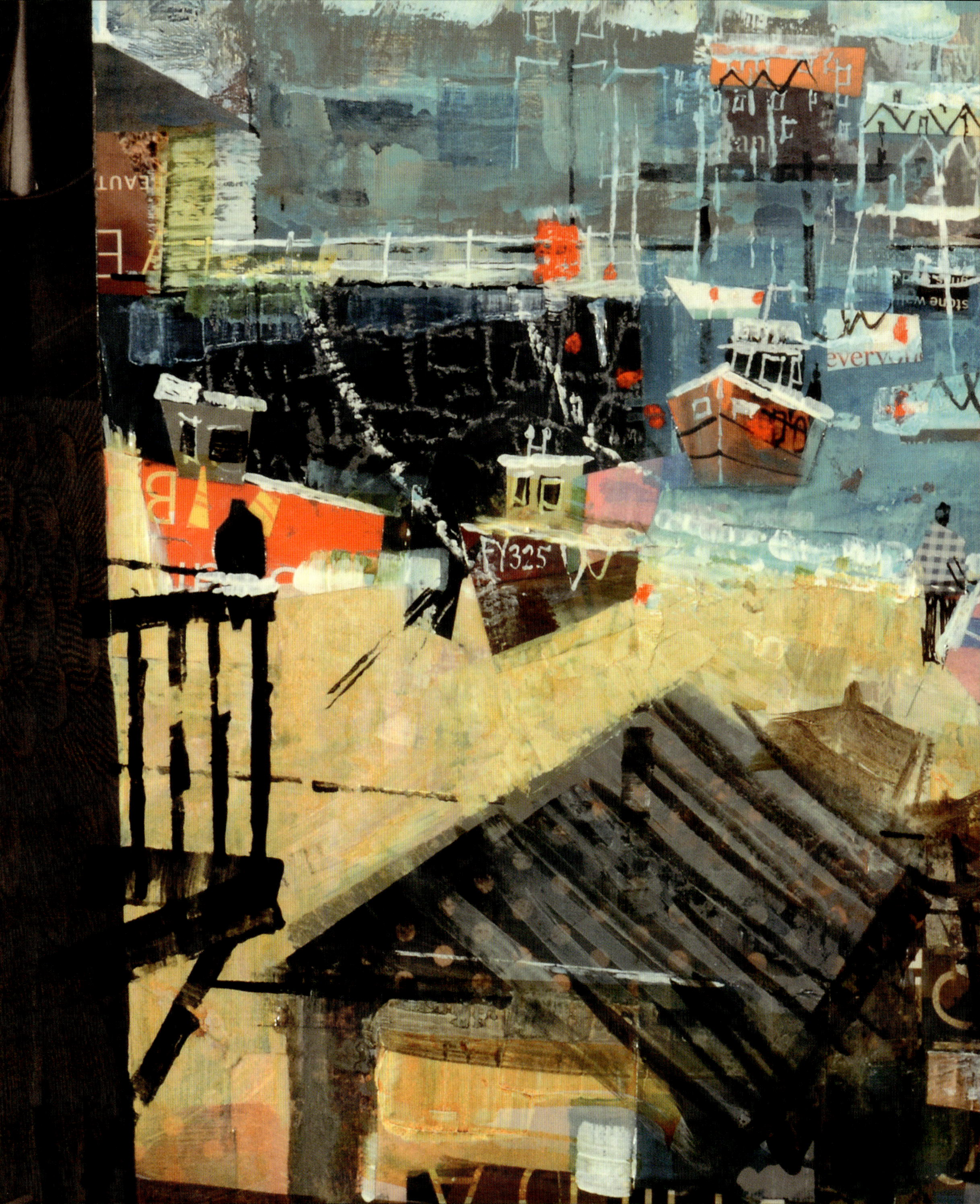

FY325

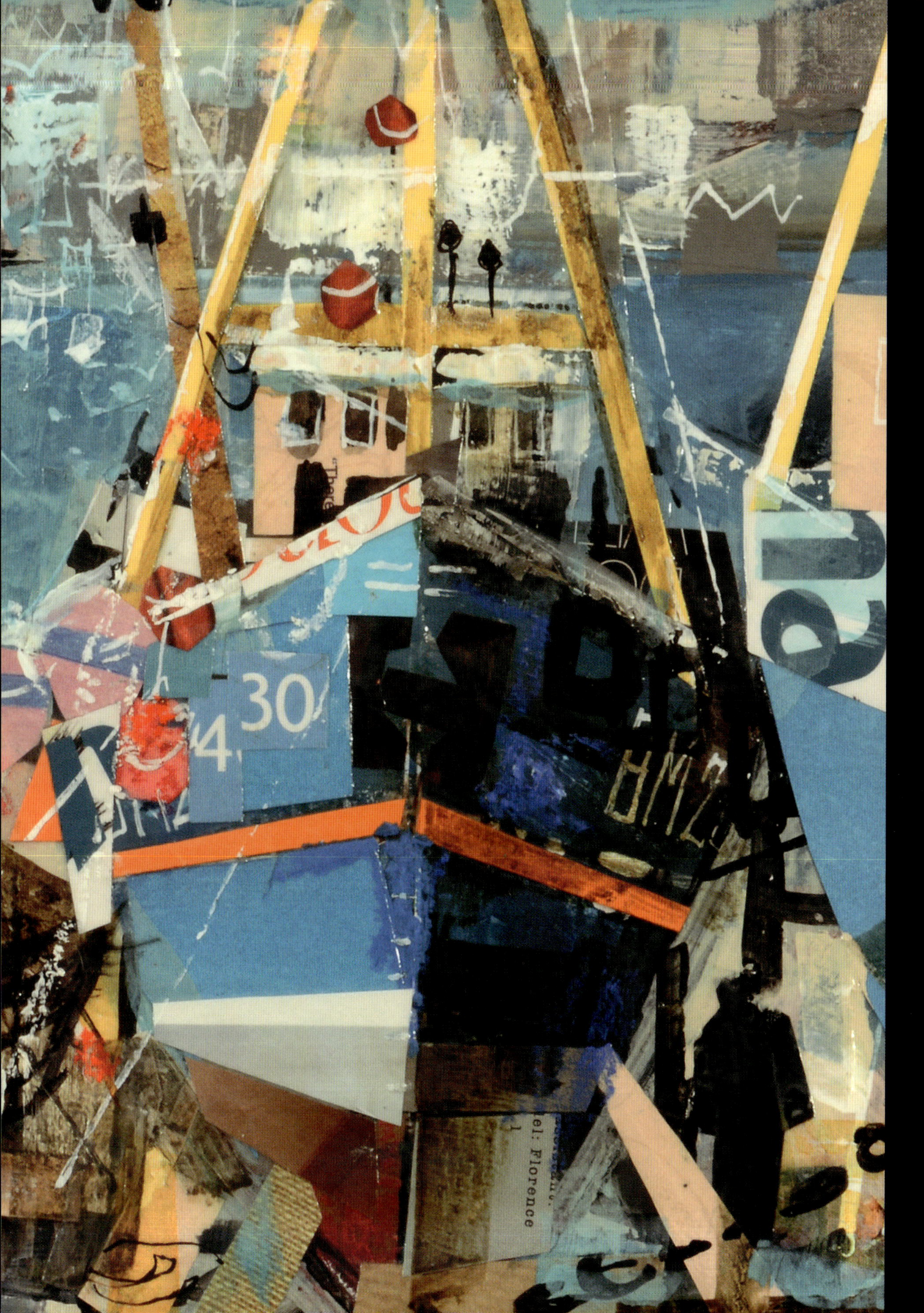

Atmosphere and Mood

From the moment you start, there are decisions to be made at every stage of the painting process. For instance, colour, texture, placement of collage, proportions, tonal contrasts, level of detail and so on. One of these considerations is the creation of atmosphere or mood.

Although mood and atmosphere are important elements in all paintings, they are, like so many aspects of my work, not something that I plan from the start. The mood and atmosphere begin to emerge as the painting develops. So in the early stages, I concentrate on getting as much freedom into the work as possible and, according to the decisions I make as I work, a sense of mood is fostered. This includes creating arbitrary shapes, torn edges, crumpled paper and random runs of paint and similar spontaneous, unplanned techniques. As the work progresses, I start creating interest – working out the most important aspects of a scene and ways of enhancing these, while establishing a sense of mood. Throughout the process, I seek a balance between deliberate and considered effects and those that happen by chance.

Playing with your knowledge of basic colour theory, such as complementary and analogous colours, can be especially helpful in creating a sense of mood or capturing the atmosphere of a place.

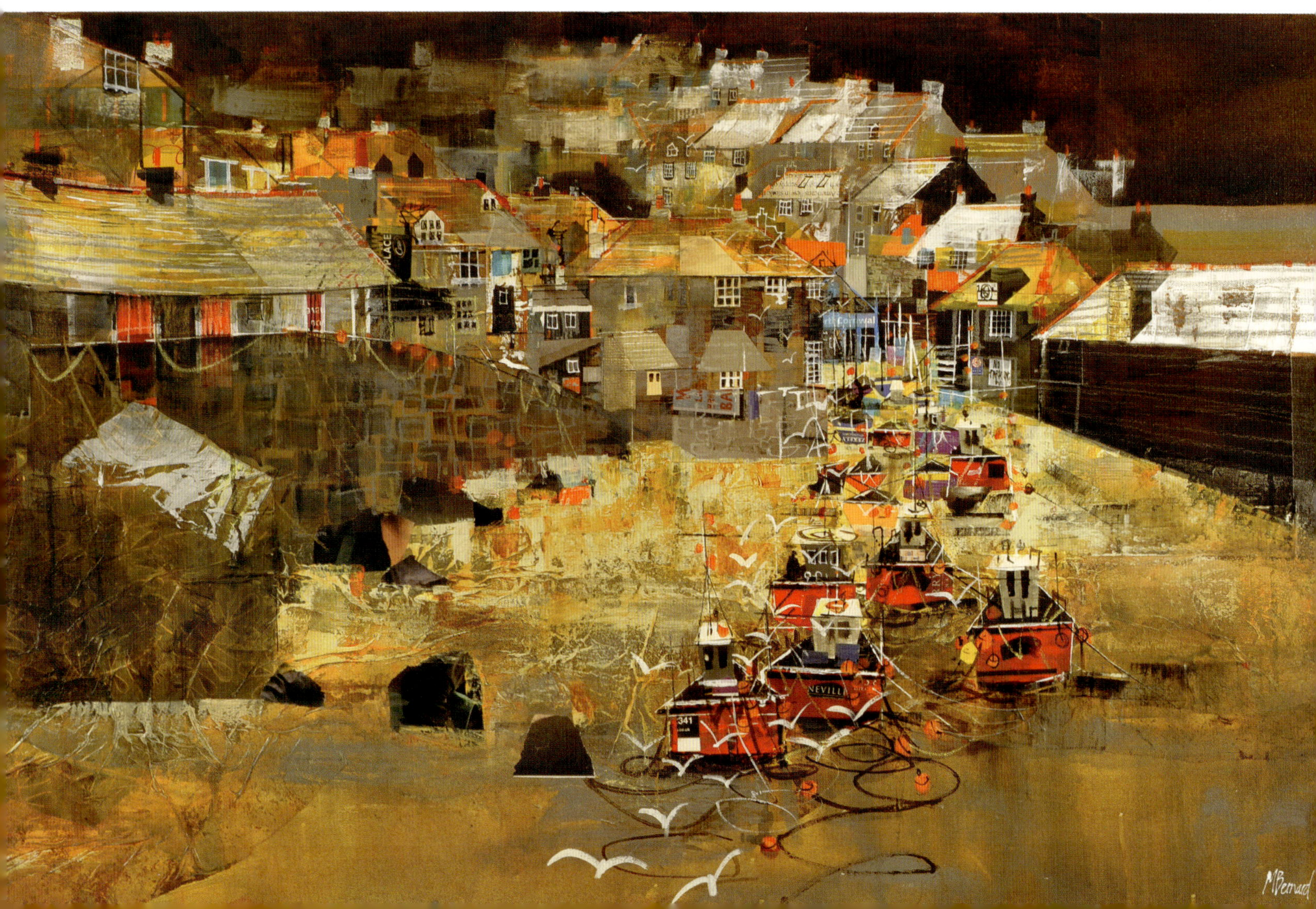

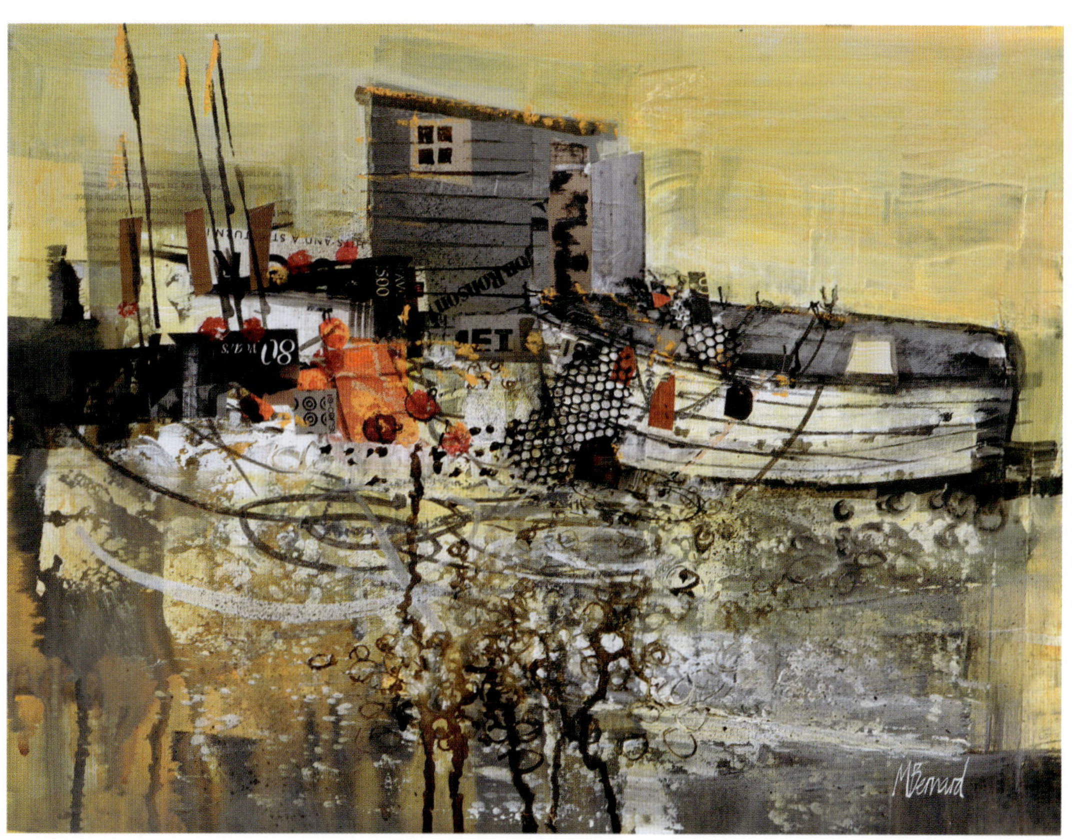

4

Colour and light

My use of colour is evocative rather than illustrative.
For me, colour should be used in an imaginative way
to work alongside texture and other more abstract
elements as you create a likeness, but also incorporating
abstraction and atmosphere. Usually the colours I use are
quite random, which forces me to work in fresh ways to
capture a resemblance while still bringing in other ideas.

As I work, I am conscious of the strong role colour
plays in my overall design and in determining the mood of
the image. For example, in *Autumn, Port Isaac*, the colours
convey the sense of the season; the mood that comes
with autumn when the leaves change colour and the
sun becomes more mellow.

Experimental exercises

Before you start to work with colour, it's a good idea to try out some tonal work. These thumbnails were made from coloured photographs as I tried to observe and match the tones in each area, that is, the darkest, middle and lightest highlights. You can do something similar by photocopying a coloured photo or changing a photo on your computer, phone or other device; it's all useful to note the relative values. Drawing, of course, makes you concentrate more and so become acutely aware of where the darkest and lightest values are in a scene.

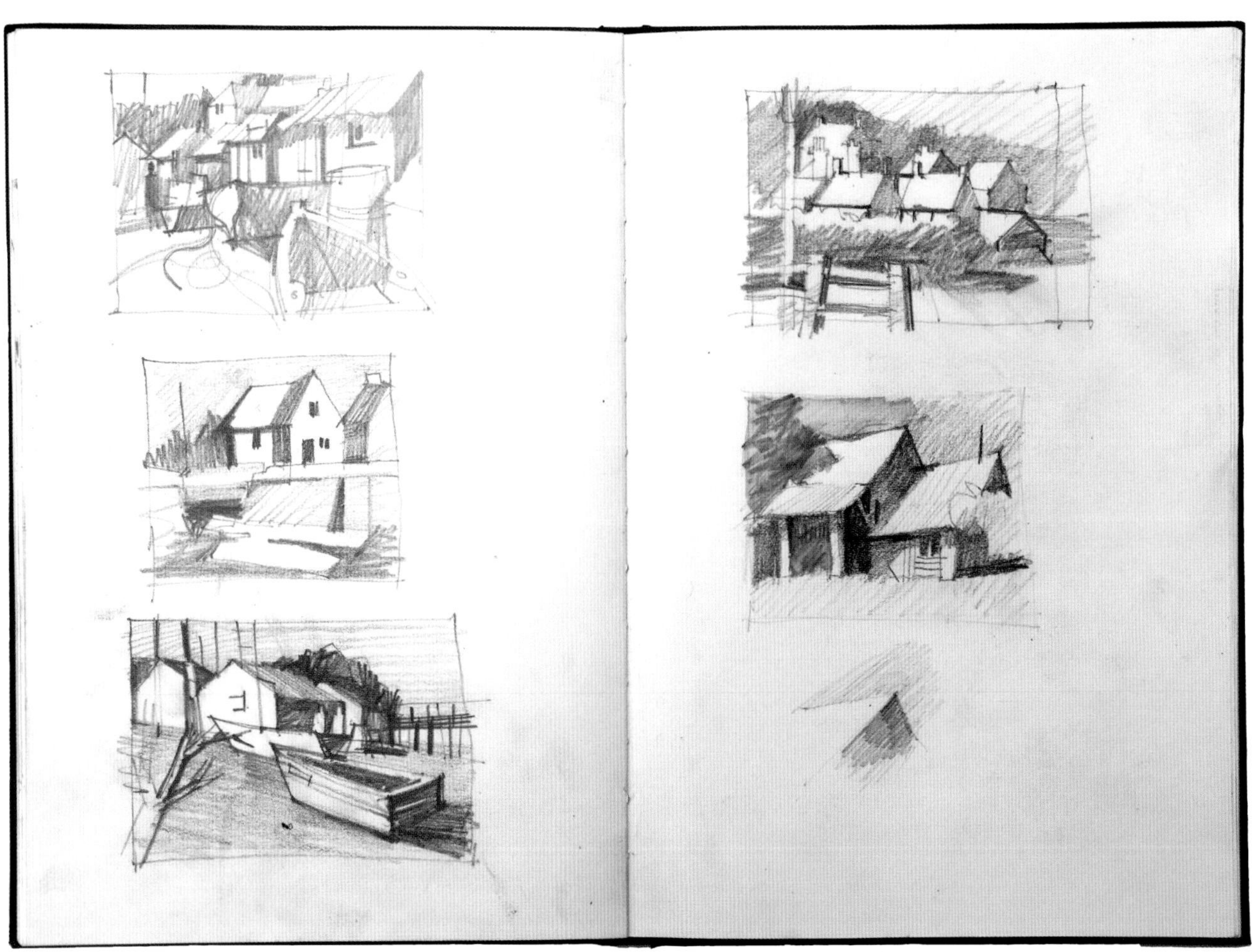

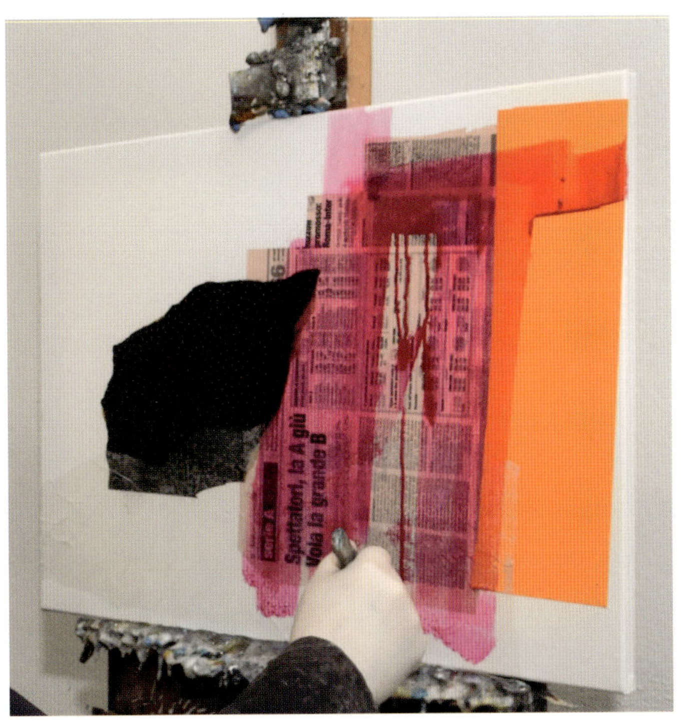

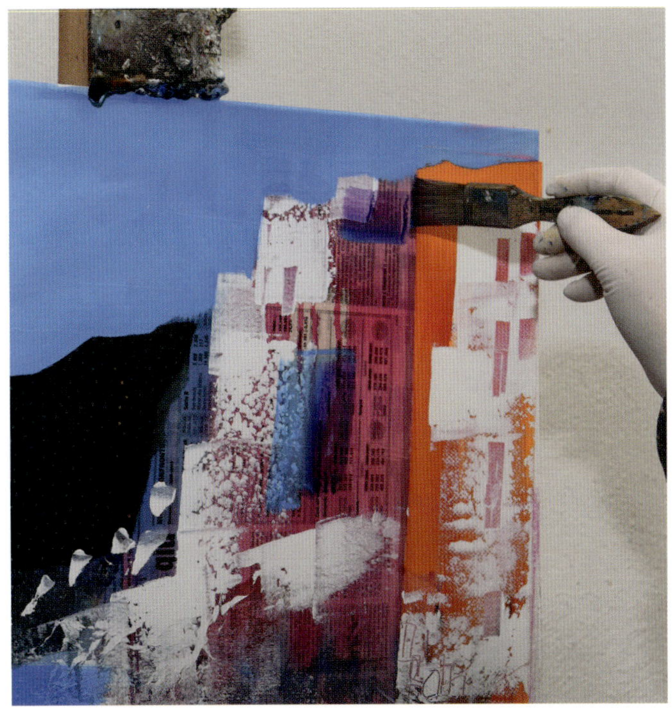

Often, I allow my two chosen colours in my paintings to mix by themselves, randomly on the paper. Rather than mix them on a palette, I apply them wet-into-wet and see how they run into each other. As you can see here, I am using a large brush to drag some transparent wet ink across an underlayer of magenta. This was the start of my painting *Riomaggiore* (see pages 56–59). I did what I could before I started the work to create a sense of spontaneity. Later, as I worked, I employed another regular technique in which I allowed the underlayer to dry and then glazed some wet paint over the top. Both of these techniques are extremely useful and worth practising.

Another way of exploring colour is to select two colours, any two, perhaps red and blue. Then find as many examples as you can of those two colours in magazines or anywhere else – tissue paper, wrapping paper and so on. Once you have collected several examples, glue them all down together: that is, the blue with the blue, the red with the red. I think you'll be amazed at how many different shades of each colour you have found. This is always useful in a painting, whether you achieve the alternative colours through collage or paint.

As well as colour, shape and contrasts, I am inspired by light. Light can create a sense of mood and atmosphere all on its own, so it's a useful element to be aware of the whole time you are working. As I work, I look for shapes, both general and detailed, but across the design I pick out the lightest and darkest tones to convey weight and depth. On the whole, I allow each image to evolve its own personality as it progresses, to avoid it becoming either over-representational or overpowering, but light and colour are two of the main ways in which I can create a sense of atmosphere.

Evoking mood

While the mood of an image is not always planned, I usually find that, as a painting takes shape, a mood or atmosphere begins to present itself. Sometimes this is created by me deliberately conveying certain times of day. As with most of my paintings, this is rarely planned specifically, but often, as I'm working, a sense of the time of day (or night), and frequently weather effects as well, starts to emerge. When that happens, I nearly always try to enhance and exaggerate it in some way. If, when I start, I already have an idea about depicting a certain time of day, perhaps sunrise or twilight, for instance, I deliberately choose my two colours to reflect this.

Not all of my outcomes are left to chance. Often as I start, I will have a certain look or idea at the back of my mind that I want to achieve, and sometimes my decisions, such as composition and colours, are deliberate.

Sometimes, for instance, I know that one particular colour will evoke a mood or atmosphere and I select this colour consciously to use in my pared-down palette. Colour always creates emotional impact and I am conscious of the types of impact certain colours and colour combinations will create. Often, I base my colours on a warm and cool contrast, or I will make it predominantly cool or warm, dark or light, subdued or bright and so on, depending on the effects I want to suggest. Also, the amount of white in a painting or the amount of definition or ambiguity I convey will make a difference to the overall atmosphere a painting evokes.

A glance at any painting by the Impressionists will show you how colour can dictate atmosphere or mood. Known for using limited palettes and colours in shadows rather than just greys, the Impressionists suggested all kinds of moods and ambience. While you should be inspired by

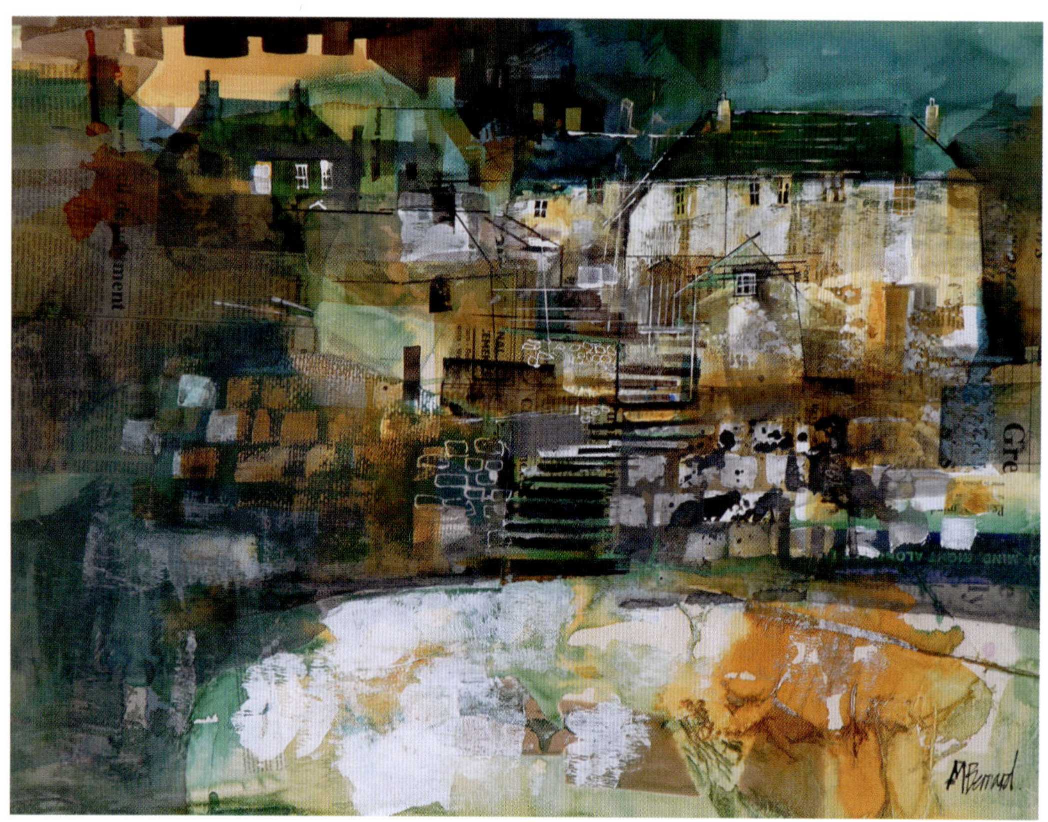

Harbour Steps, Coverack
Mixed media,
40 x 58.5cm (16 x 23in)
Using just the two colours of Indian yellow and turquoise, as well as opaque white for texture, I created this richly coloured image. The steps lead the eye into the composition.

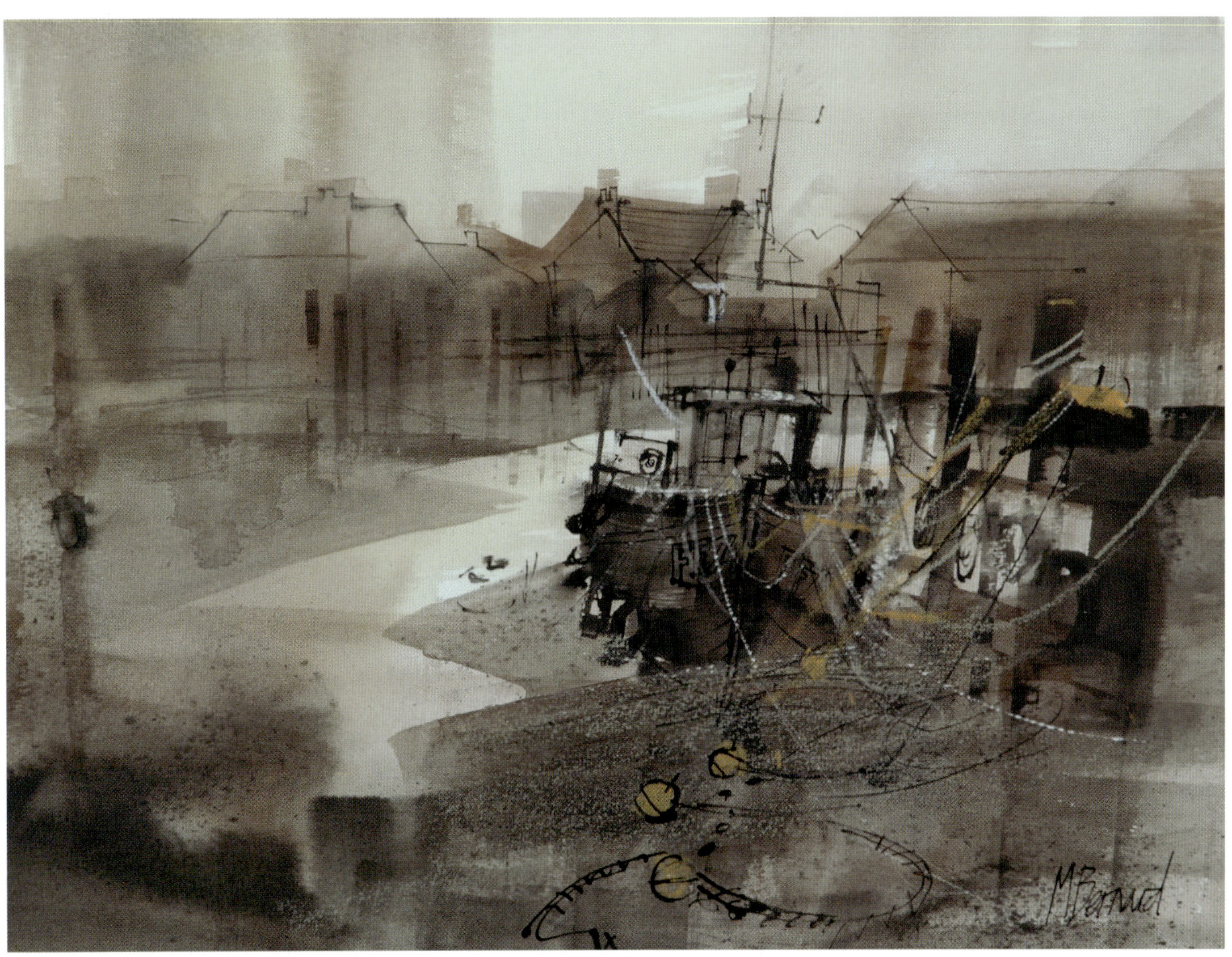

Fading Light, Emsworth
Mixed media, 30 x 38cm (12 X 15in)
With this view, I was attracted by the fading light as the sun – that couldn't be seen that day anyway – was setting. It left a mysterious, almost haunting, monochrome scene that I've tried to capture with the diluted ink. Only brown and black are used here, with touches of yellow ochre.

these artists, you do not have to slavishly copy them – or any other artist for that matter. They inspired me originally to work with a limited palette of colours that I reduced down even further to usually just two colours in any one work. I had been strongly aware when working outside, directly in front of a subject, that the colours I saw dictated how and what I painted, but following exactly what I saw did not necessarily evoke the mood or atmosphere I was after. I found that if I made notes and sketches, and then distanced myself from the subject when I was painting it in the studio, I could use colour in a more detached yet personal way.

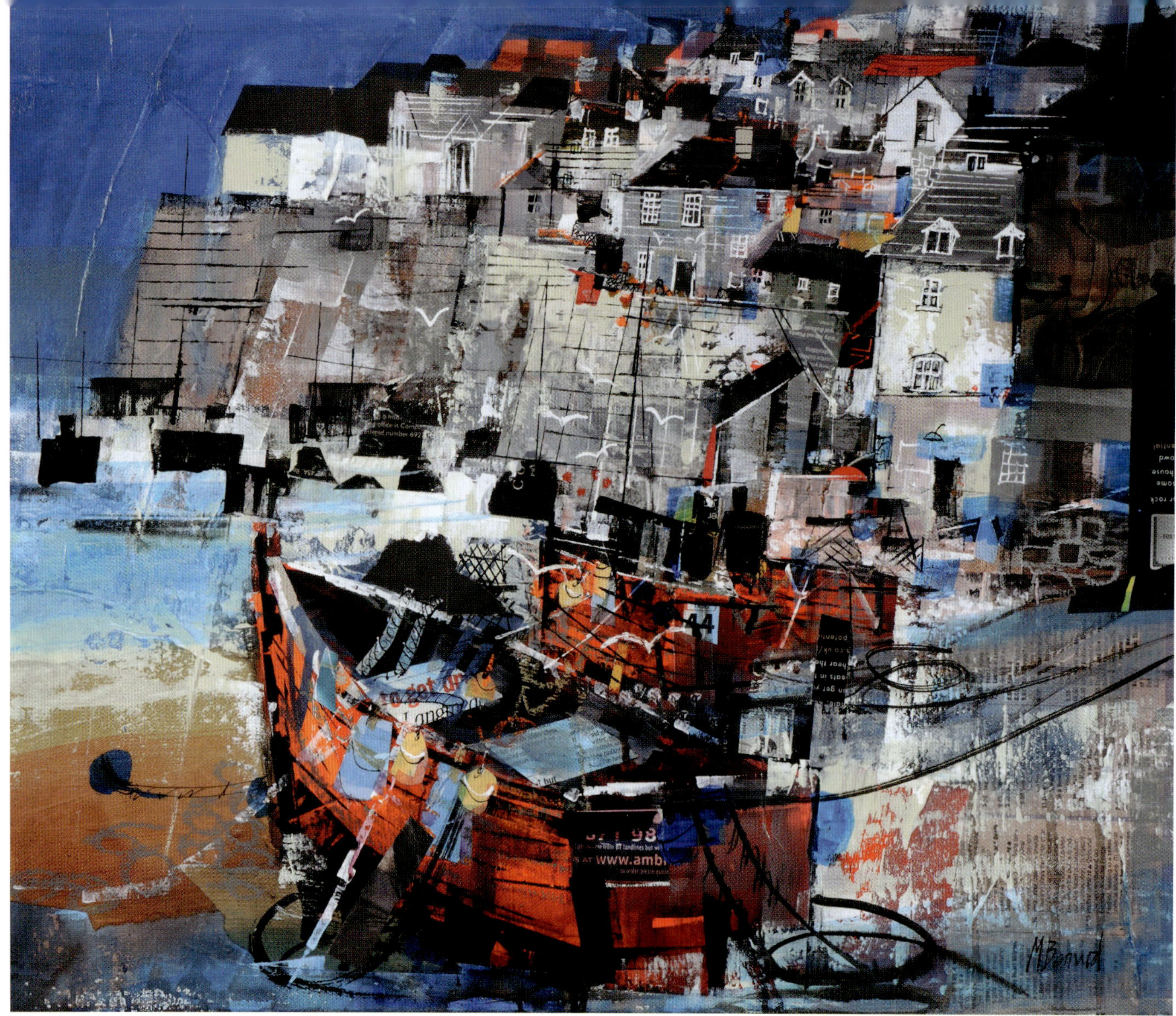

Contrast and viewpoint

Strong contrasts between colours, shapes and tonal values, or light and dark tones, will ultimately create a mood or atmosphere. This will be seen by every viewer before he or she even comes close to your work. For instance, a painting with a lot of blue and touches of pink or orange can seem cool and calm with hints of warmth. A predominantly orange-toned painting will suggest heat and perhaps afternoon light. Dark grey and pale yellow might suggest late evening or a cool day, and yellow and green or blue and white will convey a summer's day or cool winter respectively. One of the most striking ways in which I express a mood is by creating strong contrasts of dark and light tones. Sometimes this is balanced across an entire landscape, while at other times, the dark passages outweigh the lighter areas or vice versa.

Another factor that affects the conveyed mood is whether your viewpoint is close-up or distant. For some of my paintings, for instance, *Bay Road, Ireland*, I paint with the view in the distance, while in *Red Boats, Port Isaac*, close-up works well to create the sense of bustle, daytime, people and summer. For other images, such as *Deserted Beach in the Hebrides*, or *Evening Lights, Salcombe*, distance and deep

Bay Road, Ireland

Mixed media, 51 x 76cm (20 x 30in)
Here, the composition for me is created
by the patterns formed by the fields in the
distance, the houses in the middle and the
flowers in the foreground.

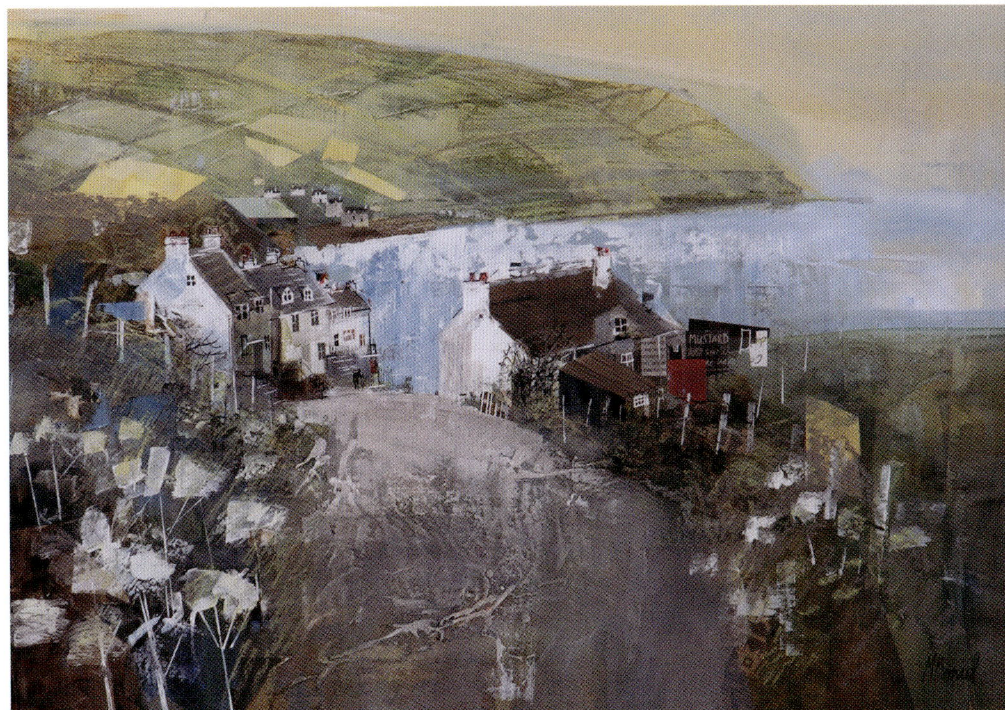

Left: **Red Boats, Port Isaac**

Mixed media, 61 x 51cm (24 x 20in)
I enjoyed making the boats in the
foreground large in comparison
to the background view. The
close-up creates drama and the
distant view sets the scene.

**Deserted Beach
in the Hebrides**

Mixed media, 40 x 40cm (16 x 16in)
From a low viewpoint, I used three mainly
muted and nuanced colours. Touches of
ochre mixed with white create a sense of
the sun breaking through the sombre sky.

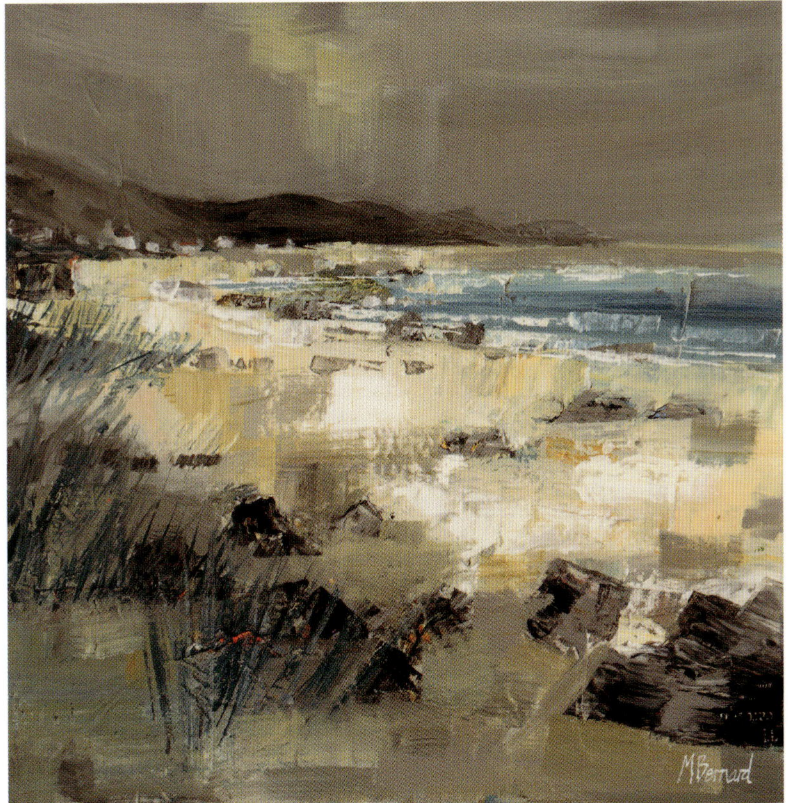

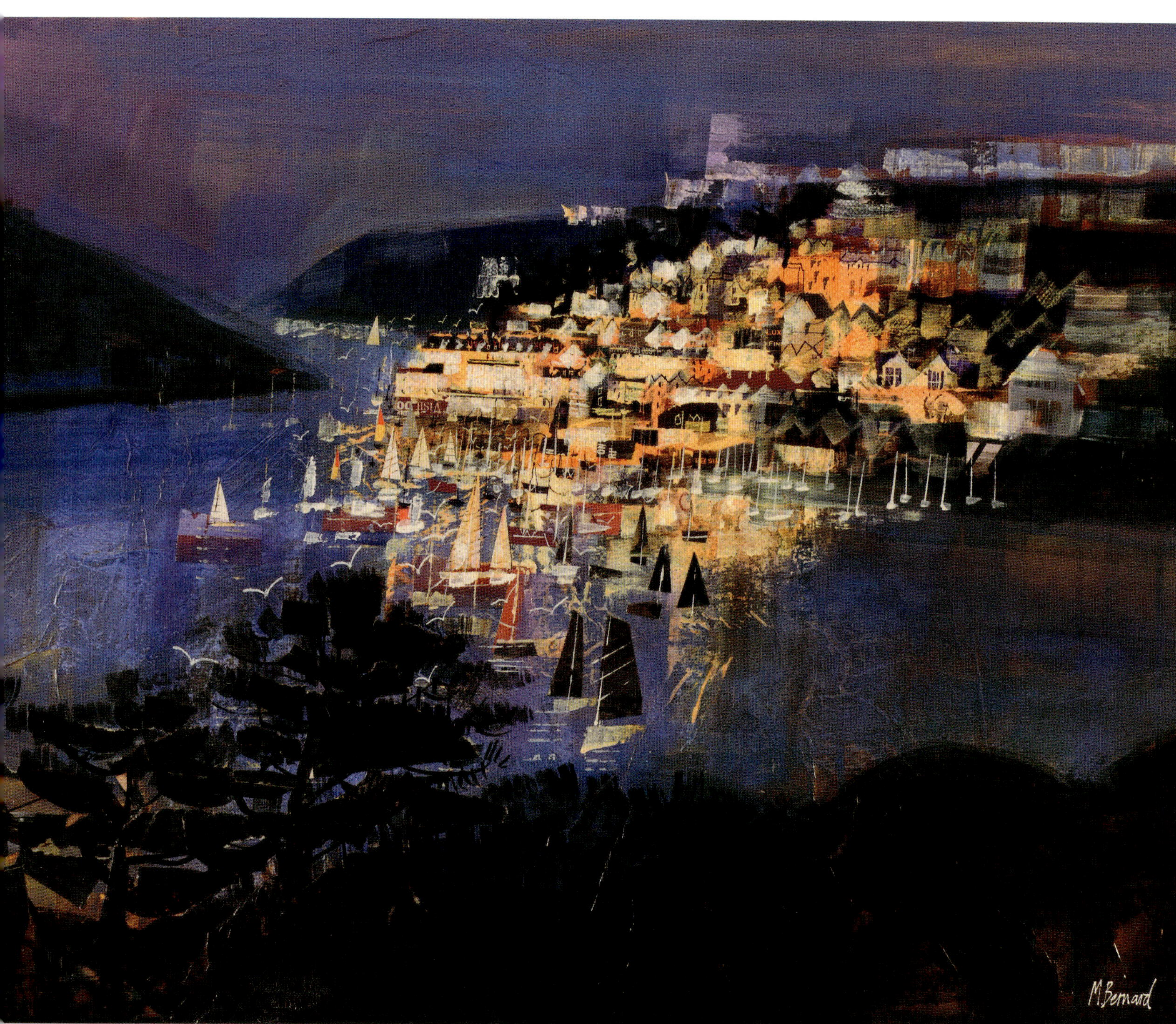

Evening Lights, Salcombe

Mixed media, 61 x 61cm (24 x 24in)

Even when my use of colour is quite descriptive, I aim for
boldness and vibrancy. The mood here is buoyant and lively.

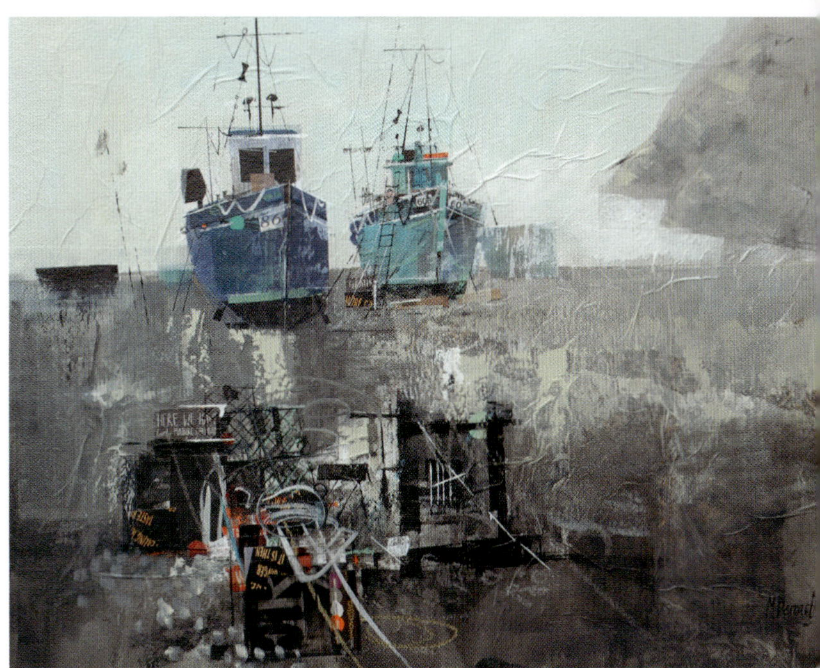

Beached Fishing Boats, Cadgwith
Mixed media, 61 x 71cm (24 X 28in)
With my cool palette of greys and pale turquoise, I was able to create a dramatic atmosphere with a sense of rainy weather here.

colour can be more emotive and ethereal. For *Evening Lights, Salcombe*, you can see that the brilliant blue sky dominates, reflecting on the water. Other colours here are yellow, red, pink and orange that, along with white and black, work as accents, enlivening the scene. In *Beached Fishing Boats, Cadgwith*, I used grey and turquoise to evoke a sombre atmosphere.

For me, using perspective and angles in various ways can also help to create a sense of atmosphere. Many of my works are painted from a bird's-eye viewpoint, that is, from high above. With its rich blues and almost spot colour, *Evening Lights, Salcombe* is painted from a vantage point that only a bird or a kite could have. Coupled with the rich, velvety colour, this creates an interesting, tranquil sense of peace. In this painting, I not only created a dramatic viewpoint and strong contrasts of colour, but I also contrasted the effects of the paint – some of the edges are hard and others are softer, more blurred. Divergently, *Fishing Boats, Ilfracombe Harbour*, is a straight-on, direct view, using the fresh, daytime colours of blue, turquoise, cream and orange. Different viewpoints allow me to play with shapes, proportion and perspective. Silhouetted and overlapping shapes become steadily smaller, creating the suggestion of depth and distance, without becoming too bogged down with technicalities.

At any one time, I can have quite a number of paintings in progress at once. One or two might be at collage stage, another couple may be being painted and yet another two or three might be about to be finished. In this way, they all remain fresh to me, and contrasting the viewpoints helps me to instantly jump back to the atmosphere I was aiming to achieve with each, from the moment I resume work on that particular painting.

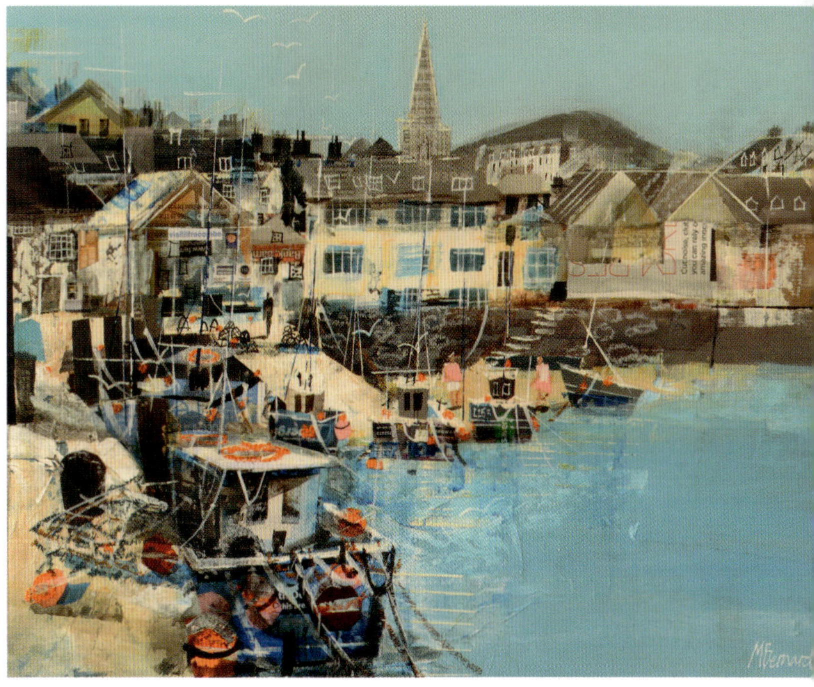

Fishing Boats, Ilfracombe Harbour
Mixed media, 43 x 56cm (17 x 22in)
Calm turquoise, blue and cream are offset by bright touches of orange and low-key browns.

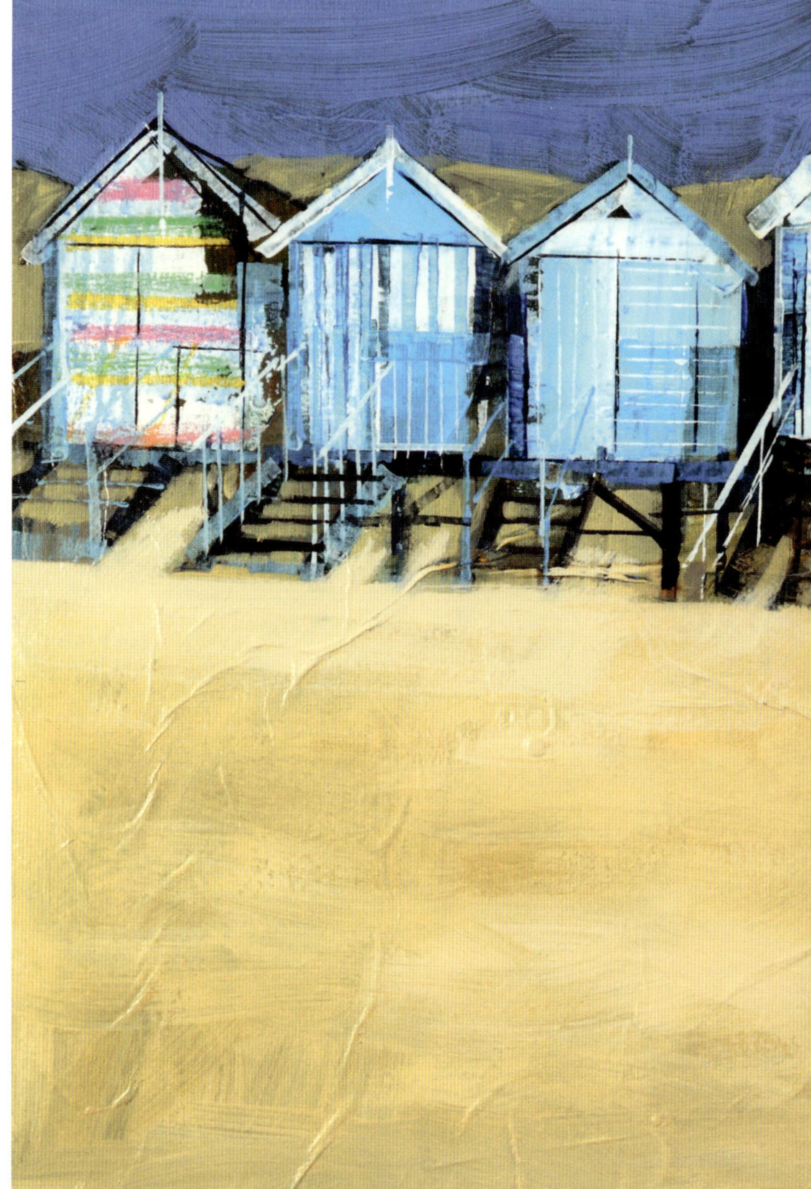

Design

Although I insist that I do not contrive to create a sense of
atmosphere and mood, there is probably nearly always an
idea in the back of my mind when I choose a subject that
will appear as I work. Choice of colours affects the mood,
but so also does the composition. While colour always
creates an emotional reaction to an image, composition
does too. Dramatic viewpoints create a theatrical or
spectacular, intense mood, and high viewpoints are often
helpful in setting the atmosphere that might not be so
dramatic from where I make my initial location sketches.
Between my initial sketches on location and starting a
large painting, I often create compositional sketches to
work out where I will place things, how large or small
they will be, whether there will be any foreshortening,
if there will be several figures, a few or none, and if my
perspective lines will lead the eye into and around the
scene. My compositions are complete when I can see
that there is a pleasing pattern, unified by a harmonious
palette and with enough abstract elements to retain an
atmosphere of spontaneity, freshness and freedom.

Thick and thin paint

Paint textures can be used to literally create a sense of
how things feel, or they can invigorate paintings, or they can
calm an image. Thick, impasto paint can convey the idea that
objects are close to the viewer, as the textures on the paint
often express real textures on objects. Similarly, thin veils of
paint or ink can create the sense of larger areas, aspects of
the image that are further away. I like the contrast between

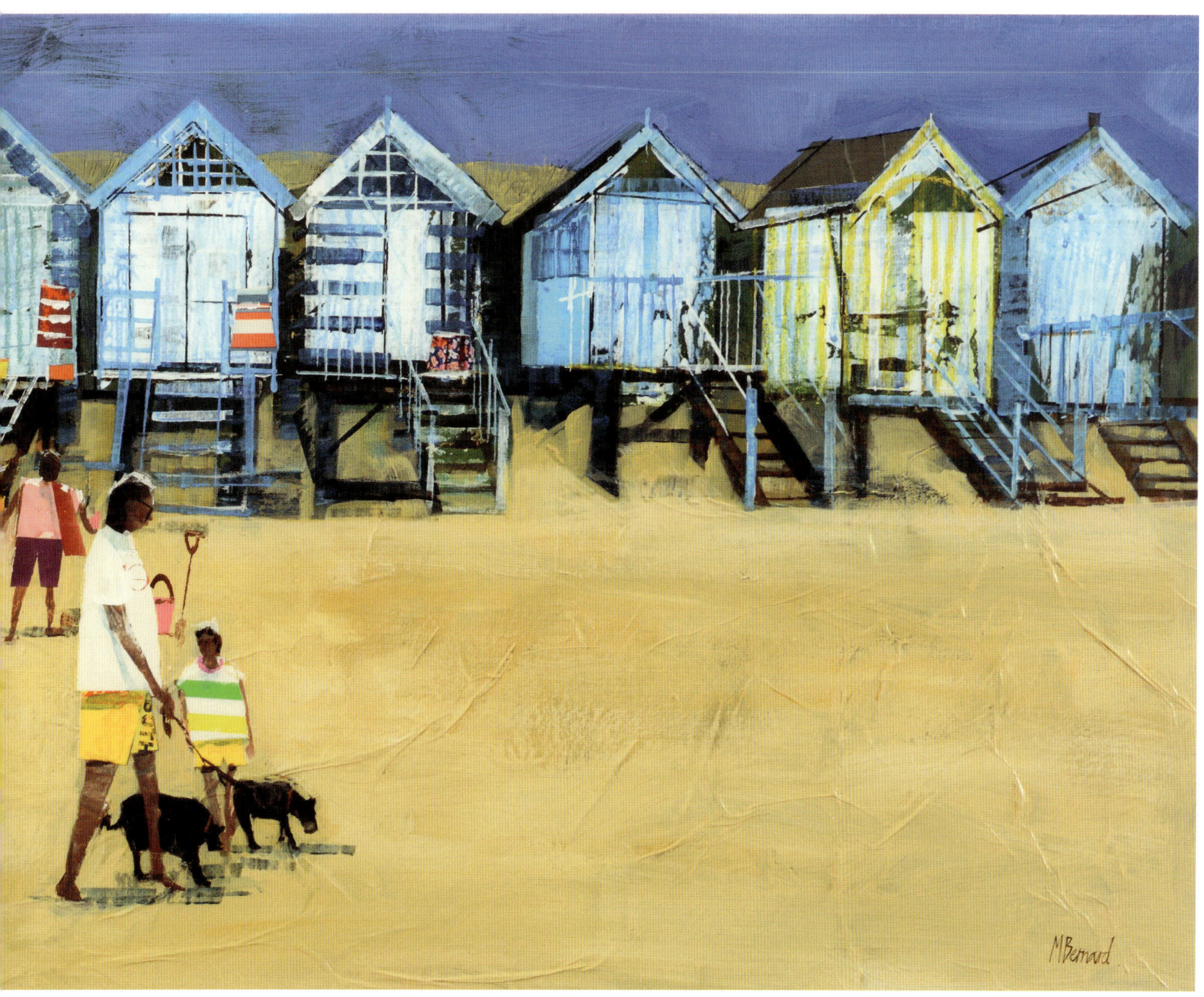

abstract qualities and representational elements. With textures, this means that some are included to add interest and are subsidiary to subject matter, while others are more evocative and expressive of actual things. Whether for such things as sky, water, rocks or boats, the use of thick or thin paint or inks creates a different idea of atmosphere and mood. In general, I concentrate on specific textures and details around the focal point of the composition, with more expansive, thinner or transparent paint or ink used to describe areas that are further away. My impasto aspects of the painting are often created with acrylic paint, with successive layers of acrylic ink or oil pastel.

The materials I use to apply paint can also have a strong effect on the atmosphere. So, for instance, when I apply it with card, I use either the thin edge or the thicker flatness of the card itself. Sponges and rollers create different effects again, as do brushes held vertically for stippling or the ink used dry and dragged across the painting.

Applying paint inventively

For *Beach Huts, Wells* (pages 96–97) and *Red Boats, Port Isaac* (page 92), I used the card and acrylic ink method to suggest textures on the buildings and harbour wall. To do this, cut your piece of card to whatever size suits you. Make sure it's easy to handle, firm enough to use vertically and to drag over the painting, and practise before you use it. Usually, I work with fairly large pieces of card in the earliest phases of a work in progress, often up to about 10cm (4in) in length. Rather like a palette knife, I load the card with paint or ink and then, holding it against the painting, I pull, push or drag the colour over the areas where I want it to be. The effects left will vary, with the underlying textures of the collage having an effect. Sometimes I use the card almost upright and create the thinnest lines, or use the corners of cards, dipped in paint or ink, to make dots, tiny dashes, and other small marks.

When using rollers, I tend to use 7.5cm (3in) lino-printing rollers. My favourite method is to apply white acrylic paint on my palette, then I smear thinner acrylic ink on the actual roller. I roll this across the white and then across my painting. As with the card, depending on the textures of the collage or painting surface, unexpected patterns and marks will appear by doing this. The thicker the collage beneath, the more texture will be made, and the different types of textures will evoke different moods and atmospheres. Whether smooth or random and broken, the textures will give an instant 'feeling' for your viewers. Once these have dried, I often apply coloured, semi-transparent glazes over the top.

To create other interesting textures and to evoke even more moods and atmospheres, I often use clingfilm, sponges and brushes – all in different ways. I place the clingfilm on an area of wet acrylic ink in part of the paint, leave it to dry and then remove it. This rather satisfying technique leaves a random pattern that evokes an instant look, such as water or rocks, and immediately helps to create a mood. Or try dipping a small piece of sponge into acrylic ink and dab it on certain areas of your work.

In summary, to create atmosphere quickly and effectively, use your paint wet, dry, diluted or thick, and drag, dab, roll, scrunch and stipple, using whatever implements you feel comfortable with. The main thing is to be open to those happy accidents in whatever type of image you are creating.

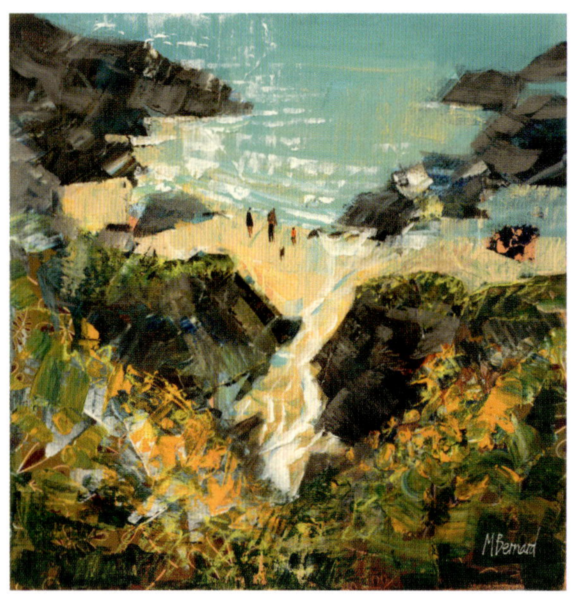

Palace Cove, Lansallos
Mixed media, 40 x 40cm (16 x 16in)
Paint dragged on with a piece of card creates angular marks in the rocks but also the lines of sea spray.

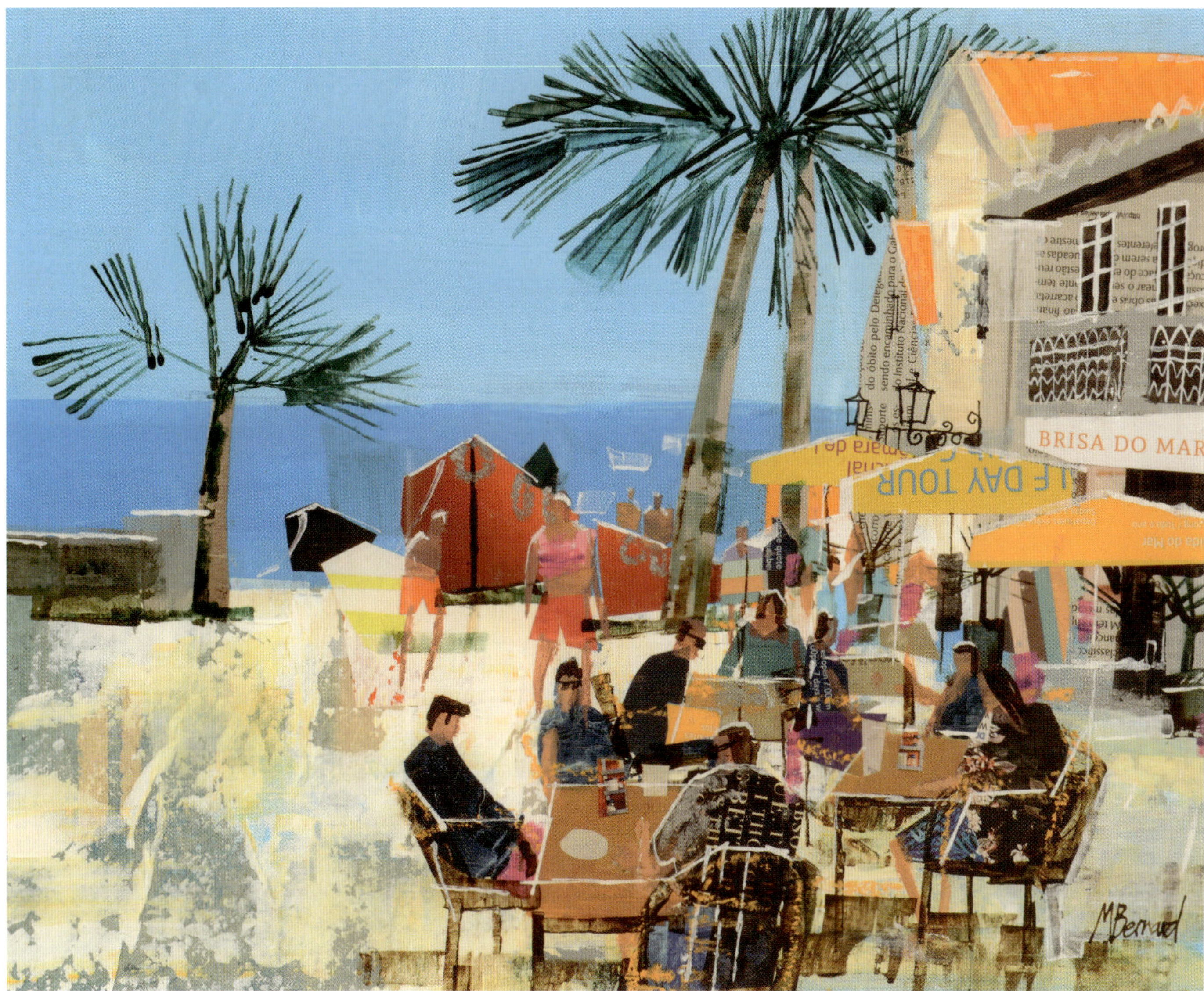

Texture and underpainting

One of many decisions to make at every stage of the painting, is about the kinds of textures to actually make or to convey. Often the underpainting or the collage create a sense of texture, which can portray different moods. For instance, in *Beachside Café, Tuscany*, the lively textural effect was created by applying colourful collage materials and opaque white paint over underlying scrunched paper. In *Autumn, Port Isaac* (see page 86) I worked with plenty of white acrylic ink mixed with yellow ochre and the edge of a piece of card to create textural effects in the sand and to apply various textures across the scene.

Beachside Café, Tuscany
Mixed media, 30 x 40cm (12 x 16in)
The suggested rather than detailed figures and the palm tree leaves created with the edge of a piece of card and paint all come together to create a dynamic-looking scene.

I aim to keep my work as free and flexible as possible, while still often moving towards a sense of atmosphere. Texture is created with both underlying collage and patches of underpainting. This underpainting is generally created with acrylics and made with one or other of my restricted-palette colours. Even before building up the subject, at these early stages of painting, I concentrate on creating some interest that will ultimately result in the evocation of mood or atmosphere. Depending on the way in which the painting develops through each stage, I begin to define the content, always being mindful of the atmosphere or mood I am creating. *Evening Light, Sidmouth* (see page 118), for example, has a warm, glowing appearance, created partly by the palette of warm orange and yellow contrasting with cool mauve, which creates an amber evening light, but also partly by my use of opaque white to build broken textures, both in the sky and water, and also in the fine lines indicating window frames and seagulls. In the painting *Crail Harbour, Early Summer*, my actual textures in the foreground flowers create a sense of atmospheric perspective, as the elements of the scene that are in the distance are less detailed and appear flatter than aspects near the front of the image.

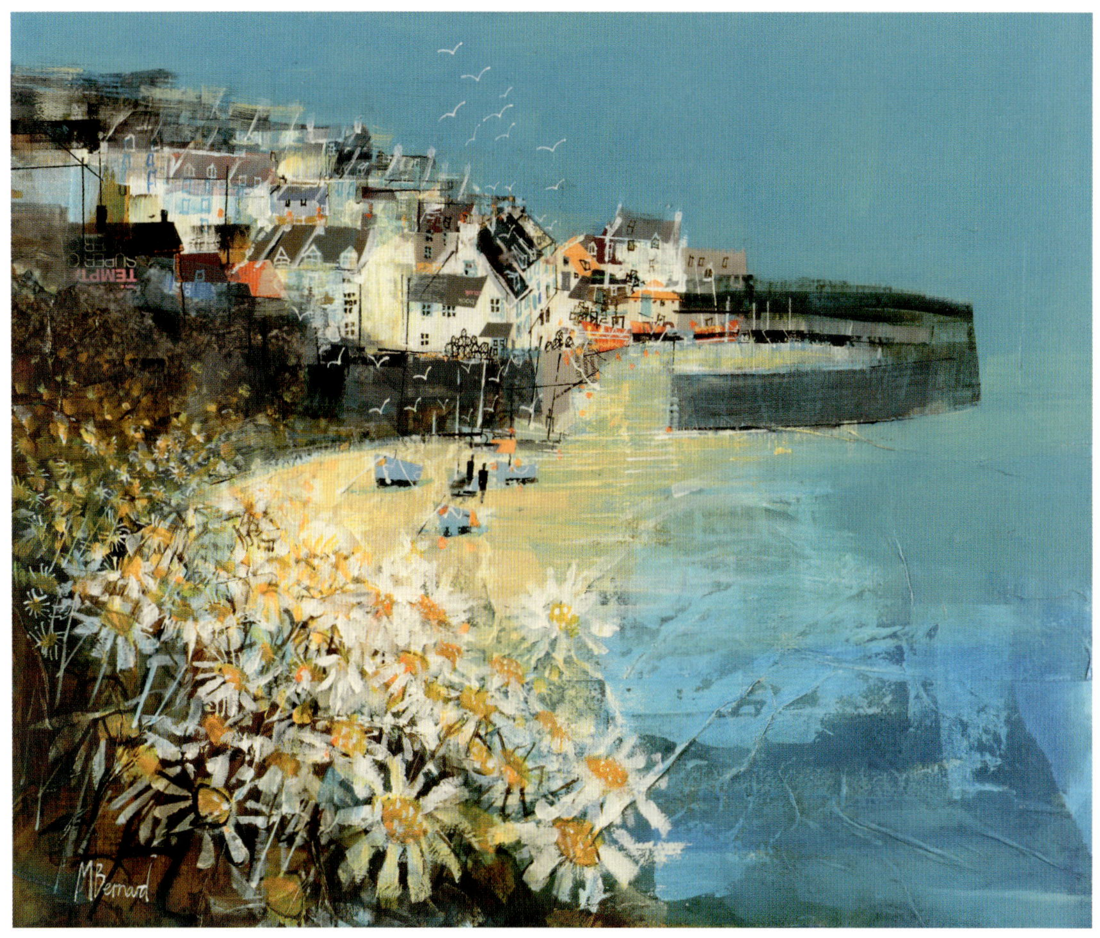

Crail Harbour, Early Summer

Mixed media, 46 x 56cm (18 x 22in)
Horizontal marks on the sea and sand evoke a sense of stillness and calm, while the angled, crowded flowers in the foreground add animation and texture.

Project – Polperro

The following five steps of my work in progress of Polperro Harbour show you how I normally develop a painting, starting with the initial foundation work in collage.

1 I build a collage by tearing pieces of paper to establish a sense of the basic design for the painting. The dark shape on the left is the first indication of the foreground sea wall. Similarly, the brown rectangular piece of paper centre-left creates a foundation texture for another section of the harbour wall. Additionally, the newspaper at the top hints at fishermen's cottages, while some wrinkled tissue paper below suggests where the water will be.

As well as thinking about the subject matter in literal terms, I am also considering ways in which various shapes interrelate and begin to create interest and balance within the design. For instance, notice that I have placed some tissue-paper shapes at the top to balance those in the foreground. Equally, I am thinking of the textures and how these might be used later on.

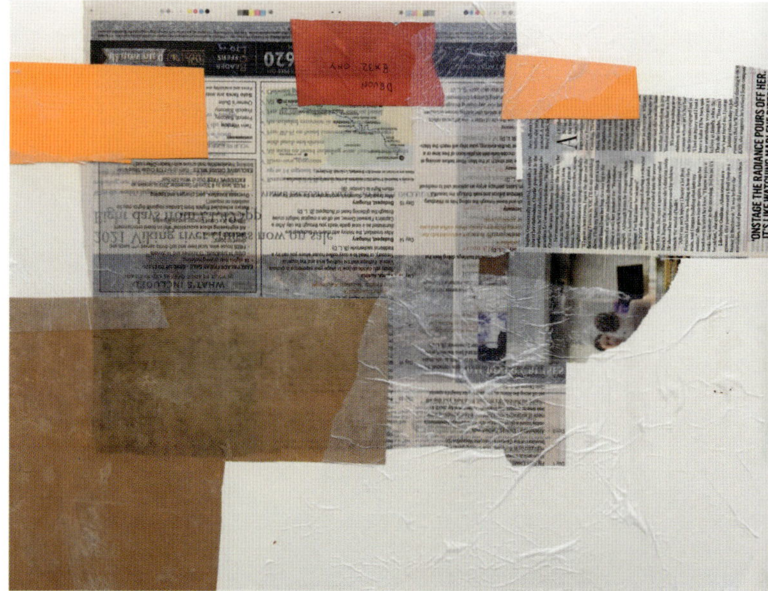

2 I sometimes develop the collage further, before starting to apply the two main colours that I have chosen for the subject. I decided to use an earth brown and black for this painting, working as usual with acrylic inks and applying them with a soft-haired 5cm (2in) varnishing brush. The collage must be dry before starting on this stage, and then I wet the paper by spraying it with water before applying the inks.

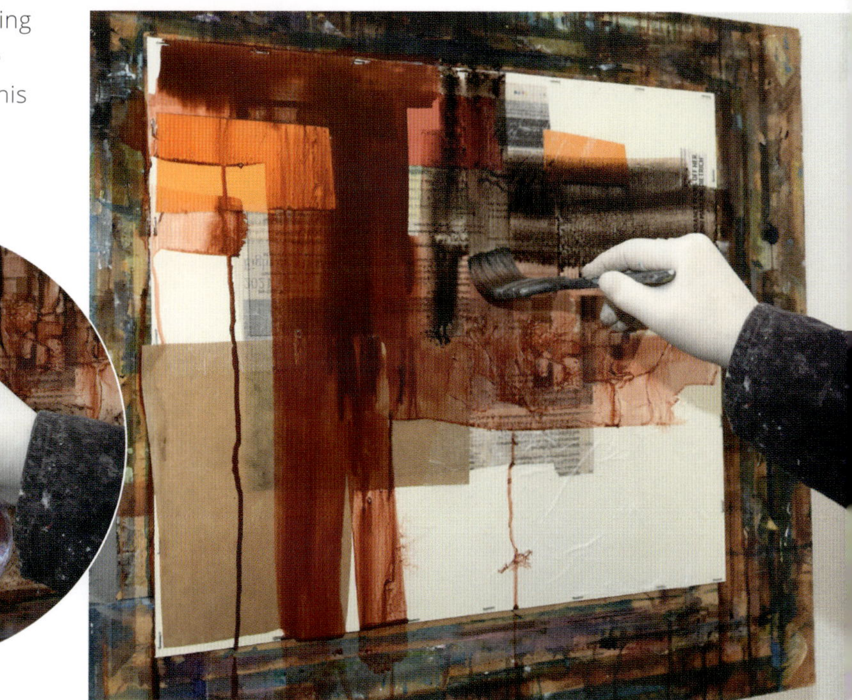

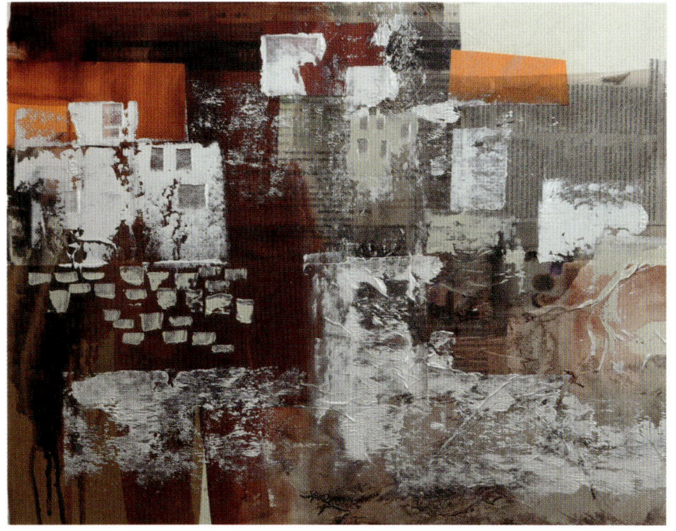 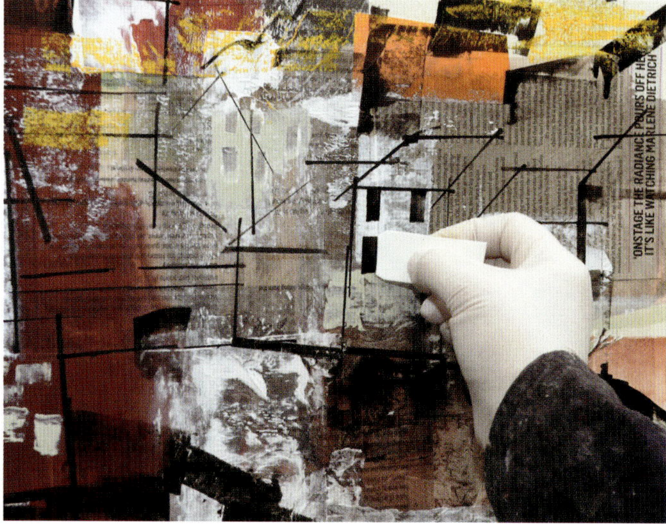

3 With the entire painting surface now covered in some way, either with collage or colour, I begin to think more particularly about textures. For those areas in which a rich textural quality will be useful, I apply Liquitex titanium white with card quite freely. Again, I aim to create a sense of unity by repeating the texture in different areas, although avoiding those passages of the initial black or earthy brown which I estimate will relate to specific parts of the subject matter. As well as adding texture, the white acrylic imparts a luminosity to the painting later on, when coloured glazes made from diluted acrylic inks are applied over it.

4 During the next stage, with a fresh look at the location drawing, and where appropriate exploiting the divisions, marks and surface effects that are now part of the painting, I start to resolve the essential elements. As you can see in the photograph, I have now defined the main house, using white acrylic paint, and with black acrylic ink applied with the edge of a piece of card I am putting in some window shapes. The challenge is to balance areas that give meaning and definition with those that are left as textural, abstract qualities.

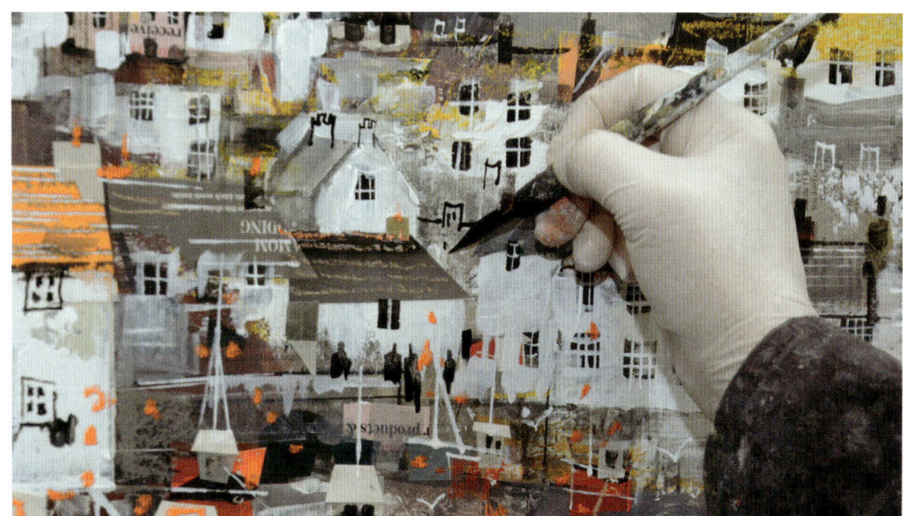

5 Finally, as shown left, I draw with a dip pen and some black or brown acrylic ink to add any further outlines and details that I think are necessary.

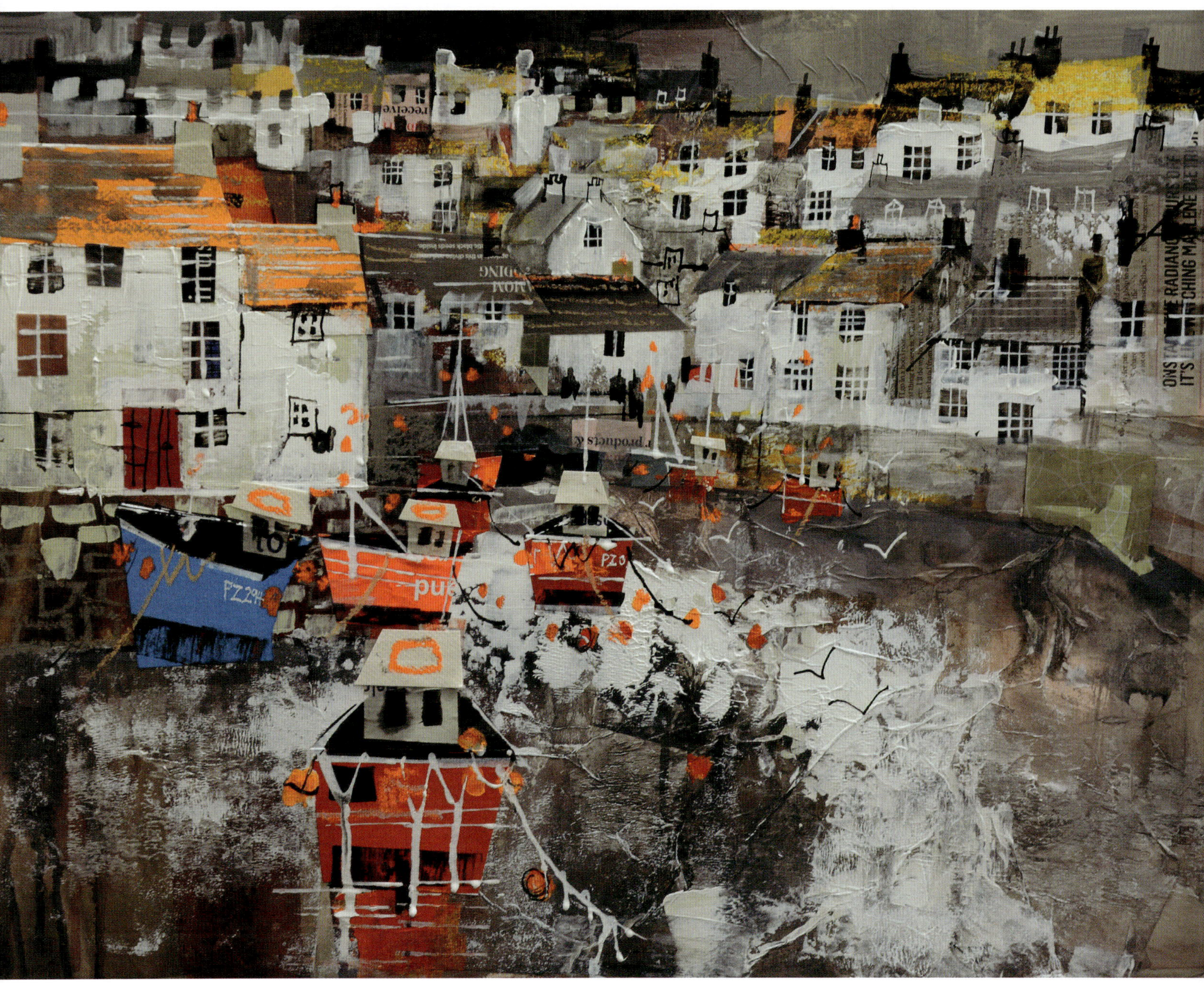

Polperro

Mixed media, 40.5 x 54.5cm (16 x 21½in)
I've enlivened the image with one bright
blue boat to create a vibrant focus in the
midst of an otherwise fairly sombre scene.

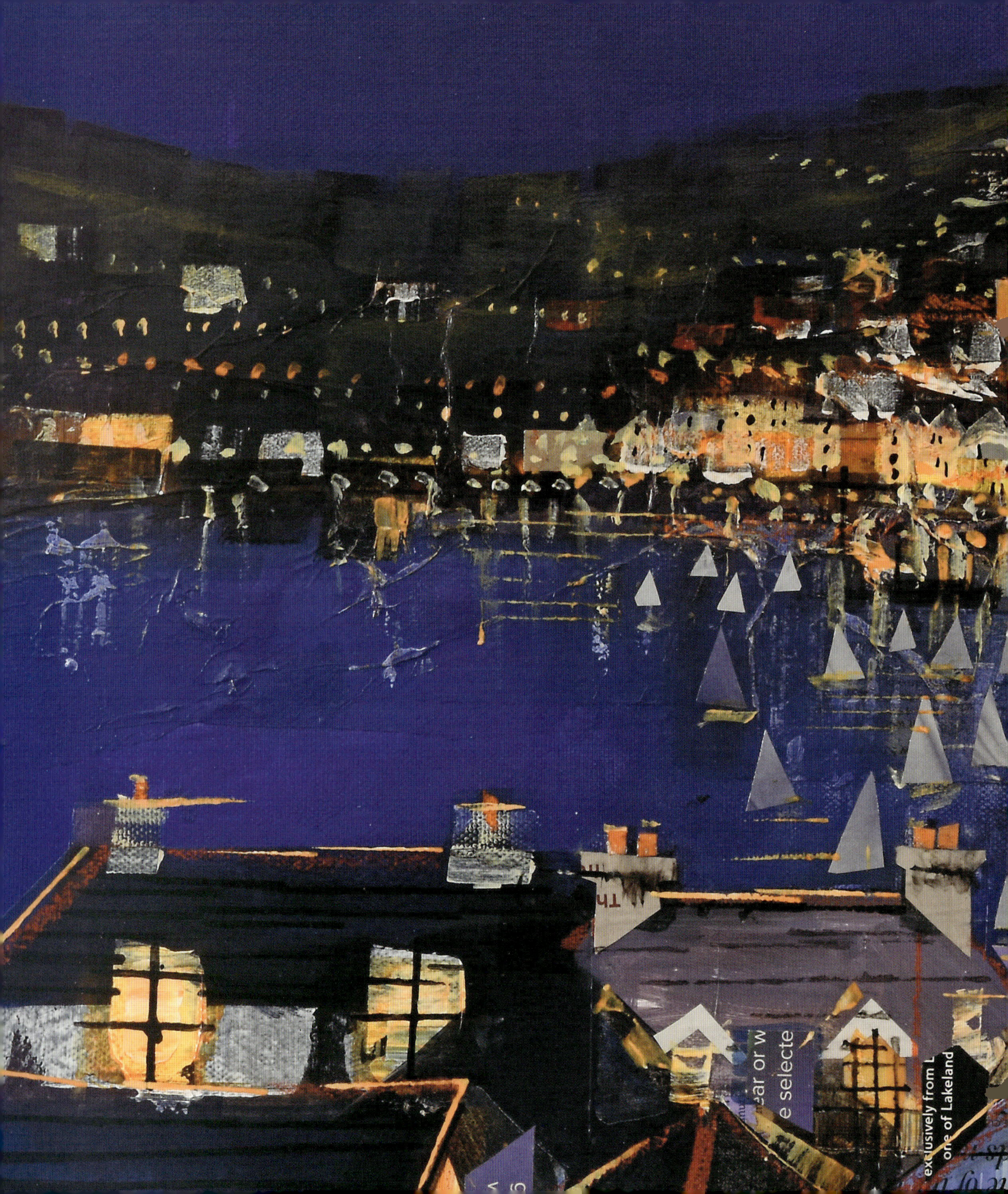
ar or w
e selecte
Th
exclusively from L
one of Lakeland

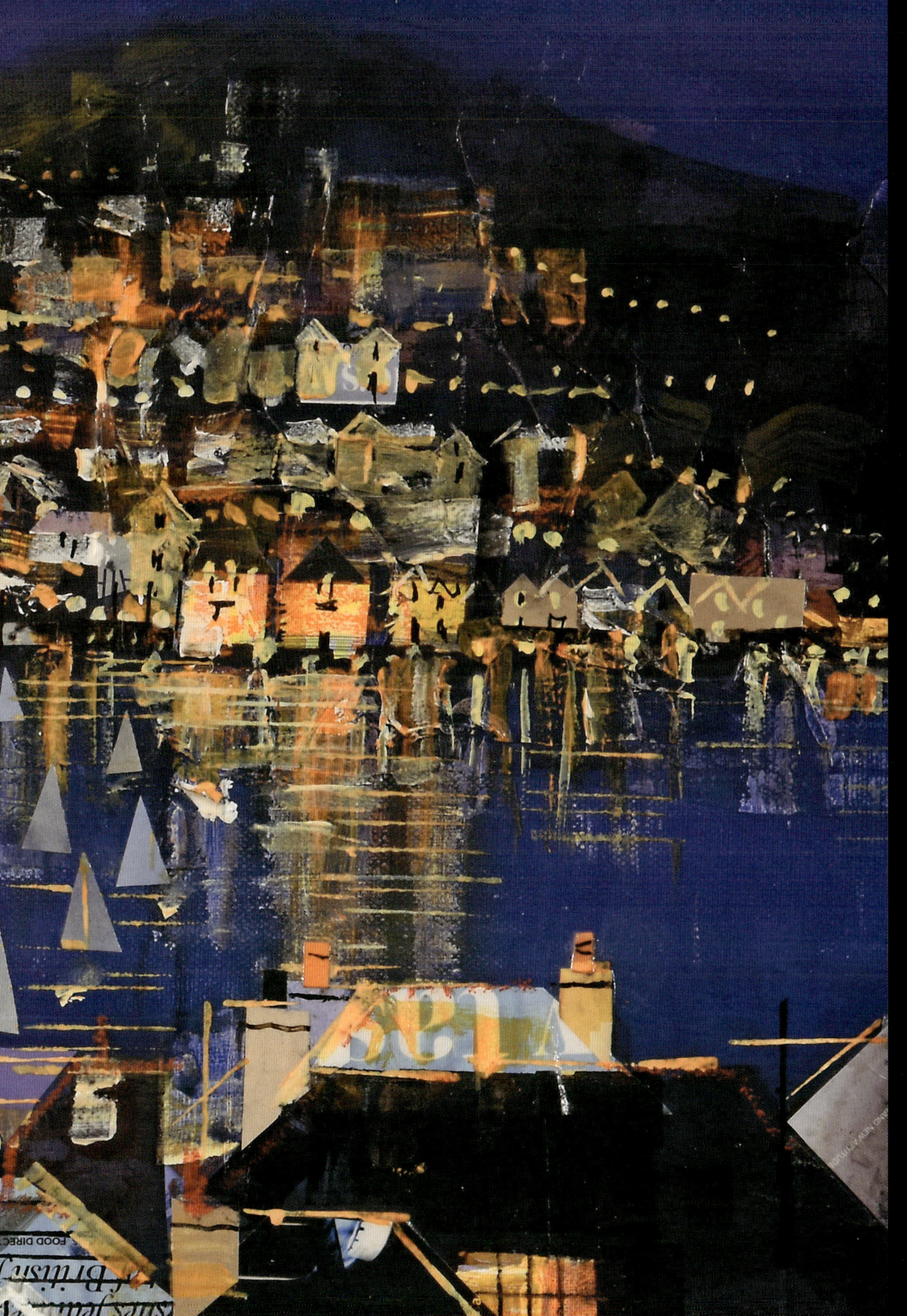

5

Going Further – Towards Abstraction

Often, some of the most appealing elements of my paintings are the abstract qualities. As mentioned, I am particularly attracted to subjects that have an obvious sense of pattern. For example, *Dartmouth and Kingswear at Night* is semi-realistic, but predominantly abstracted through the repeating patterns of triangles throughout the composition. I enjoyed almost layering the houses on top of each other on both sides of the water as they hug the coast. Then the boats, with their narrower triangular shapes, echoed and pulled this patterning together. Notice how I flattened the sense of the image by simply creating vertical, horizontal and angled lines to build a coherent pattern across the composition that results in an abstracted image rather than a realistic one.

The amount of abstraction in each image depends on several factors that are never planned exactly. Some paintings naturally end up looking more abstract than others. *Fowey Sunset*, for example, includes little that connects it to the real world. There are simply indications of lights, buildings and water. Many famous artists of the past, such as Wassily Kandinsky and Piet Mondrian, created abstracted images using this method of drastically simplifying their subjects. By ignoring the details and viewing the subject purely in terms of shapes, colours and textures rather than as specific objects, then you will nearly always arrive at an abstracted image. Of course, it will never be purely abstract if you are basing it on the real world, but moving towards abstraction will help you to become more individual, unique and free.

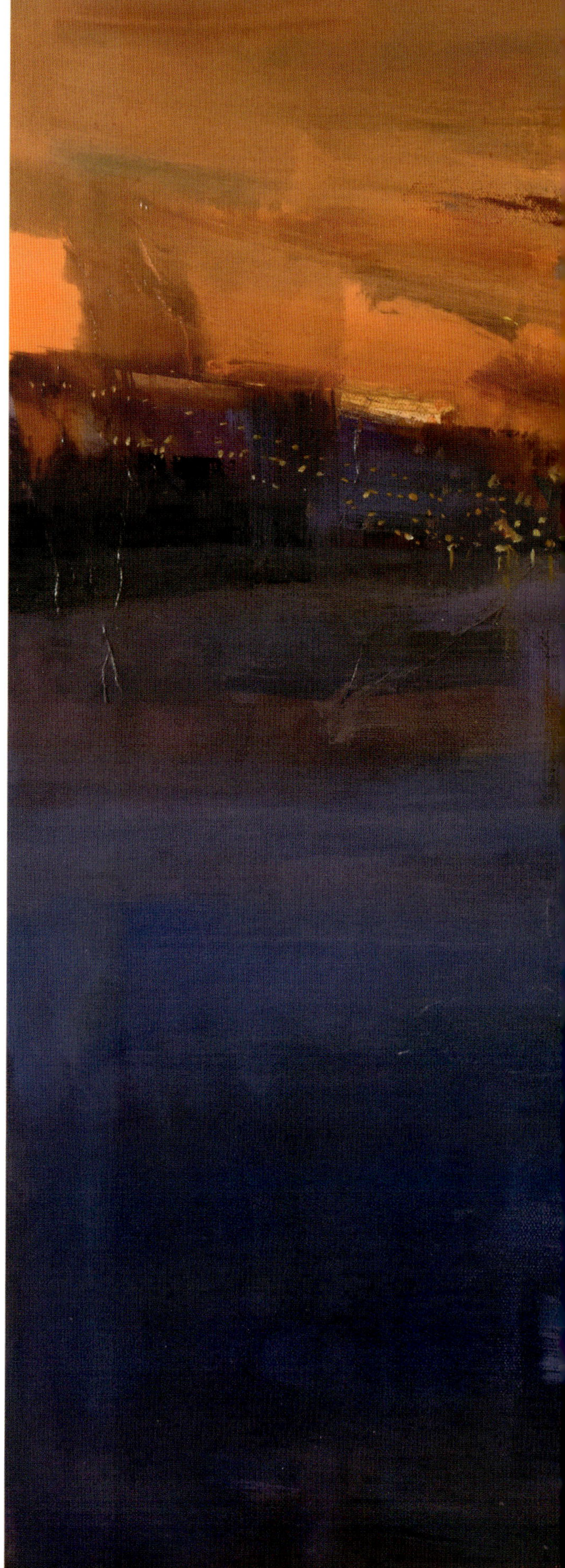

Previous page: **Dartmouth and Kingswear at Night**
Mixed media, 40 x 56cm (16 x 22in)
Even though this night scene clearly represents buildings and boats on water, it is abstracted.

Left: **Fowey Sunset**
Mixed media, 61 x 76cm (24 x 30in)
The fiery orange contrasts dramatically with the blue and violet, creating a sense of pattern as much as the landscape.

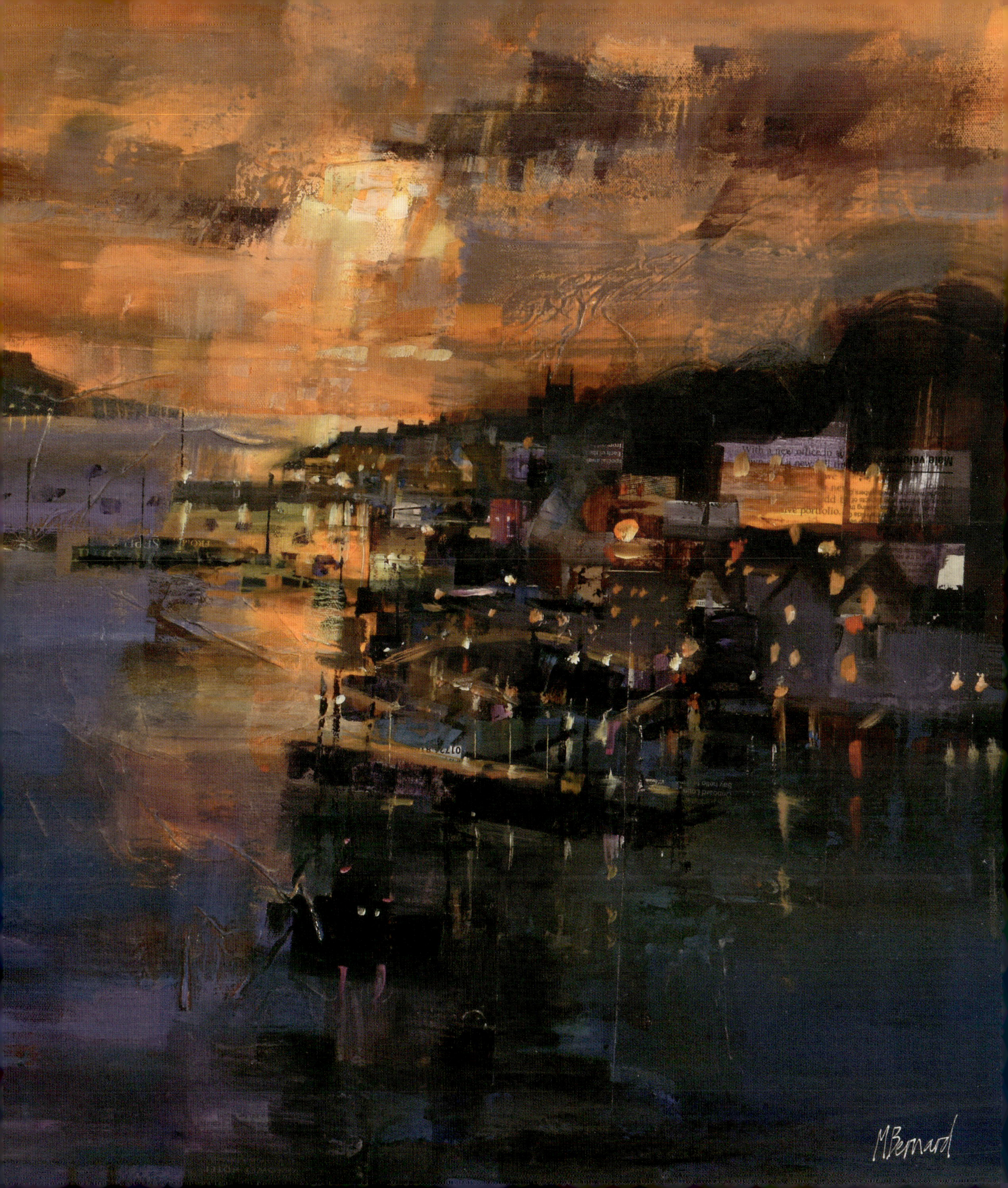
M.Bernard

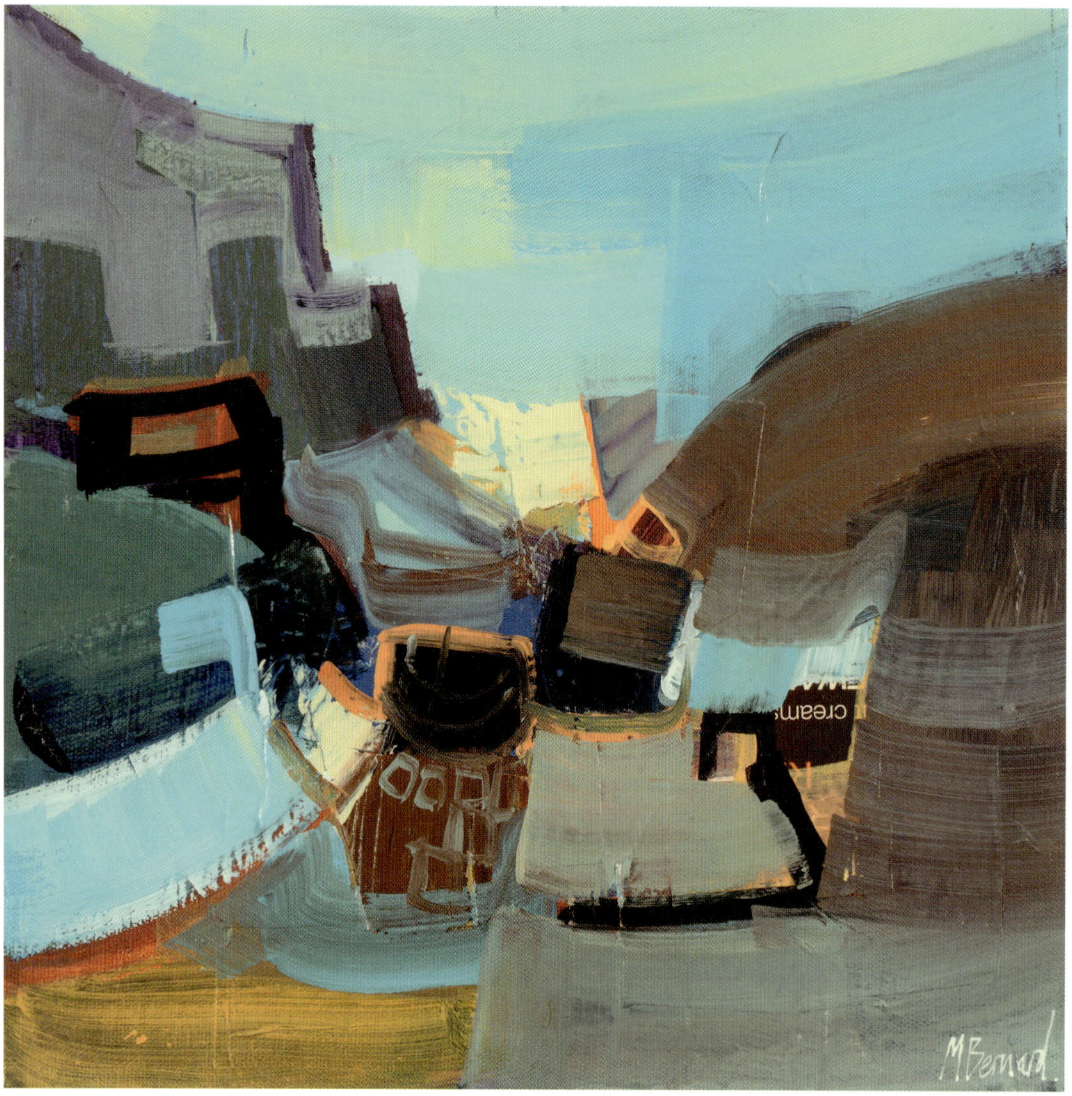

Coastal Blues II

Mixed media, 30 x 30cm (12 x 12in)
Using paint fairly fluidly, I created an
impression of a coastal scene.

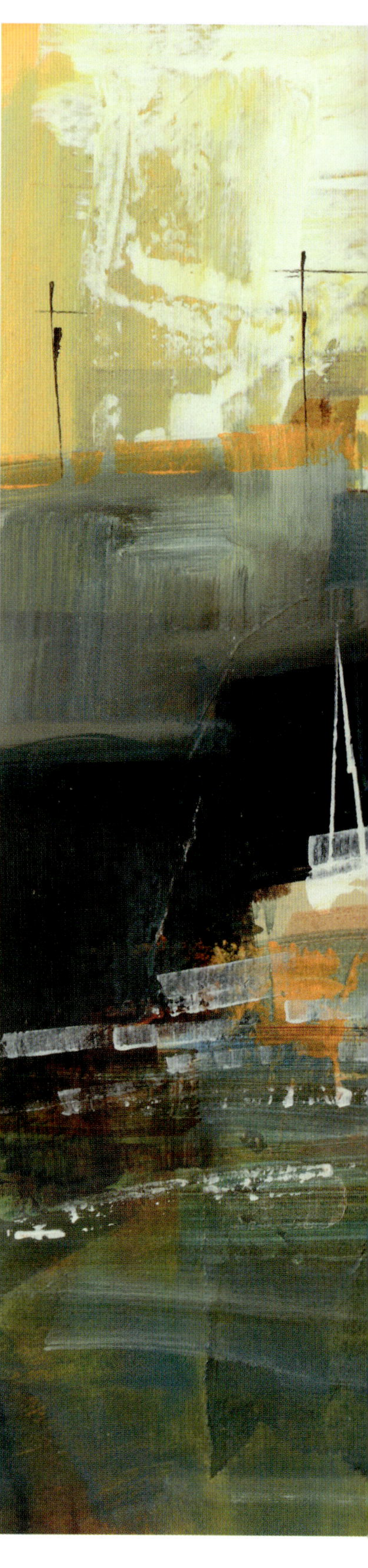

Cornish Beach

Mixed media, 40 x 51cm (16 x 20in)
Using blocks and patches of colour
and contrast, I built up a sense of
recession and distance, but because
all the shapes are so sketchy, the
image retains its abstracted air.

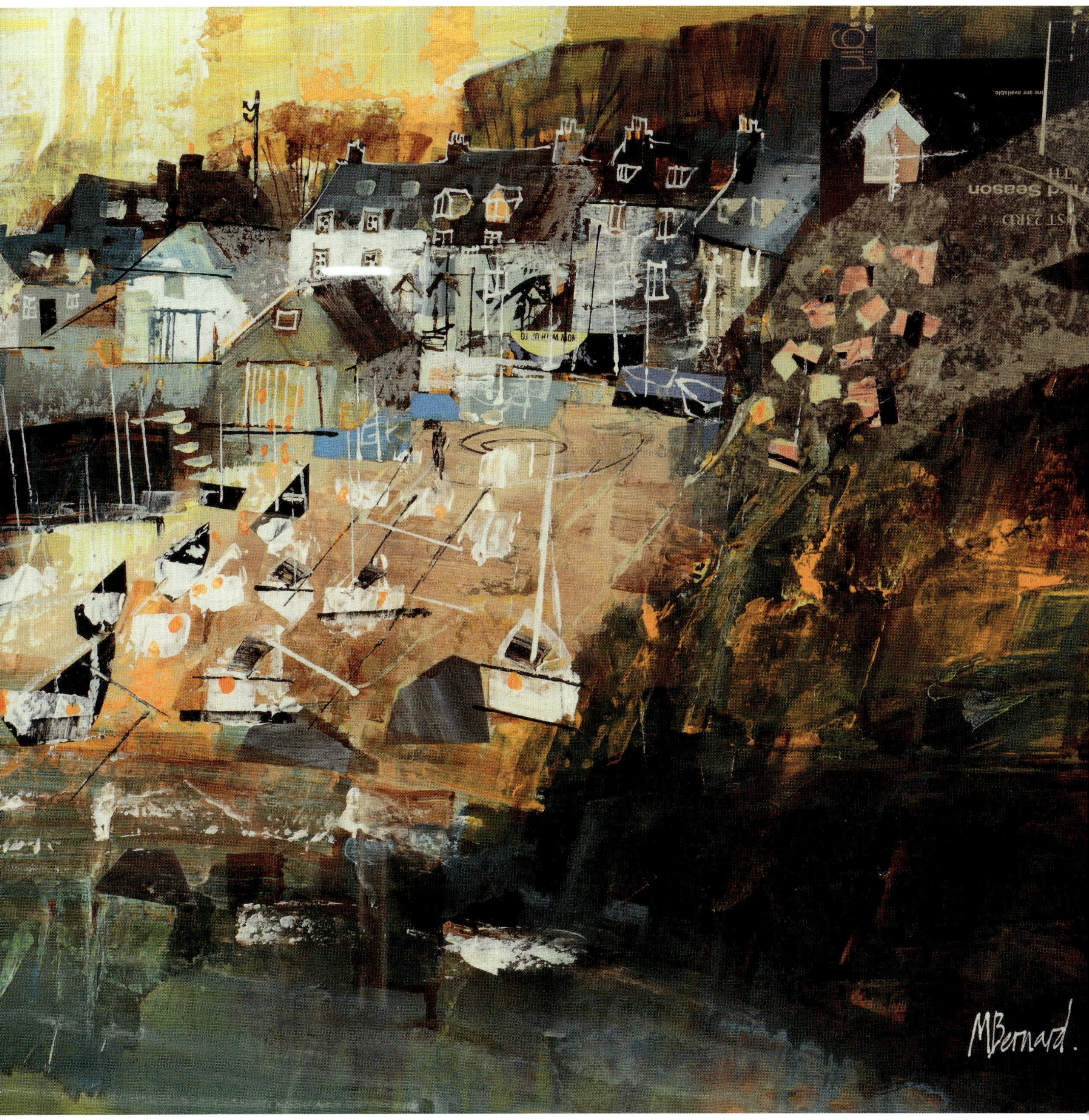
MBernard.

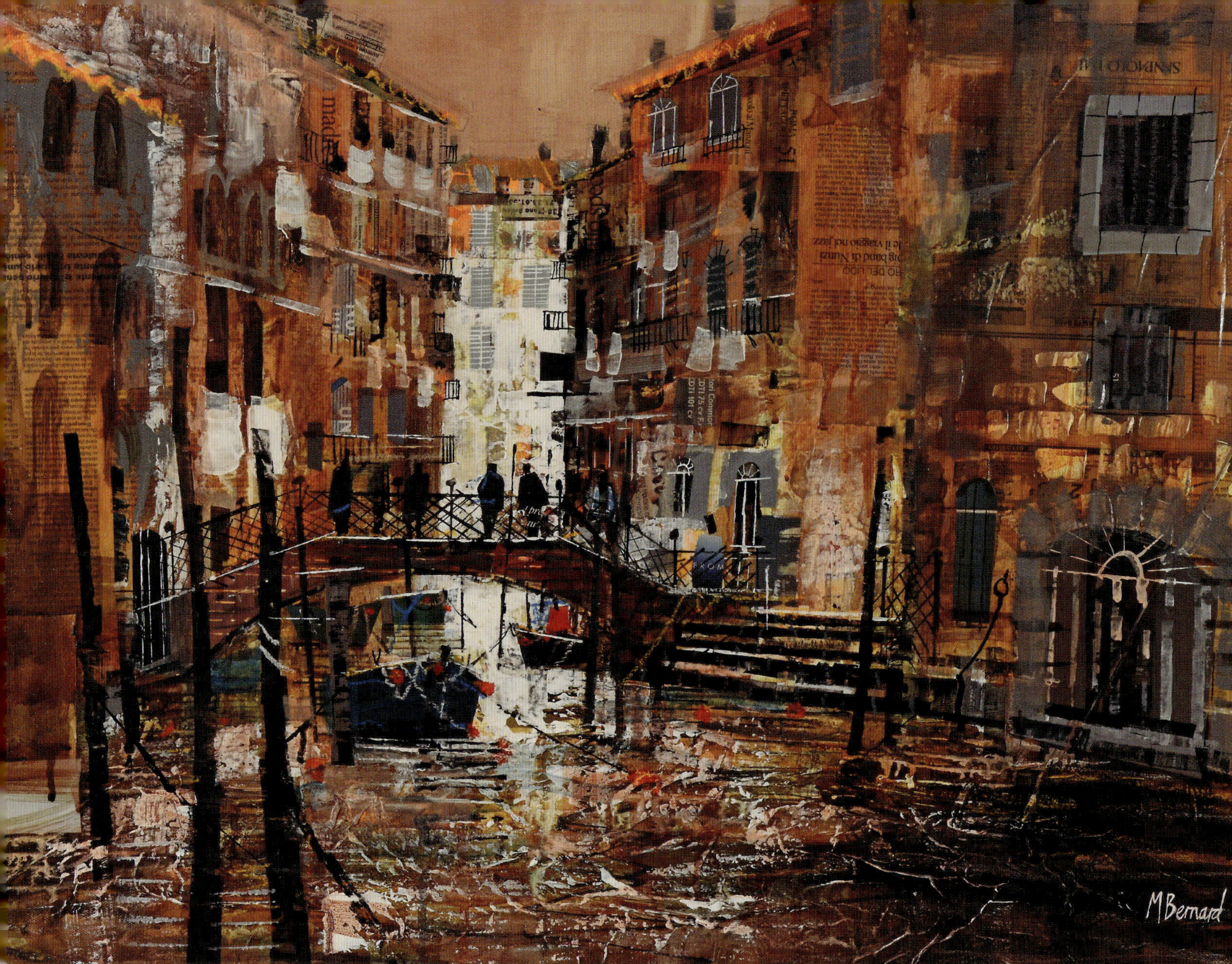

Progression

Of course, it's often easier said than done to discard all you have learned or understood about creating art. To break away from the notion that you have to make things look realistic, try working on a large scale. This is not as daunting as you might think. If you haven't done this before, build on what you have learned and try to break down the impetus that you have to make things look realistic. You can see, for instance, in *Overlooking Amalfi* and *Autumn in Venice* that there are clear elements of reality but that, through my simplifications, the scenes are becoming abstracted. By ignoring the details and viewing the subject purely in terms of shape, colour and texture, you will find those abstract qualities appear without you having to worry about them. When you are trying to create a lifelike image, you will always be considering things like perspective and tonal contrasts. When you are making things more abstract, these aspects of an image are no longer priorities. I treat objects and spaces equally; perspective and shadows lose

Autumn in Venice

Mixed media, 61 x 76cm (24 x 30in)
Here, I have incorporated angles and
reductions of scale to indicate distance, but
it is purposely not accurate perspective, to
create the appearance of abstraction.

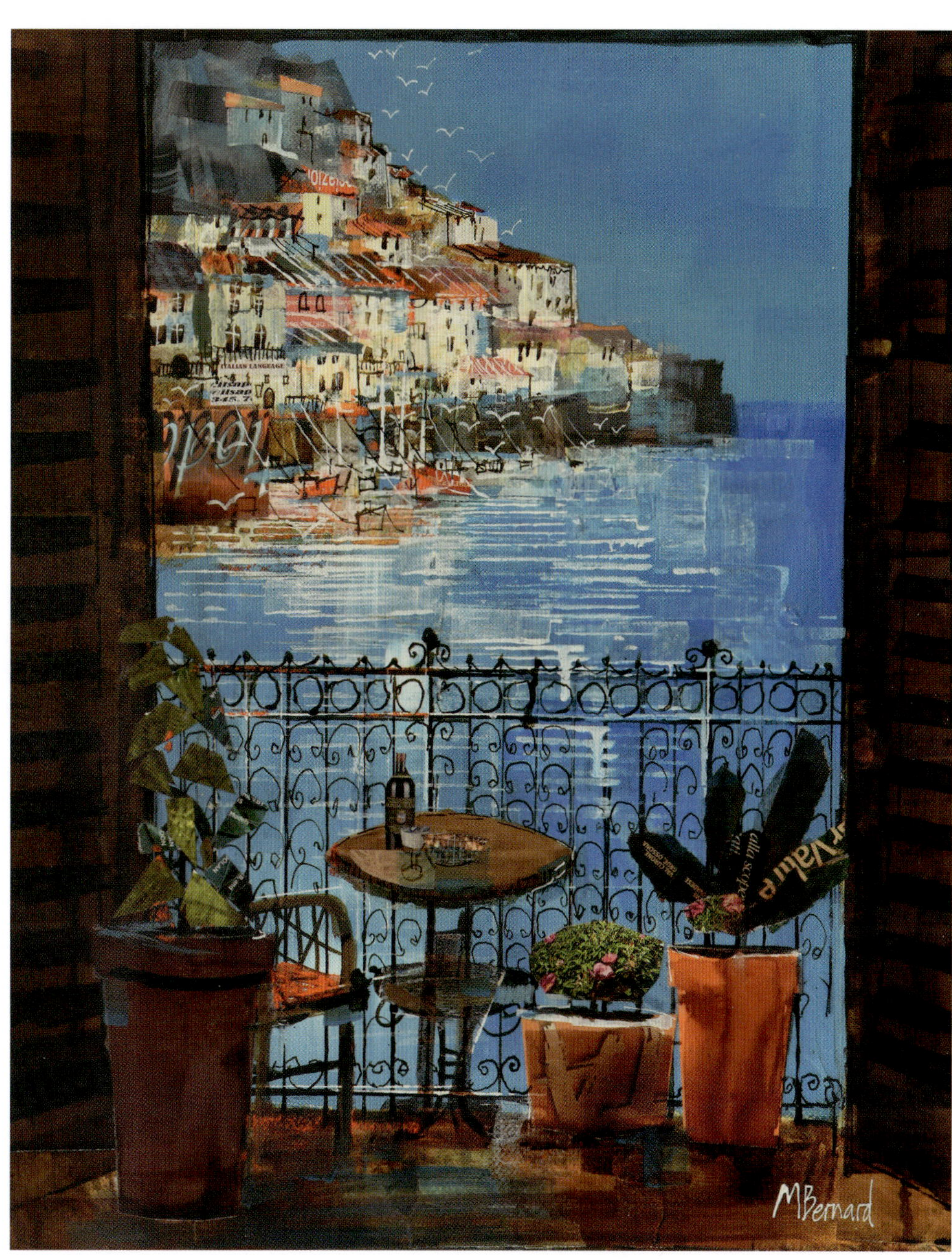

Overlooking Amalfi

Mixed media, 51 x 40cm (20 x 16in)
'Looking through' is always a
favourite composition of mine.
Here, I have deliberately distorted
the table, chair and plants and
their pots in the foreground.

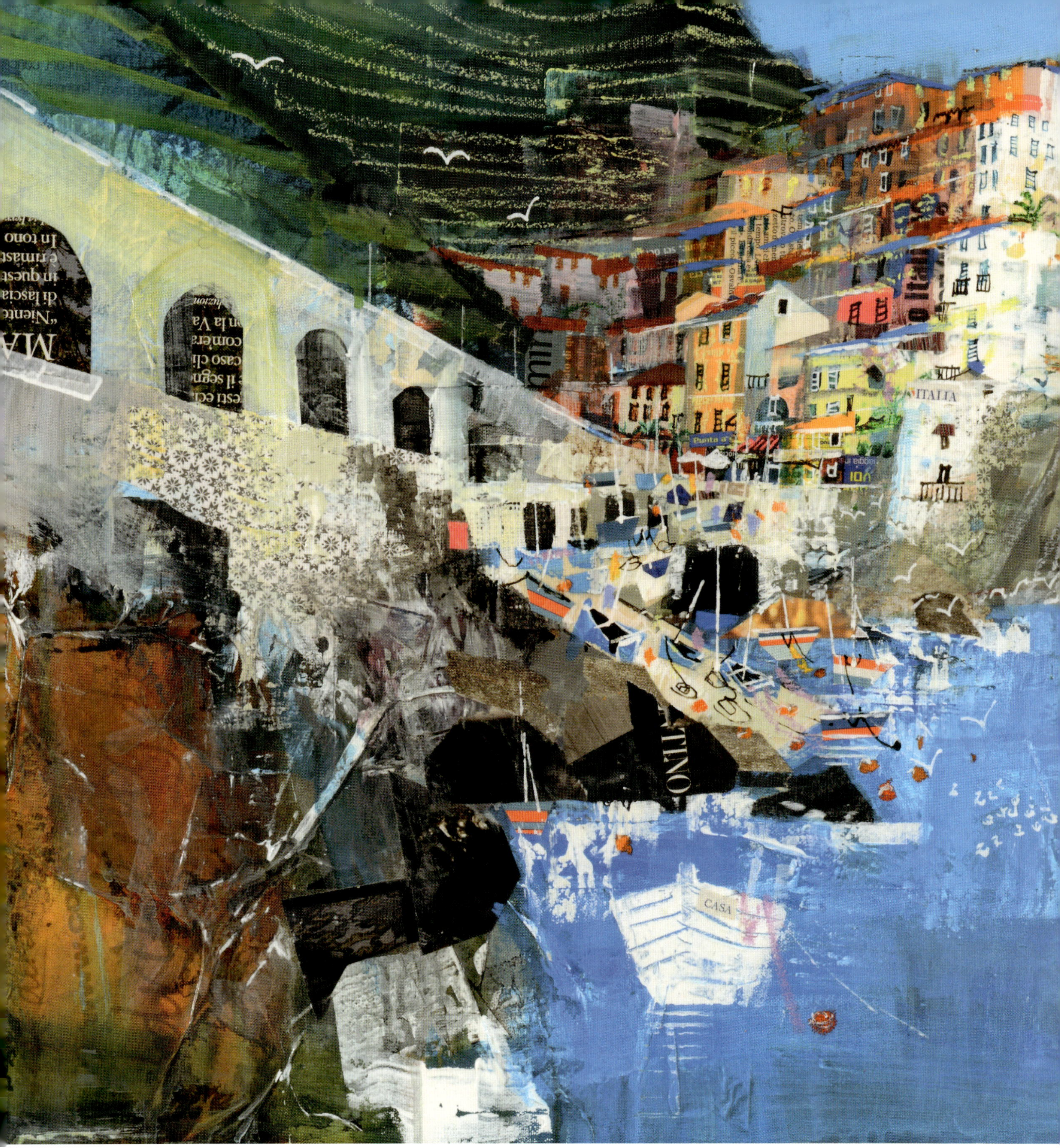

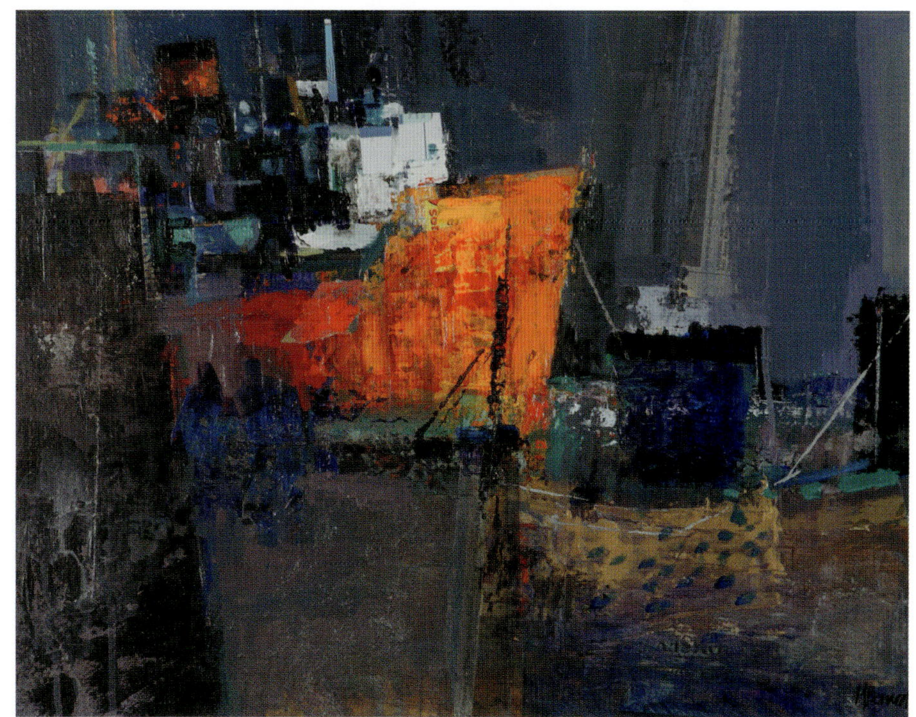

Red Ship After Storm
Mixed media, 46 x 56cm (18 X 22in)
With only a suggestion of the shapes
and forms that I saw here, this painting is
taking abstract ideas further than most.

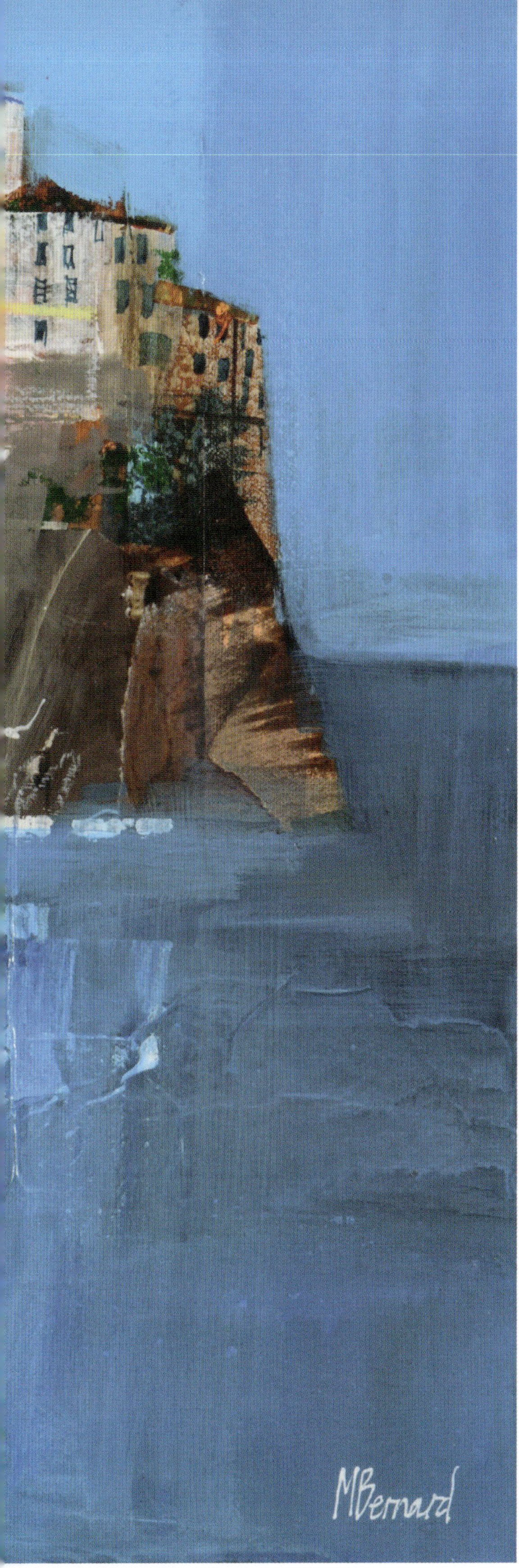

Manarola, Cinque Terre
Mixed media, 46 x 61cm (18 x 24in)
Although I worked directly at the
scene, I've reduced details quite
drastically so it is beginning to
become abstracted.

their importance. I become more focused on positive and
negative shapes, contrast or consistency, and abstraction
and representation. If you look at *Manarola, Cinque Terre*
(page 112), you will see how I've clearly worked from
a real scene, but by reducing details, including tonal
contrasts, while the image still represents a place, it is
progressing towards abstraction. The contrasts between
the expressive, simplified aspects of a subject and detailed

realism always create liveliness and interest. It may be
that you push this further and end up, as I have done in
paintings such as *Amalfi at Night* or *Seaside Memories*, which
have an even greater emphasis on abstract qualities. You
will notice, however, that although some of my paintings
take the abstract ideas further than others, I still always
retain a sense of place; there is always some association
with the real world around us.

Morning Light, Portsmouth Harbour
Mixed media, 46 x 61cm (18 X 24in)
Here, my reduced palette and simple
suggestions of lines create a pattern out of
the scene. You can see what is going on, but
my simplifications have made it more of a
sense of pattern than a descriptive scene.

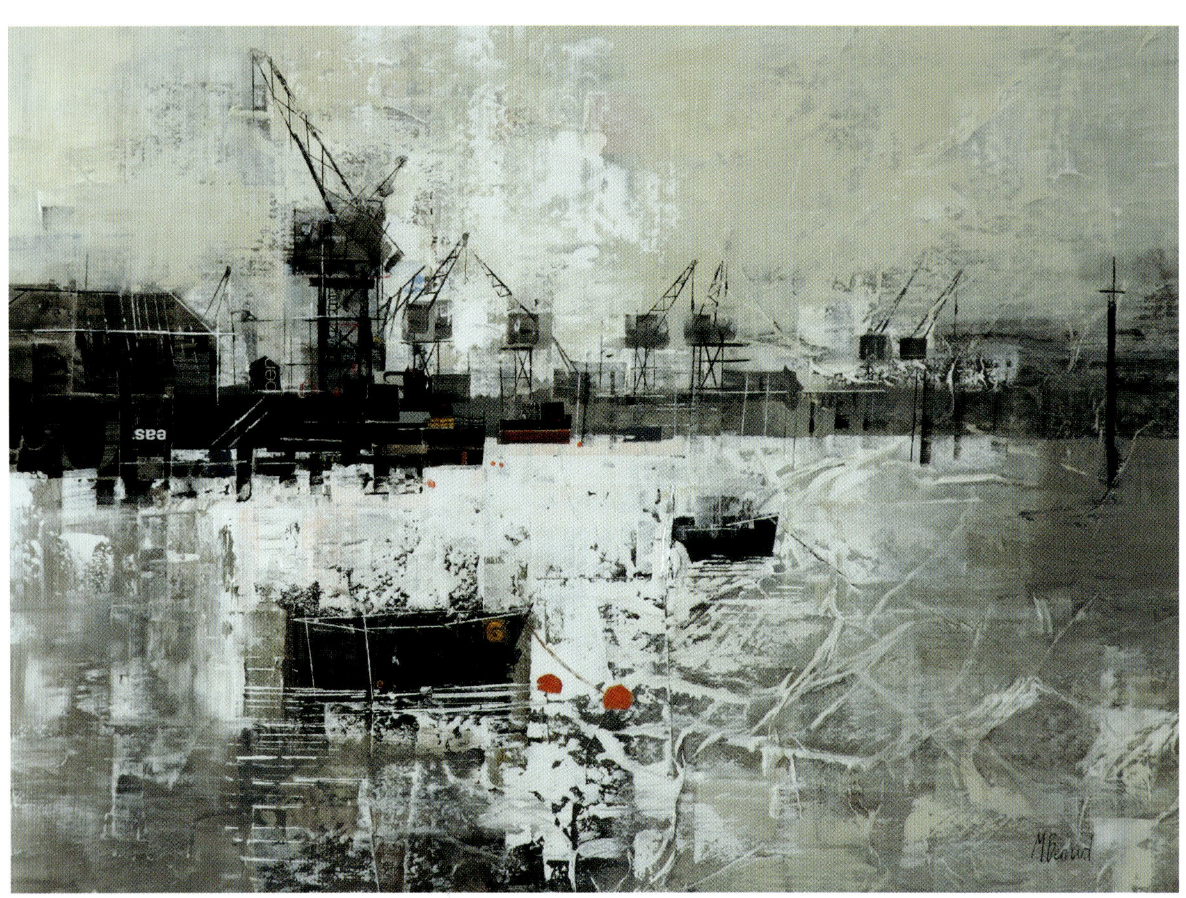

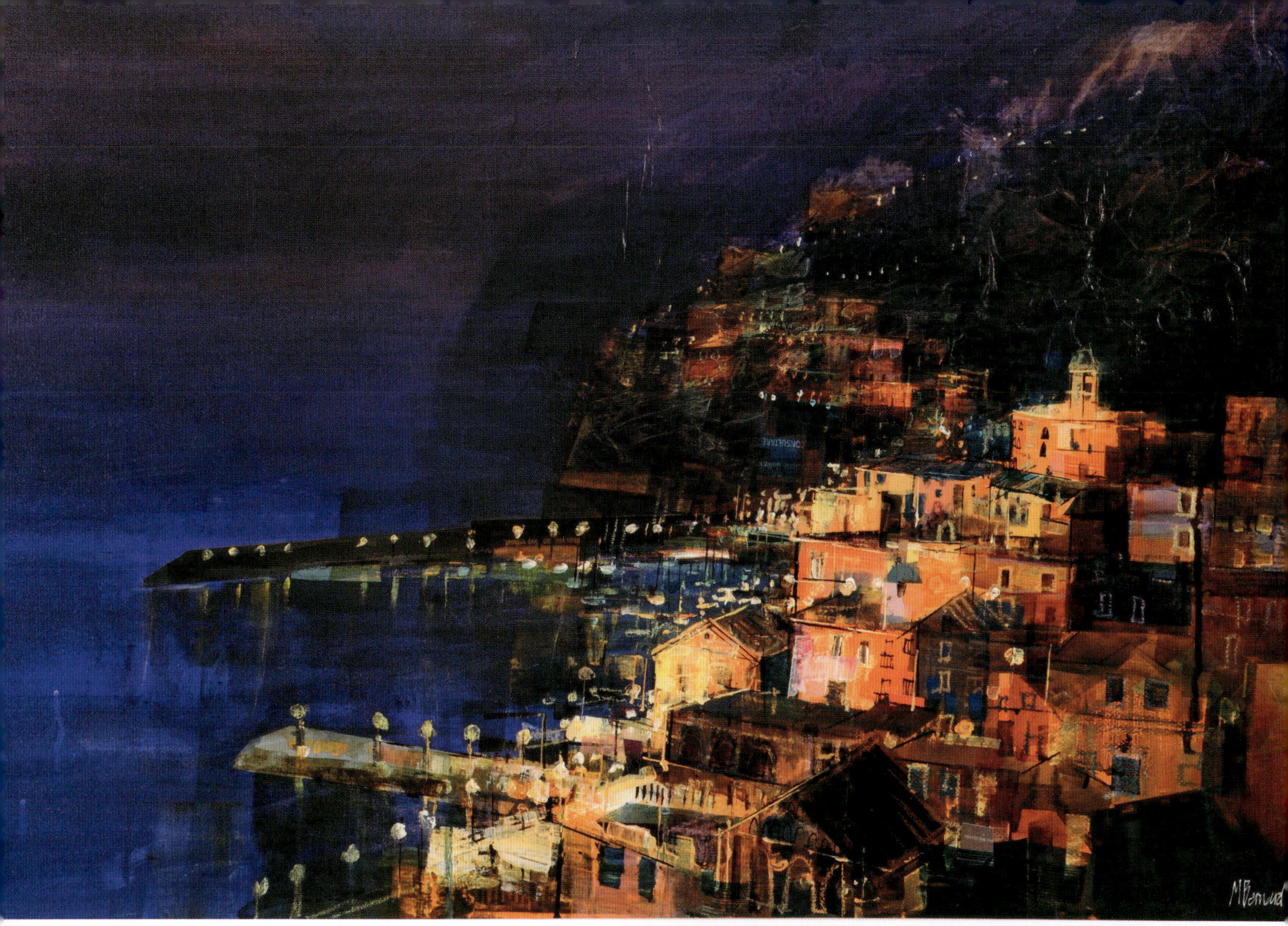

Amalfi at Night

Mixed media, 61 x 91cm (24 x 36in)
Drama and theatricality can be created
with a strong contrast of dark and bright,
light colours as here. This drama almost
becomes the subject of the work.

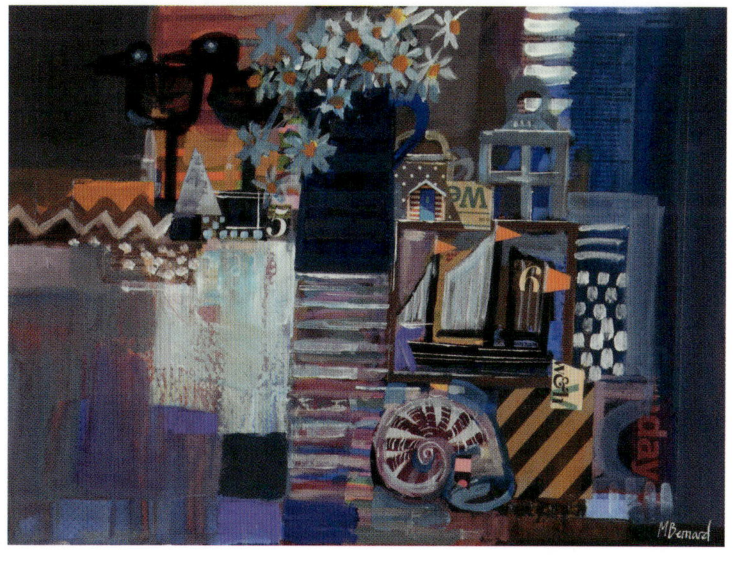

Seaside Memories

Mixed media, 40 x 56cm (16 x 22in)
Various mementoes collected from the
seaside are gathered in a still life, but I
only give a sense of what they are. My
marks and patterns are the focus.

Some practical advice

If you are still concerned about how to represent places in your paintings while moving away from reality and towards abstraction, try this. From the start, break down the image you intend to paint into shapes. I always begin with pure abstract shapes and colours and develop my paintings from that. So all my paintings start as abstract designs, with almost random shapes of collage. Then I start working towards some sort of reality. This requires determination; you are shaping abstract patterns into a real-life place. However, although you might start to include recognisable elements, stop yourself from becoming too detailed. Step back and refrain from painting for a while if you feel you are creating too much realism. You need a contrast of abstract qualities and recognisable areas.

If you work on a large scale, you will work more boldly; use large pieces of collage and strong blocks of colour.

Apply your paint or ink with rollers, knives, sponges or card, don't fiddle or fuss! Flatten everything by ignoring shadows and only suggest perspective with the sizes of your shapes – that is, make them smaller in the distance, but don't worry too much about perspectival accuracy. Where you feel things are not working, block them out with opaque white applied with a piece of card and paint or draw – or collage – over the top. Look at *Italian Harbour* on page 119. At first, it may seem to represent a place fairly closely, but look at it more carefully and you will see that I have omitted many details. The shapes and figures are simplified so that they end up as just suggestions, lines have been almost printed on over the collage and paint, using the edge of a sliver of card. Leaves and plant pots are created from cut pieces of collage and slabs of paint. I used a variety of colours and textural techniques, and you can see clear

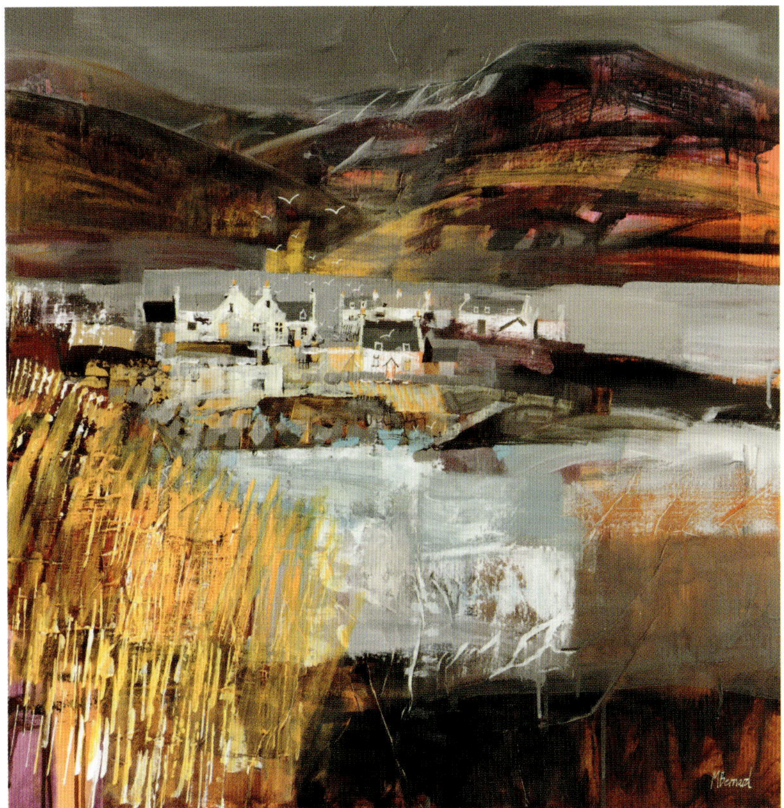

Coastal Hamlet, Skye
Mixed media, 81 x 81cm (32 X 32in)
The textures in the large expanse of foreground and the reduction of detail on the central buildings help to make this image more abstract than representational.

Kynance Cove
Mixed media, 71 x 71cm (28 X 28in)
Angles, a sense of texture and spontaneity, and a lack of details make this scene more an abstract interpretation than a precise view.

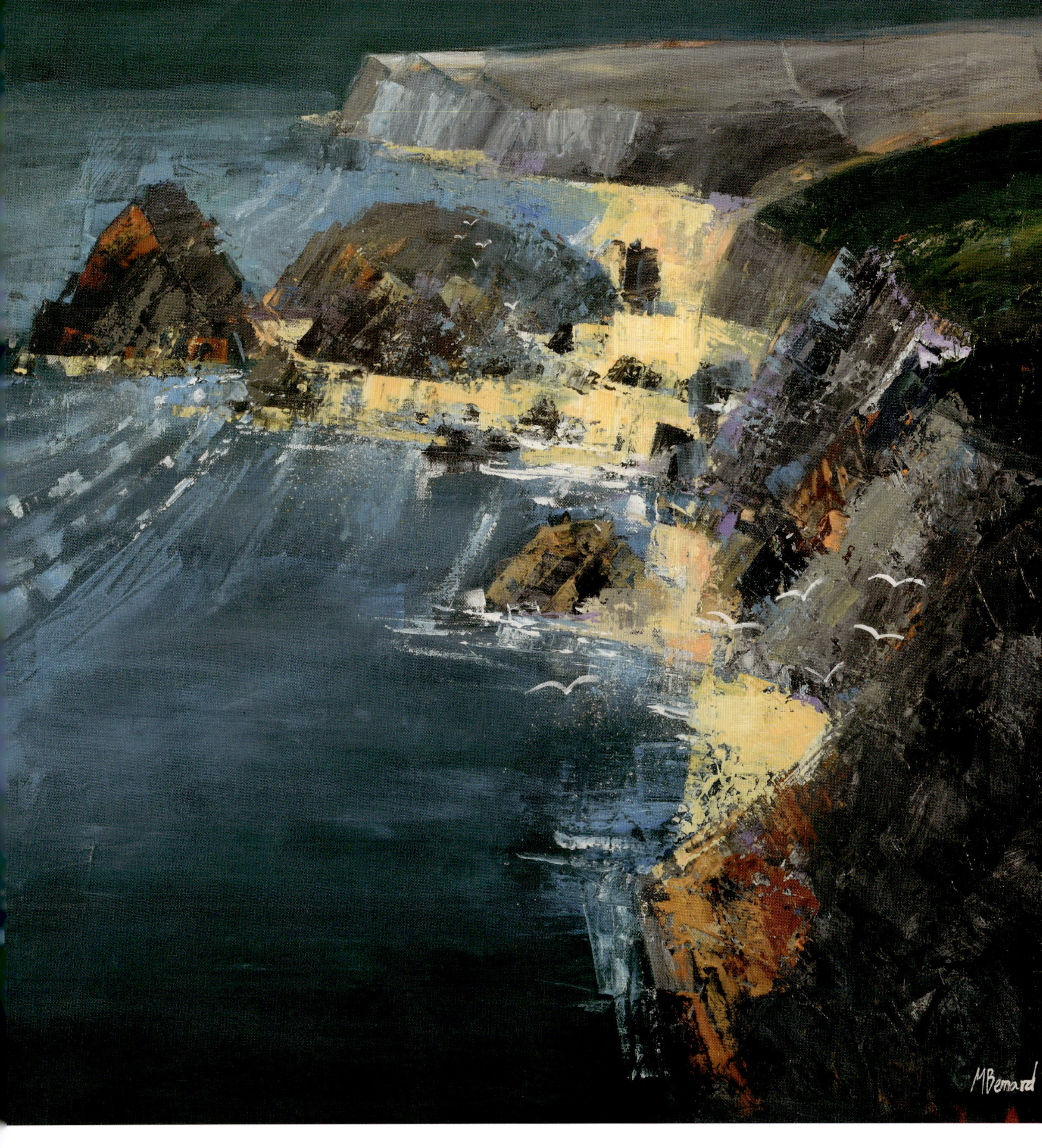

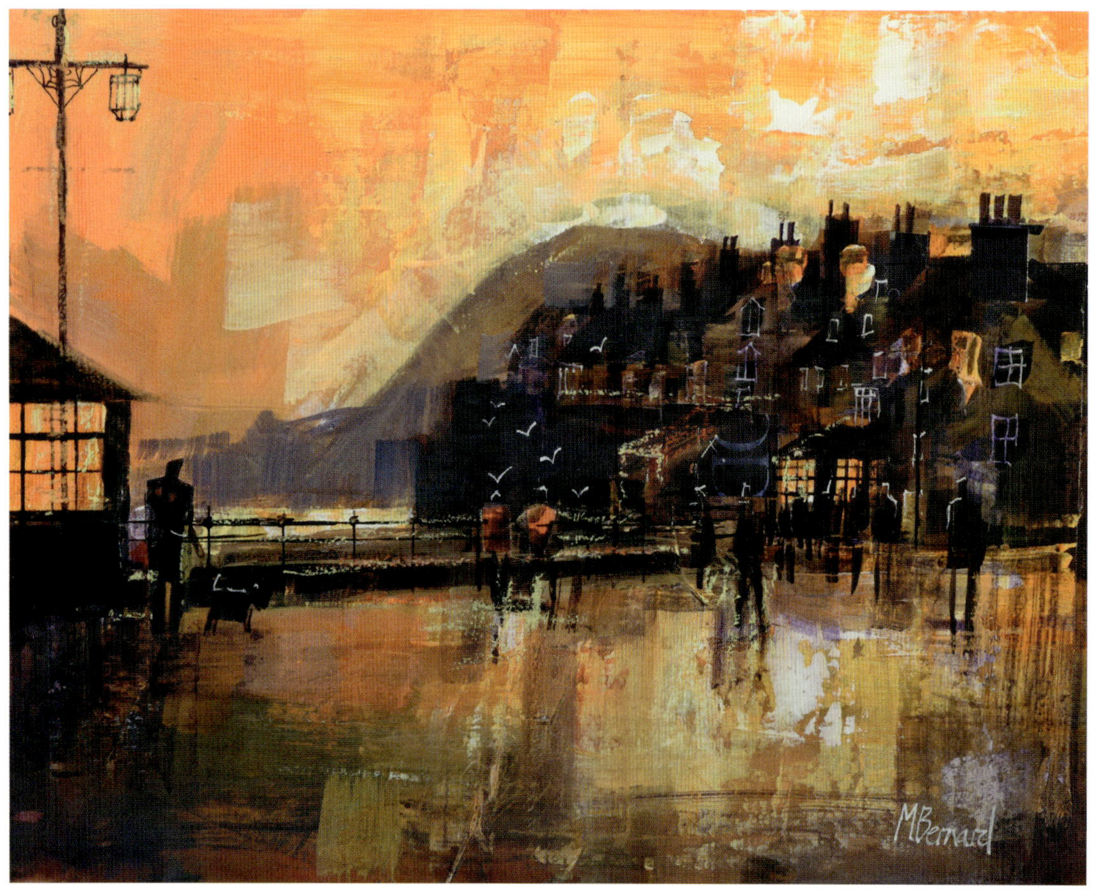

**Evening Light,
Sidmouth**
*Mixed media,
73.5 x 94cm (29 x 37in)*
I particularly like subjects
where I can create strong
contrasts between
realistic elements and
abstract shapes.

evidence of the use of a roller here and there. *Beachside Café,
Tuscany* on page 99 is similarly semi-abstract, achieved by
paper collage and little attempt at perspective or shadows.

Above all, don't allow yourself to have negative thoughts,
don't give up, keep the momentum going. However nervous
or apprehensive you may be in the beginning about making
your work more abstract, remember that this can be
achieved in many ways and it is a way of liberating you, of
giving you the freedom to work even more individually and
uniquely. At some stages in my work, I work completely by
instinct, placing and gluing, painting and dabbing, with little
concept in my head of what I'm aiming for. Once you get used
to this way of working and you find that you can bring your
painting back to a sense of reality afterwards, you will feel
liberated. Inevitably, you will be considering the view you
want to illustrate, but be determined not to follow the exact
details closely.

Italian Harbour
Mixed media, 61 x 46cm (24 x 18in)
Here I think I've managed to create an
effective balance of representational
and abstract elements.

Imagination

Obviously, experience helps in creating unique paintings, but equally, I rely on my imagination. Without that, everything I paint would probably look the same! By working intuitively, I create a sense of abstraction, but I also have to stop every now and then, take a long look at what I've been creating and consider, or reconsider, what I am doing, where I will go with it, what is working and what isn't. As I've mentioned several times, at the start of a work, when I am laying down my collage, I have little idea about how it will turn out. This is great, as it means that little can

go wrong! I will make the most of almost everything – and for this I have to use my imagination. So at the beginning, I am free to enjoy the materials and process, to stop thinking hard about what I am aiming for and simply get on with it. This initial freedom of working can really enhance what you eventually do with a painting, and how you work all the way through. The sense of spontaneity should be held on to for as long as possible. Believe in your imagination. Often your initial ideas will be the best ones, so be confident and try not to question yourself as you work. Perhaps photograph

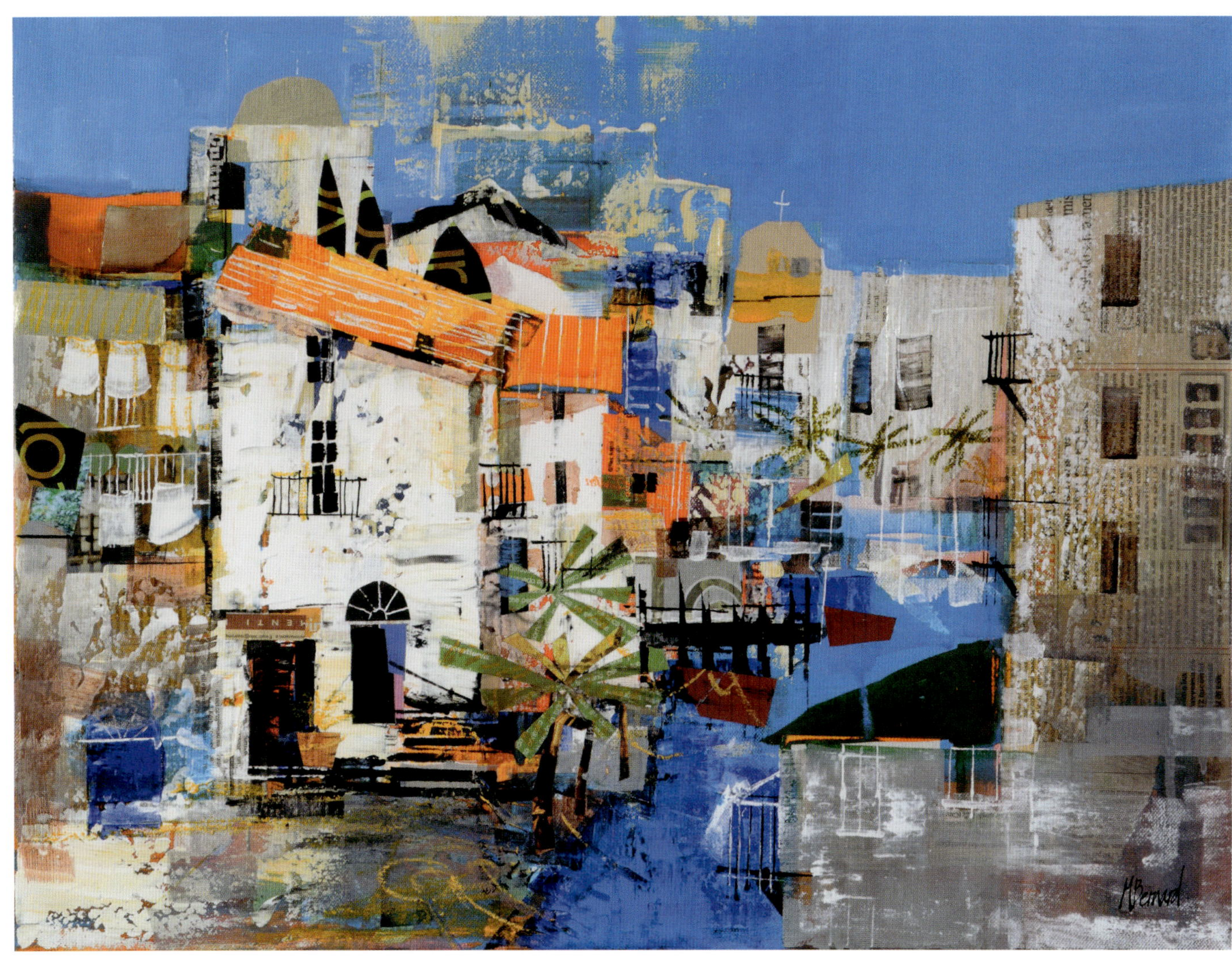

your initial workings, that is, your early applications of collage and paint. Remember what ideas you had then and, however much you may digress later, recall what ideas you had.

The way I work means that there are nearly always paintings in progress, set aside to dry or because I'm not sure how I want to move on with them. Maybe you won't have so many works in progress, but I find that this is great practice. By putting paintings to one side and returning to them with fresh eyes a few days or weeks later, you will capture several ideas that you probably didn't have when you were first working on them. When you are working on a painting, you become totally absorbed and involved, aware of every mark you make, every intention you have. If you leave it for a while, then come back to it, you will see it with fresh eyes, with a whole new perspective, which in turn should spark your imagination and help you notice something incongruous, or something great that you want to enhance, or you may even realise that you want to change it altogether. Related to this, my advice is to never throw anything away, no matter how upset you are with it. Something can always be salvaged if you allow your imagination to take over. A good way of firing up your imagination is to stare at your painting for ages; notice every aspect, every mark and piece of collage. Study it for a good long time. Then stop. Walk away or put it out of sight. When you return to it, allow your imagination to enhance it. Let your thoughts flow and expand.

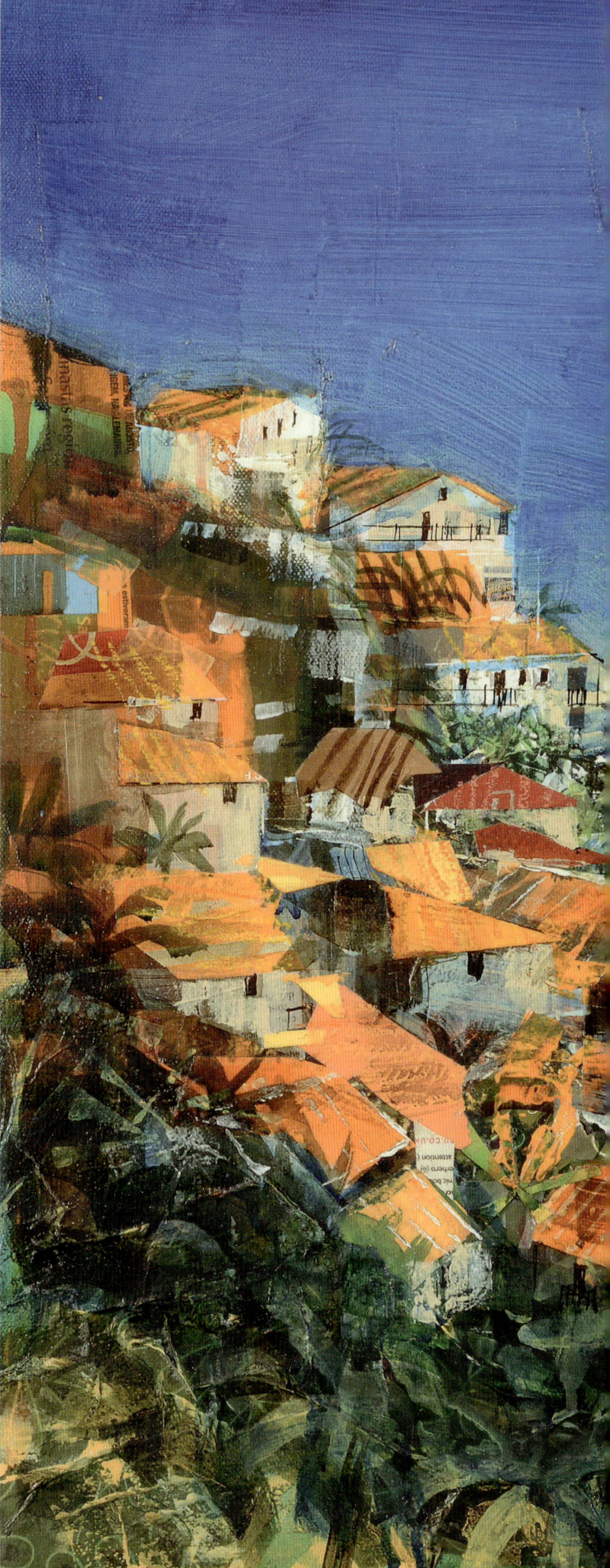

Fishing Village, Madeira
Mixed media, 61 x 76cm (24 x 30in)
Sometimes it is necessary to drastically simplify
a scene in order to create a more effective view.
In this way, although this is still clearly a view of a
village from above, I used my imagination to make
the shapes, lines and colours convey patterns.

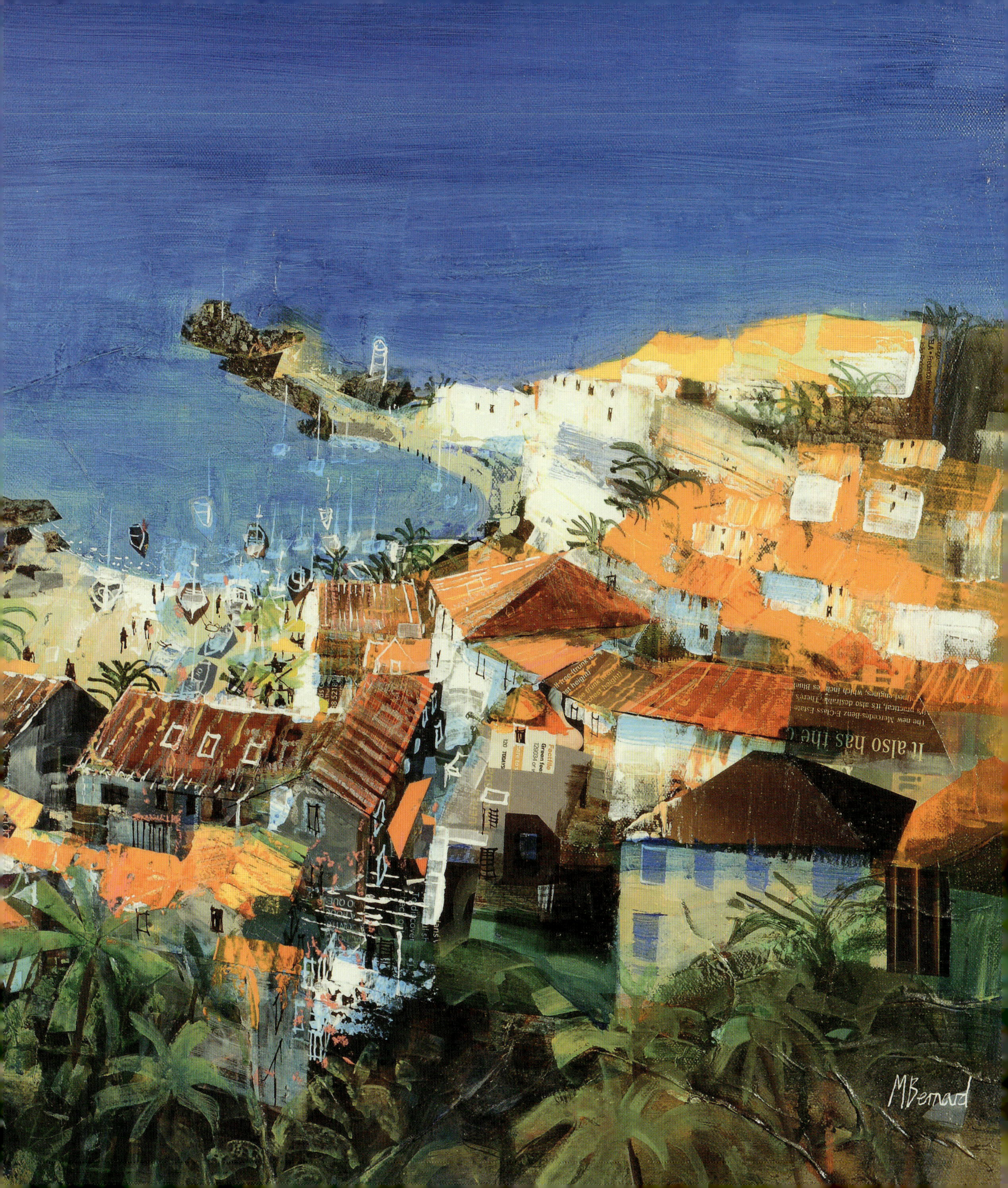

M.Bernard

When things go wrong

At every step of the way, you will be making choices as you create. Of course, I do this too, at every juncture of my painting process. With experience and hindsight (a wonderful thing), I often know what to expect, what will probably – not always – happen and how to resolve things if they go wrong. However, even without the benefit of experience, there are ways that you can control (to a certain extent) how your paintings turn out. While it is great to be spontaneous and to follow your gut instinct and use your imagination, it is also helpful often to have ways of resolving issues, to know that if things backfire for you or

go horribly or even just slightly wrong, you can fix them and put your painting back on track. While this part of the book is all about working towards abstraction, sometimes you can go too far in this direction for your liking and need to bring things back closer to reality. It's all a case of feeling comfortable with the way you work and the outcome of that process.

For example, you may have been working on a painting for several days, then you step back and notice that it all looks a bit too flat; that you want to include some sense of recession or tonal contrast. To see whether you need

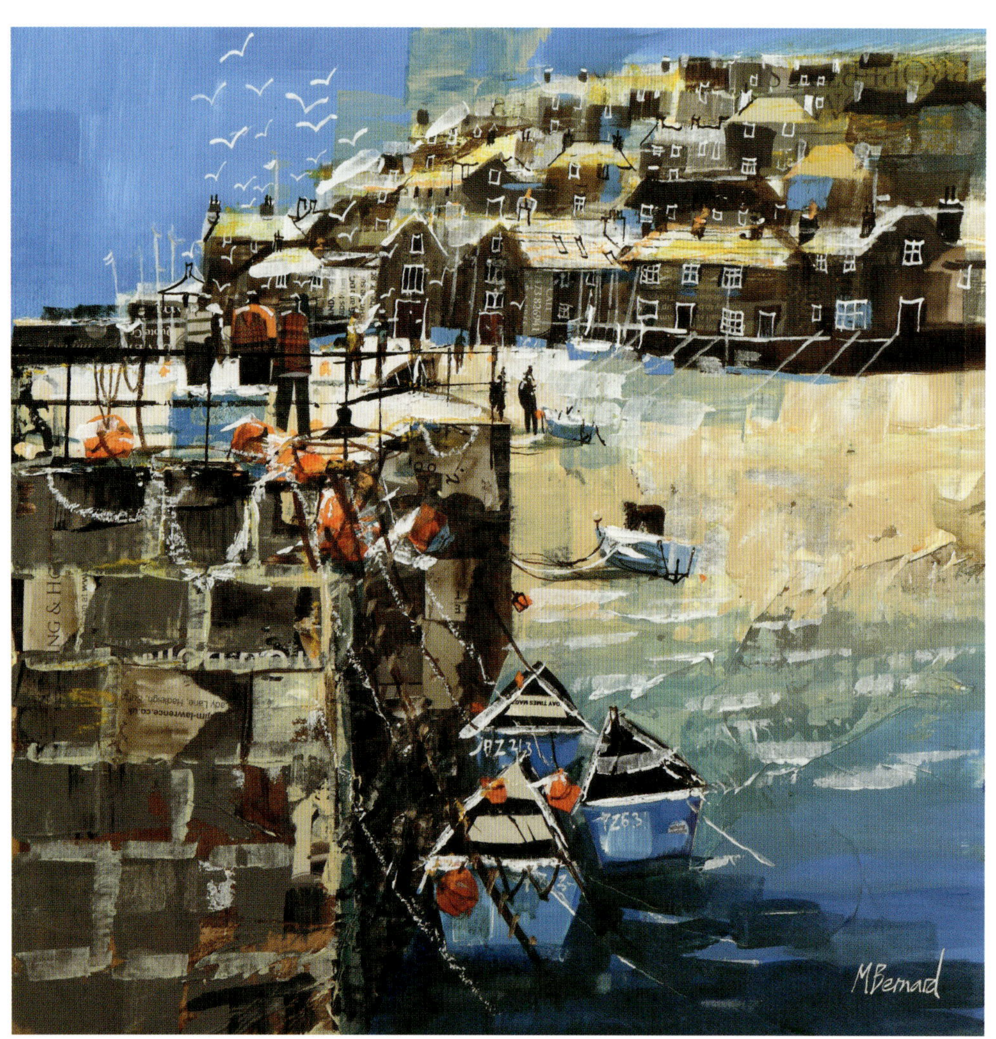

Harbour Wall, Mousehole
Mixed media, 35 x 35cm (14 x 14in)
I had originally intended to make this wall less of a feature in the composition, but it was all part of my aiming to break the rules and to experiment.

to do this, try standing back, looking at your work overall, and squinting. Squinting enables you to visually simplify the values in the scene, to eliminate the perception of reflected light, and to better see the whole image. By looking at your work with half-closed eyes, you will see greater definition of values and shapes. What jumps out at you? What seems to stay static and too flat-looking? You might think that you need a splash of colour, or alternatively to reduce the brightness of the work. You might find that one shape dominates too much. Or that you need to create more definition in certain areas.

As well as looking at your work after not seeing it for a while, or standing back from it, try looking at it in a mirror. This is a way of making mistakes jump right out at you. If the pattern or design is not harmonious, for instance, this will show up more in its mirrored reflection that it does when the painting is sitting in front of you on an easel. All these choices about what to put in and what to leave out should be made with the idea in your mind that you are moving towards abstraction. Often this will involve ideas about key features and whether to make them stronger, larger, brighter, or to reduce them, or even to blot them out entirely. Remember that overworking will stifle your creativity and individuality and often move things away from the idea of abstraction in your work, which is what will make it more unique and personal than just a straight, painted view.

Every decision you make, however small, will have an impact on your painting as a whole. You can change the time suggested, the weather, the emphasis or the atmosphere, for instance, depending on which features you develop. One decision to avoid at all costs, however, is the decision to aim for perfection. This will stifle the personality, creativity and excitement of your work. For example, in *Harbour Wall, Mousehole*, I changed my viewpoint as I was working and reduced the number of buildings in the image to create a simpler, more impactful scene. Having a large chunk of the harbour wall blocking the view in a large part of the left-hand corner was a gamble that paid off.

Experimentation

Perhaps you're thinking, 'It's easy for him to tell me to simply discard details, but how do I know which details to discard? How can I create impact and actually move towards abstraction without losing a sense of the place I'm depicting?'

Well, one of the ways that you can do this and find your own sense of confidence is to think of your painting as a journey, not a destination. Don't concentrate on the final result, but try out different ideas and techniques as you work. I've already mentioned that you should try out and investigate materials and processes before you begin, and similarly, once you have started, don't pressure yourself about the end result; experiment and explore ideas as you go, enjoy the process and just see what happens. Allow yourself to work freely with no pressure and you will almost certainly surprise yourself with some interesting and effective outcomes. Sometimes, experiments don't work for whatever reason, but usually, even if the actual painting fails – or you feel it has – the ideas and the knowledge you gain from this experimentation is worth the sacrifice. Although I've given you details about the paints and other materials I like to use and that I feel work for me, feel free to experiment with your own. There are so many different products on the market these days, so many colours and textures to choose from and so many ways in which you can use different materials, that you owe it to yourself to experiment with some of them and find out what you like best.

It may be an apocryphal story, but it is said that Wassily Kandinsky painted his first abstracted works after seeing one of his own representational paintings upside down in his studio; before he realised what it was, he decided that paintings without subjects from the real world, or that were abstracted in some way, were more powerful than purely representational paintings. From then, he experimented for the rest of his career. So you're in good company if you experiment, as I do, with every image you produce. You will inevitably make some mistakes, but on the whole, what you discover will inform not only the painting you are working on at the time, but also your future work and your total development as an artist. Good luck!

Index

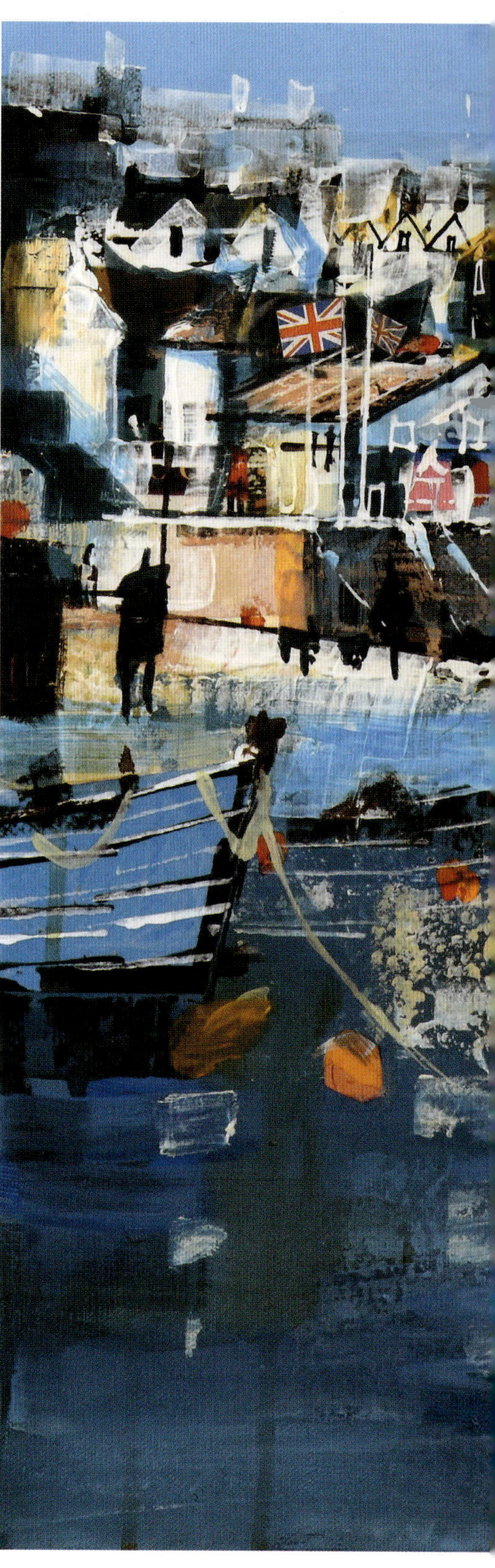

Quayside View, Salcombe
Mixed media, 40 x 56cm (16 x 22in)
Now you know all my 'secrets', you should be able
to spot repeating shapes and marks that act like
stepping stones to lead you on a merry path.

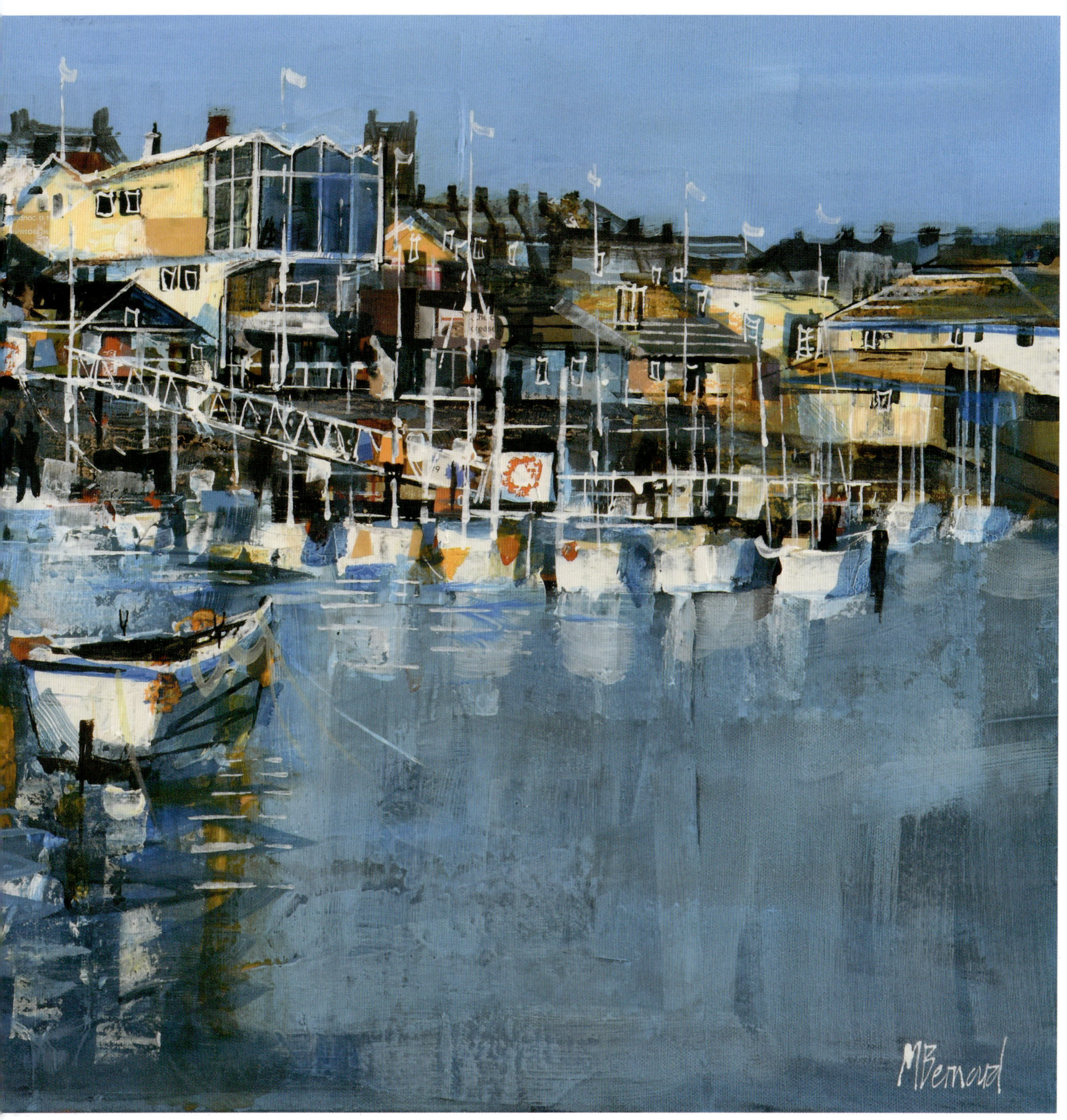

MBernard

Mike Bernard is a pioneer of mixed-media work,
especially collage work. His various art studies include
time at the Royal Academy schools. He has exhibited at
the Royal Festival Hall and the Royal Academy Summer
Exhibition in London and was elected member of the
Royal Institute of Painters in Watercolour in 1997. His
awards and prizes include the Stowells Trophy, the
Elizabeth Greenshields Fellowship, the Silver Longboat
Award and the Laing Award. He is the author of the
hugely successful *Collage, Colour and Texture in Painting*.

Susie Hodge, MA, FRSA, is an award-winning author,
art historian, artist and journalist with over 160 books
published for both adults and children, mainly on
art history, practical art and history. She also writes
magazine articles, and web resources and booklets
for museums and galleries, and gives workshops and
talks and lectures at schools, universities, museums,
galleries, festivals and societies around the world. She
regularly contributes to radio and TV programmes and
documentaries.